OMAR PASHA.

GREECE
AND THE
GOLDEN HORN

GREECE,

AND THE

GOLDEN HORN.

BY

STEPHEN OLIN, D.D. LL.D.,

LATE PRESIDENT OF THE WESLEYAN UNIVERSITY.

WITH AN INTRODUCTION,

BY REV. JOHN M'CLINTOCK, D.D.

NEW YORK:

J. C. DERBY, 8 PARK PLACE.

BOSTON: PHILLIPS, SAMPSON & CO.

CINCINNATI: H. W. DERBY.

1854.

Greece and the Golden Horn.

TO THE FRIENDS

OF

The Wesleyan University.

THIS VOLUME,

WRITTEN BY A PEN FOREVER LAID ASIDE,

Is respectfully dedicated.

A CORDIAL WELCOME FROM THEM, MAY GIVE IT POWER

TO AID AN INSTITUTION, FOR WHICH A SAINTED

SPIRIT LABORED AND PRAYED.

Introduction.

The work now presented to the reader was left in manuscript by the lamented author. His "Travels in the East," which has been for some years before the public, has gained the rank of a standard work upon the lands of the Bible; indeed, it is in many respects the best work on those countries, for general readers, that has yet appeared. This is eminently true with regard to Dr. Olin's account of Egypt, which brings together the best account of the policy of Mehemet Ali and of its results in the condition of the country, that can be found anywhere, to our knowledge, within the same compass.

The present volume is characterized by the same excellent qualities that have marked all Dr. Olin's writings. His mind was singularly comprehensive; but, at the same time, had a rare faculty of accurate and minute observation; and these qualifications, combined with a severe and conscientious truthfulness, fitted him admirably to write books of travel. He does not, indeed, give us romance; but reality is better; he tells what he saw, not what he dreamed. It is true, that amid associations such as those that haunt the hills of Athens, his calm mind grows imaginative, and, to use his own language, "finds it easy to repeople scenes that have been consecrated by the highest examples of genius and virtue;" but his judgment, ever cool and collected, does not fail him under any degree of intellectual excitement, and his words may always be taken for true in their full meaning.

It must be remembered, however, that these pages were not prepared for the press by Dr. Olin. It cannot be expected, therefore, that they will show the fineness of finish, or even the fullness of detail that would have been given them by his final revision.

The countries of which they treat have always been full of interest; but now men's eyes, in all lands, are turned with straining anxiety to "GREECE AND THE GOLDEN HORN." Within the territory indicated by those titles, will be found the earliest seats of empire, the scenes of God's nearest approach to man, the ground hallowed by the feet of the Saviour, the sites of the Apocalyptic churches—in a word, all the sacred localities of the Bible. Within that territory the noblest races and the highest acts of mankind have originated and flourished. It has been the seat of more *history* than any other portion of the earth's surface; and this day, its strangest history, perhaps, is enacting before our eyes. The Mussulman and the Giaour have often met in deadly combat; for ages there has been hereditary strife between them. It has been thought that prophecy, and policy, and wisdom have all alike called for the overthrow of the Ottoman, and the rescue of the holy places from his sacrilegious hands. But now a new crusade is preached within the coasts of England and through the valleys of France,—not to drive the Turk from Byzantium and Jerusalem, but to keep him on his throne, and to preserve the integrity of his dominion. The CZAR is, by profession, a Christian monarch; the faith of his people is that which formerly was preached in St. Sophia; but France and England unite with the Sultan against the Czar. How is this change to be accounted for?

The reason is not far to seek. The old names do not mean the old things. The CZAR affects to consider Turkey moribund, and wishes to be in at the death and take the lion's share of the spoil. To secure his ends he has exhausted every artifice of fraud and dissimulation, and now resorts to force of arms, seeking to call out the fiercest ferocity of his savage hordes by baptizing his ambition with a Christian title, and declaring, unblushingly, to all the world, that he is fighting the old hereditary battle of the Cross against the Crescent. In all this he commits at once a great mistake and a great crime. His mistake is in supposing Turkey to be dying at the very time when she shows a most unconquerable vitality, and is, indeed, taking to herself new powers and a new lease of life, by dropping her old and worn-out forms of life. One great principle of political vitality it has always had —a principle which will prevent too rapid changes, and at the same time make all needful changes possible without revolution— namely, municipal privileges and a free provincial distribution of authority. Neither in extent of dominion, in resources, nor in spirit, is Turkey either dead or dying. Michelsen gives the following statistics:

"The Ottoman Empire extends over a part of Europe, Asia, and Africa, embracing an area of about 913,000 square miles.

"Including the tributary provinces, the population is as follows:

EUROPEAN TURKEY (RUMILI).

Thrace	1,800,000	
Bulgaria	4,000,000	
Moldavia	1,400,000	
Wallachia	2,000,000	
Bosnia and Herzegowina	1,400,000	
Rumelia	2,600,000	
Servia	1,600,000	
Islands of the Archipelago	700,000	
		15,500,000

ASIATIC TURKEY (ANADOLU).

Asia Minor	10,700,000	
Syrians, Mesopotamia and Kurdistan	4,450,000	
Arabia, (Mecca, Medina, Habesh)	900,000	
		16,050,000

AFRICAN TURKEY (GARB).

Egypt	2,000,000	
Tripolis, Fezzan, Tunis	1,800,000	
		3,800,000
		35,350,000

Dividing the population into races and tribes, the result is as follows:—

Races or Tribes.	In Europe.	In Asia.	In Africa.	Total.
Ottomans	1,100,000	10,700,000	......	11,800,000
Slavonians	7,200,000	......	......	7,200,000
Rumanians	4,000,000	......	......	4,000,000
Arnauts	1,500,000	......	......	1,500,000
Greeks	1,000,000	1,000,000	......	2,000,000
Armenians	400,000	2,000,000	......	2,400,000
Jews	70,000	100,000	......	170,000
Tartars	230,000	.....	......	230,000
Arabs	......	900,000	3,800,000	4,700,000
Syrians and Chaldeans	......	235,000	......	235,000
Druses	......	25,000	......	25,000
Kurds	......	1,000,000	......	1,000,000
Turkomans	......	90,000	......	90,000
	15,500,000	16,050,000	3,800,000	35,350,000

Taking the population according to religious creeds, the result is:

CREEDS.	In Europe.	In Asia.	In Africa.	Total.
Mohammedan	3,800,000	12,950,000	3,800,000	20,550,000
Greeks and Armenians	11,370,000	2,360,000	......	13,730,000
Ro. Catholic	260,000	640,000	......	900,000
Jews	70,000	100,000	......	170,000
	15,500,000	16,050,000	3,800,000	35,350,000

Here is a so-called Christian population of fifteen millions; and besides these, there are foreign Protestants to the number of many thousands, with Protestant missionaries from England and America planted in the most important centres, and engaged in spreading evangelical Christianity. The simple question necessary to be answered, in order to decide on which side lies the *Christianity* in this quarrel, is, whether these Christian populations and Protestant missionaries can enjoy greater privileges and liberties under the Czar than under the Sultan? The claims of the

Czar are maintained by some parties in England; and even in America, Bishop Southgate at least has declared his "every feeling of truth and equity convinces him that the claim of Russia is just and moderate, and that it ought to be sustained." Let us see.

It is believed that no copy of the Scriptures has been printed in the vernacular language in Russia since 1823. ALEXANDER favored the Bible Society, and even established presses to print the sacred book; but NICHOLAS has changed all that, and now, according to a statement made by Lord Shaftesbury in his place in Parliament, *no printing presses are permitted for printing the Bible in modern Russia*, nor is a single copy of the Bible in that language allowed to circulate. There are two millions of Jews in Russia, but the Czar will not permit a single copy of the Hebrew Bible to pass his frontiers for their use. His policy is to keep his people everywhere in the worse than Asiatic superstition that characterizes his so-called Greek church, and to let them know nothing better than a form of worship, compared with which Jezebel's worship of Astarte could almost be called rational and respectable. He represses evangelical missions with an iron hand, not merely when they seek to make proselytes from the Greek church, but even when they attack only the heathenism of his outlying provinces. The Moravians had gathered 300 converts among the Calmucks, but the Imperial edict forbade their baptism, and the mission was disbanded. The Scottish mission in Russian Tartary was compelled to end its labors just as they were beginning to be productive. The missionaries of the Basle society were ordered to quit the Russian empire in 1833. And in 1841, the mission of the London Society in Siberia was suppressed by an order from the Russian Synod, under the plea "that the mission, in relation to that form of Christianity already established in the Russian empire, did not coincide with the views of the church and government." It would not be difficult, moreover, to show, that while Russia rejects all ameliorating religious influences from without, the exercise of its own power degrades the moral and religious condition of every province that it touches.

On the other hand, it can be shown "that the Turks have for

many years been in reality—no matter under what compulsion, no matter from what motives—the protectors of nearly all the genuine Christianity that exists in Eastern Europe and in Western Asia, while Russia is slowly, surely, terribly, moving down to destroy, as the frozen mass of a glacier makes its way, year by year, to overwhelm the homesteads of the valley." In more than fifty towns and villages of Turkey there are Protestant congregations, many of them composed of seceders from the Greek church. A correspondent of the London Christian Times gives the following comparative statistics:

Number of Protestant clergymen in Constantinople and its suburbs in		1830	0
Ditto	ditto	1854	19
Number of Protestant sermons preached on every Sabbath in different languages, in ditto		1830	0
Ditto	ditto	1854	26
Number of Protestant schools in ditto		1830	0
Ditto	ditto	1854	14

These statistics refer to Constantinople and its immediate environs alone. In the entire empire (including Constantinople) there are now sixty-five Protestant preachers. Did Nicholas reign instead of the Sultan, there would not be *one*. The facts of the case fully justify the strong remark made by Lord Shaftesbury (in the speech before referred to), that "Turkey had done everything to advance, and Russia everything to prevent the progress of Christianity among the millions of mankind." The Turkish system allows free scope to Christian missionaries, whether Protestant or Catholic, to carry on their operations by preaching, teaching, printing or circulating the Scriptures. There are presses at Constantinople, Bucharest, and elsewhere, at which the Bible is printed in almost every Oriental tongue, including the Turkish. "There are forty depôts for the sale of the Bible in Turkey, and at this moment there are colporteurs and native agents engaged in every province."

Let Turkey succumb in the approaching conflict, and Russia

obtain the power she seeks, and all this will be changed. The Muscovite system of absolute exclusion will prevail, and all Protestant missions must come to an end. The war, even at this early period, has benefited the Protestant missions, and its successful prosecution on the part of Turkey will be accompanied by still further concessions to his Christian subjects. Islamism, as such, is of course opposed to such concessions; but the advances of Turkey for the last twenty years have all been made at the expense of Islamism. The defeat of Russia will secure to the Christian population of Turkey a more independent position and a higher influence than they have ever yet enjoyed. "They have long been obtaining concessions of civil liberty. Their religious liberties are secure. The great officials of the empire help them to build their churches. One stigma after another has been removed. They are rising in the social scale; and it is to be hoped that when they have attained that true equality which is now fairly in view, they will not forget that there was a time when the shelter of the Ottoman Empire was sought by Christians under Christian persecution, by Jews, and by all who were driven from Christian lands for liberty of thought, religious or political." In view of all these facts, Christians—and most of all, Protestant Christians—owe their sympathy and their prayers to Turkey, England and France, in the present war.

The views expressed by Dr. Olin with regard to the new Greek kingdom in the following pages, evince his keen political discrimination and foresight. Thirty years ago English and French fleets blindly fought the battle of Russia against the Turk. Aptly does Dr. Olin ask (p. 252), "What good has been done by the battle of Navarino? Greece, too weak to be independent, and too corrupt and ignorant for freedom and self-government, has become virtually a province of Russia, under a stupid king, whose rule is decidedly more oppressive than that of the Turk."

One word may be proper as to the pecuniary results of the present publication. The Wesleyan University, at Middletown, Conn., of which Dr. Olin was President, lay very near his heart. In his will he made provision that, in case he should leave no children, the copyright of his "Travels in the East" should be given to the University; and moreover, that on the death of Mrs. Olin, and in default of children to inherit, the whole of his property should fall to the University. His wife and son survive him—and long may they remain—but the present volume is dedicated, in the spirit of his last will, to the object he so dearly cherished. *The whole profits of the book will accrue to the Wesleyan University*, to whose Trustees the copyright has been assigned.

J. M'CLINTOCK.

April 27, 1854.

CONTENTS.

CHAPTER I.

CHAPTER II.

CHAPTER III.

CHAPTER IV.

CHAPTER V.

CHAPTER VI.

CHAPTER VII.

CHAPTER VIII.

CHAPTER IX.

CHAPTER X.

CHAPTER XI.

CHAPTER XII.

CHAPTER XIII.

CHAPTER XIV.

CHAPTER XV.

CHAPTER XVI.

CHAPTER XVII.

CHAPTER XVIII.

CHAPTER XIX.

CHAPTER XX.

CHAPTER XXI.

CHAPTER XXII.

CHAPTER XXIII.

CHAPTER XXIV.

CHAPTER XXV.

CHAPTER XXVI.

CHAPTER XXVII.

CHAPTER XXVIII.

CHAPTER XXIX.

CHAPTER XXX.

CHAPTER XXXI.

CHAPTER XXXII.

CHAPTER XXXIII.

CHAPTER XXXIV.

CHAPTER XXXV.

CHAPTER XXXVI.

CHAPTER XXXVII.

CHAPTER XXXVIII.

CHAPTER XXXIX.

CHAPTER XL.

Greece.

GREECE AND THE GOLDEN HORN.

CHAPTER I.

THE IONIAN ISLANDS.

Corfu is the first Greek town we have seen. It is said to contain three thousand five hundred inhabitants, and is situated upon the eastern side of the island, opposite to Albania, from which it is about two miles distant. Near the middle of the channel is the small island of Vidi, consisting of a few acres of rock, out of which has been excavated an impregnable fortress, not yet entirely complete. This fortress quite commands the channel, which is deep enough for ships of the line on the Albanian side, as well as towards Corfu. There are also strong forts in the city opposite to Vida, and it appears hardly possible for an enemy to disturb this stronghold of England, which, along with Gibraltar and Malta, must secure to her the dominion of the Mediterranean, so long at least as she maintains her naval superiority. The bay, perfectly shut in by mountains, is of great extent and depth of water, but is said to be exposed to winds from the Albanian mountains. The entrance is by a narrow winding channel that seems to be quite blocked up with mountains, when you look back to it from the city. There was but little shipping in the harbor—mostly small Greek vessels employed in the coasting trade. The island of Corfu, seen at a distance, seems only a mass of desolate mountains. It, however, contains many fertile valleys, which produce olives in great abundance. These constitute the agricultural wealth of the island. Corn is imported from the Black Sea by the government, and sold to the people at cost. Vegetables, some vines, and lately potatoes, are the other products.

The city of Corfu is built upon a point of land, just opposite to Vida, and though not perfectly flat, is not, with the exception of the citadel and the streets near the governor's palace, greatly elevated. The houses built of stone or brick, and plastered and whitewashed, have a neglected and decaying appearance. The streets are very narrow, and, with a few exceptions, the shops are small, poor, and dirty. Only a few of the coarsest articles are exhibited for sale, and though the streets are several of them crowded, there is but little appearance of business. Multitudes of people stood or sat idle, laughing, talking, or smoking. Nothing could be more picturesque and un-European than the whole scene. It was decidedly oriental, and the more striking for being the first oriental town I had visited. The flowing and various costumes of the Greeks, Turks, and Albanians, were mingled in gay confusion.

With very few exceptions, all was marked with the impress of squalid poverty. The boatmen, who seem to be active and expert, generally speak a little English, as do many of the shop-keepers, several of whom are, in fact, Englishmen. The aspect of the people is decidedly Greek, and it is only here and there that, with the exception of the military, a man is seen dressed in the European fashion. Corfu, which is the key to the Adriatic and the Archipelago, may be expected to increase in size and importance. The expenditure of the army and for public works is a source of prosperity. The fleets of England are often here, and considerable trade is carried on with the neighboring coast of Turkey. The High Commissioner is said to have the prosperity of these islands much at heart, and the native legislature, though by no means an enlightened body, concur to a good degree in his views. Good roads have been constructed, a thing unknown in other parts of the Levant.* A

* A fearful hurricane burst on the island of Corfu on the night of the 19th of February, 1853. The country was everywhere ravaged, and the most lamentable misfortune was occasioned. The houses were agitated as if by an earthquake; doors and windows were torn from their fastenings and hurled through the air, and the roofs of houses fell crashing into the streets. The town of Corfu suffered severely. Several houses were blown down; all the ships at anchor suffered, while many were wrecked; upwards of one hundred trees on the Esplanade were uprooted, and a portion of the walls supporting the land was demolished by the sea. One account says that twenty-nine lives were lost in the environs, and another eighty. One village is spoken of as entirely destroyed. A letter dated the next day after the hurricane says:

"The magnificent forest of olive-trees, which was the pride and wealth of Corfu, is entirely destroyed. The country is literally sacked. The few trees which remain standing may be counted, but college, which is well attended, has been endowed. The professors were mostly educated in Italy, and some of them are Italians. An Englishman was appointed to one of the chairs, but upon an alleged interference with the religious prejudices of the country, was compelled to retire, and a statute forbids the appointment of another. There is a growing attention to common schools, which are also established by the government. The land of the island is held in small estates, which are valuable in proportion to their number of olive-trees. The Ionian islands pay annually for the British connection, £36,000, beside maintaining their own local institutions and improvements. The governor receives £5,000 per annum. Intercourse with the eastern part of Turkey is embarrassed by a rigorous quarantine.

Upon leaving Corfu, the Albanian shores continue bleak and mountainous, with scarcely an interruption, for I should think more than a hundred miles. The same is true of the island, though the mountains are less lofty and abrupt. Ithica, which we passed before 5, on the morning of the 21st of November, has a similar appearance, as has Cephalonia, of which we had a more distant though distinct view. These, with many smaller islands, are masses of mountains apparently

it is impossible to reckon the thousands which are torn up and broken to pieces, Never have I witnessed such a deplorably desolating scene, of whose horrors description is impossible. All the roads are blocked up by trunks of trees; the country no longer has the appearance of a land inhabited; it has the aspect of a chaotic overthrow."—*Ed.*

consisting of many rocks and peaks of a gray ashey color, nearly destitute of verdure, and quite without trees. Many of the valleys and some small plains have great fertility, though but a thin soil.

We entered the bay of Patras between 9 and 10 A. M. The shores on either hand are still bounded by mountains of considerable height, and almost perfectly bare of verdure. Not a tree is to be seen, and the eye rests upon boundless sterility. Nearer Patras the hills recede a half a mile from the beach, and a strip of level ground, apparently fertile, stretches along the coast for several miles. Back of this narrow plain, the elevation is less than elsewhere, and appeared to be planted with olive-trees. The town is built close to the water, extending back to the foot of a high hill which is surmounted by a citadel that quite overlooks the town, and, though constructed with little solidity, might resist a sudden incursion of undisciplined foes. It is not kept in repair, nor has it any garrison at present.

The town is entirely new, and with the exception of five or six houses, is built in the most slight, wretched manner. The walls are, many of them, of bricks dried in the sun—some of small shapeless stones, laid in mud. A large majority are mere cabins of the worst possible kind, not more than four or five feet high, without floors, filthy and without furniture. The people, who seemed all to be in the street, or in the front of their open shops, were, with few exceptions, meanly dressed in the coarsest clothes, many of them dirty, ragged, without stockings, and slipshod. Still their costume was picturesque. Considerable quantities of cheap coarse goods were displayed in the shops, and the market was well supplied with vegetables, chiefly cabbages and onions. We saw no antiquities at Patras, though ruins of a temple of Ceres are said to exist there. It has been the site of a city for several thousand years, has a favorable situation for trade near the entrance of the Gulf of Corinth, and there is said to be a fertile country in the vicinity, though it was hid from our view by the mountains. I heard that there are four or five English merchants resident here, who carry on a direct trade with Great Britain. The few ships in the harbor were of small dimensions, and, with the exception of two brigs, not fit for any but coasting voyages. The population is variously reported at from five thousand to eight or ten thousand. It gives one but a sad idea of the progress of this new kingdom, to be told that Patras is one of its three most important and commercial towns.

November 21st. The boat was detained here till near midnight, taking in coal, which is deposited here for the supply of the Austrian line of steamers. The night was dark and rainy, and the sea very boisterous. At sunrise we had not advanced in our voyage above twenty-five or thirty miles, and upon going on deck I found the boat struggling against a powerful head-wind, just off the shores of Zante. The violence of the wind continued to increase for three hours more, till, our vessel becoming quite unable to make head against it, the captain, with the entire approbation of the passengers, who were mostly becoming sick, resolved to seek the nearest port, and for this purpose turned directly back for the harbor of Zante.

The island, as we coasted along the shore at the distance of not more than half a mile, appeared—though, like all the islands and coasts of Greece, composed of mountains—to be much less elevated and precipitous than those we had previously seen. The hills were verdant with olive-yards. White cottages contrasted beautifully with the evergreen foliage. Everything bore the appearance of culture and civilization, and the whole scene, aided no doubt by the bare and desolate regions at which we had for some time been looking, had an aspect of signal and picturesque beauty. In a little more than an hour, we came in view of the city, and congratulated ourselves upon the unexpected opportunity of visiting the loveliest place we had yet seen in Greece.

Several of our company were forming a party to visit the Opera, which is said to be good, not doubting but the friendly storm would continue for at least twenty-four hours. These anticipations of pleasure were soon disappointed. The harbor, which is a mere roadstead, quite unsheltered on the side of the sea, was in great agitation. There was no safe anchorage, and it would have been quite impossible to reach the land in a small boat. It was soon announced that we were to proceed about thirty miles more in our retrograde course, to seek shelter in the more secure port of Cephalonia. We passed very near to the town, and had a good view of its beautiful site and environs.

The city of Zante is built upon the edge of the sea, mostly upon a level area, but partly upon rising ground at the base of the hill, or rather mountain, by which it is bounded on the land side. This gives to it a showy, amphitheatrical appearance. Viewed from the sea, it seems to occupy the whole open space upon the beach, and to extend back a considerable distance along a gorge of the mountain, which allowed us to see, above the tops of the houses, an extensive region of high hills and rugged cliffs—an imposing, wild background to this beautiful place. The loftiest pinnacle of the mountain is occupied by the citadel, which must command perfectly, not only the city, but all approach to it at least by sea. To the left of the town are seen several sugar-loaf hills, covered to the top with luxuriant olive trees. On the right, the mountain declines a little into a high table-land, clothed likewise with a noble forest of the same beautiful evergreen, extending as far as the eye could reach. It is a large town of apparently two or three thousand inhabitants, commercial, wealthy, and prosperous—a contrast to nearly everything in this blighted region.

A company of Germans left us at Patras to proceed by land to Athens, by the way of Corinth, Thebes, and Delphi. There being no roads in this country, they of course travel on horseback. For this I was previously prepared, but no report of travellers had made me understand that it was necessary to have an escort of armed soldiers in every part of Greece, but such it seems is the fact. This company, I believe eight in number, were well armed with double-barrelled guns and swords. They were advised by their consul at Patras, that it would be unsafe to proceed without the additional security of a guard of soldiers. This is regarded as quite indispensable in journeying in the interior.

November 22d. We anchored last evening, at five, in the harbor of Argostoli, having been tossed about by a violent tempest for six or eight hours. The engines of the boat, two of fifty horse-power each, are quite unequal to such a time. The boat, with the assistance of a sail, was nearly unmanageable. About three in the afternoon, our danger of being thrown upon a rocky and precipitous shore was imminent. The captain was manifestly alarmed. The old sailors gathered round him with their advice, and altogether it was a time of anxiety to the passengers. These men seem not to possess the skill and courage of our American sailors. There is a familiarity between the captain and the sailors which is little favorable to discipline, and it is altogether impossible to feel the same confidence that is inspired by a higher degree of dignity and decision. We were all glad to anchor in the well-sheltered harbor of Argostoli, and I hope some were thankful for their escape from imminent peril. The harbor is formed by an arm of the sea, which, for several miles, has the appearance of a river from a mile to a quarter of a mile wide, which seems to terminate a little above Argostoli, where it is crossed by a low bridge of wood. It is perfectly sheltered by the hills that rise like an amphitheatre in all directions.

Here we are at anchor, with little prospect of sailing again at least for a day or two. The sky is alternately black with angry clouds, and bright with a most brilliant sun. At intervals of every half-hour our deck is inundated by violent showers of rain. Gusts of wind from different points of the compass rush down upon us from the mountains, with great though transient violence. But for these clear indications of the bad weather which prevails at sea, it might not be easy to keep our patience or even good-temper in exercise.

We were to have been in Athens to-day. So far from this, we are forty miles farther from that desired goal than we were two days since, and we must sail nearly four hundred miles along a bad coast, must double Cape Matapan, must in all probability be tossed three days and nights more before our arrival in this city—a city which contains, it is said, the only good hotels in Greece.

To render this delay the less tolerable, to say nothing of our anxiety to see a city of so many attractions for the curious and classical traveller, we are subject to want and inconvenience of a grosser sort. Our fare on board the boat, bad from the first, is now much deteriorated. Towels, napkins, table-linen, are all thoroughly soiled, with, I fear, no hope of a fresh supply. The little attention which was paid to cleanliness at the beginning of the voyage has quite subsided, and our table utensils, cabin, and every article of food, seem to *vie* with our Italian stewards and their apparel in disgusting filth. These people seem to think that cleanliness is no longer of any importance after their passengers are well on board and the anchor is weighed. The same thing is observable in the hotels of Germany and some parts of Italy. An apartment is put in such a state as not to disgust a traveller at first sight; but after he has once taken possession, everything is neglected. The floor is not swept, the bed-linen is seldom changed, snuffers, candlesticks, tumblers, are left in *statu quo*.

One hardly knows whom to reproach with the bad management and filth with which we are now afflicted —I mean what people. The boat is Austrian, the master an Ionian Greek, I believe, from Cephalonia, the crew is Dalmatian and Greek, the *gens de service* Italian and Greek. From the observations I have been able to make, no injustice would be done by charging all these races with a great deficiency in the virtue—it has been called, and I am not *now* at least inclined to detract from its dignity—in the virtue of cleanliness. In passing from Holland into Hanover, the grievous contrast in this respect is the first thing that strikes the traveller. In Prussia one at first is less disgusted with dirty habits. A more intimate acquaintance with the people, for which he need not go beyond the best hotels in Berlin or Potsdam, does not fail to remove any favorable impressions which he may have too hastily received. Leipzig, Dresden, Prague, Vienna, much more the provincial towns, merit the same reproach,—some of them even to a much higher degree than Northern Germany. Trieste one hardly knows whether to consider an Austrian or an Italian city. The streets, like those of Vienna and Dresden, are well enough, but the interior of the hotel soon admonishes the *voyageur* that he has little to hope for on the score of cleanliness from this blending of German and Italian habits.

The Dutch are certainly entitled to be considered the most cleanly people proper in the world. It is a perfect monomania with them—a perpetual annoyance to all who are so unlucky as to come within reach of the pumps and scrubbing-brushes. The English are perhaps before the French in this respect, though I could not say that their hotels are better kept generally than those of the same grade on the opposite side of the channel. In their farm-houses and cottages, this claim is much better supported. The French, however this question may be decided between them and their insular neighbors and rivals, are indisputably before the Italians in this mark of advanced civilization. In comparing the Italians with the Germans, it may be said, I think, that the latter are more attentive to out-door cleanliness. Their streets are swept and kept with greater care. The eye is seldom offended with the disgusting exhibitions which in Italy, and too often in France, are sure to meet you the moment you walk over the threshold of the hotel. But in the more important matters of clean beds, clean tables and table furniture, and all the *et cetera* of the interior economy of a lodging-house—taking my own experience as a guide—a decided preference must be given to the Italians. These discussions upon the borders of Greece, do not bespeak a very lofty and absorbing classic enthusiasm. Our circumstances just now are not very favorable to high imaginings. The animal nature of man has its claims, and is sometimes fairly entitled to assuage its griefs by uttering complaints. Another day will be more favorable to the dominion of classical meditations, and will make oblivion of sensual grievances more easy.

Nov. 23d. At 9 A. M. we are still in the harbor of Argostoli, with the wind in the unfavorable quarter, (the south,) and the clouds still threatening—at least so it seems to my unpractised eye. The force and fury of the elements have, however, partially subsided, and ships are busy in getting up the steam and making other preparations for again attempting the passage to Athens. Though we are quiet enough in this sheltered harbor, the sea is very far from being calm, as is manifest from the perpetual roaring of the waves, whose mighty voice, as they dash against the shore several miles from us, and separated by a high promontory, is perfectly audible. In the stillness of the morning at day-break, it was almost terrific. I doubt much whether we shall be able to proceed to sea. I think the captain does not expect it, but feels bound to make the trial, to guard himself against blame with the company at Trieste.

We have not been allowed to land at Argostoli, though we have been for forty hours within a quarter of a mile of the shore. We have, however, obtained some supplies of provisions and fuel. In despair of carrying us through upon the first courses, the steward has at last given a change of napkins and towels, and we are upon the whole in circumstances a little more favorable for passing a day or two longer at sea with some tolerable comfort.

We have from the deck a very fine view of Argostoli and its environs. Its situation favors this view greatly. Like the other towns which we have seen in Greece,—Corfu, Patras, and Zante,—it is built upon the beach, and extends back along the base and side of the mountain, which, verdant with the evergreen olive, forms a striking, picturesque, and lovely background, seen high above the houses, and stretching away till it is lost in the distance or in the clouds. This is a peculiarity belonging to the cities upon the Mediterranean, to which there is nothing similar in America, or, as far as I have had opportunity of observing, in the more northern parts of Europe. There, as in the United States, the shore, though sometimes sufficiently elevated, is generally flat, and the city is upon the same level with the surrounding country. Dover, and some other less important places, may be regarded as exceptions to this remark; still even they have none of that surpassing beauty of position that belongs to these Grecian towns. The noble amphitheatre of hills and mountains, rising one above another, as far as the eye can reach, is wanting. So also is the green foliage of the olive and the orange, embosoming lovely villas often to the very summit of the mountain. The whole scene of enchantment is often crowned with extensive monastic establishments and churches which occupy the pinnacles of the mountains. These edifices, as well as the country-houses and cottages that occupy the declivities below, are kept perfectly white, and seen in a clear day and by the rising or setting sun, are dazzling.

This very imperfect description applies to all the towns we have yet seen in Greece, as well as to most of the maritime cities of Italy and the south of France. Nearly the whole shore of these seas is a wall of mountains rising abruptly out of the water, without leaving space even for a road. Occasionally in some quiet bay an alluvial plain of small extent has been formed at their base by marine deposits. The declivities in such situations are usually more gentle than elsewhere; and the city built, the commercial part of it upon the narrow plain of the shore, and the residences of the more opulent and tasteful upon the ascent above, with the cottages, groves, villas, and churches, which always constitute the back-ground, is always beautiful when beheld from the sea, or from some of the heights in its neighborhood, though upon a closer inspection of the interior, one may find little or nothing that seems fitted to contribute to the agreeable impression produced by the whole. The narrow streets, the wretched hovels, the paltry shops and merchandise, and, above all, the filthy, ill-clad, and wretched multitude that throng the public squares, seldom fail to dissipate whatever illusion may have been produced by the goodly and gorgeous *tout-ensemble* which was seen at a distance.

Not having been allowed to take this nearer view of Argostoli, we shall leave its neighborhood with very agreeable impressions. It has the appearance of being well built, and of being kept in good repair. The number of vessels in the port, certainly more than a hundred, of all sizes, though generally small, indicates an active commerce, at least with near neighbors. The land appears to be more susceptible of culture here, and to be better tilled than the other regions equally mountainous which we have observed. The rugged sides of these mountains are covered with a thin soil. Some ploughed fields, said to be sown in barley, are visible upon the more level parts. The olive, which seems to thrive best in the worst soils, occupies the more bare and rocky portions; and, above all, the Corinthian currant, the chief product of this and the other Ionian islands, as well as of the Morea, is extensively cultivated.

CHAPTER II.

FROM ZANTE TO HYDRA.

November 24th. We set sail this morning at ten, the wind still adverse but less violent. Our progress was very slow, scarcely three miles an hour—the sea, though not unnavigable, was much agitated, and our passage excessively uncomfortable. It was after dark before we passed the harbor and town of Zante, and ten o'clock when we reached that part of the coast of the island from which we turned back on Friday. Our course had been hitherto partially sheltered from the violence of the wind by these islands, and much anxiety was felt lest upon entering the open sea, we might again find ourselves unable to proceed, and so be compelled to retrace our laborious and disagreeable course to Argostoli—the only harbor during the prevalence of the Sirocco.

We were happy to find that the boat was still able to proceed, though slowly. This would have been quite impossible had not the wind declined, as it did perceptibly, a little before we passed the last headland of Zante. We retired to rest with a good hope of being able in the course of a few days at least, to reach the port for which we were embarked. The time had already elapsed by one day, when we had at first expected to be released from the discomforts of our seafaring life. The delay has been attended with one advantage. We have seen much more of the Ionian islands than falls to the lot of travellers who are so fortunate as to meet with fair weather and a smooth sea.

Nov. 25th. I arose this morning and went upon deck at half-past four, as we were told we might expect to see Navarino before day-light. This sluggish boat, however, is sure to disappoint the most reasonable and moderate expectations. It was nine o'clock before we came in sight of Navarino Vecchio, and this was several miles short of the modern town. The citadel, the only remains of the ancient city visible to us, occupies the top of a lofty hill, at whose base the town and harbor are situated. It is a conspicuous and noble object, as seen from the sea. It perfectly commands the town and all approaches to it by sea, but is said to be itself commanded by higher elevations within cannon shot. It is in ruins, as well as the town, of which not a house remains. A few cottages on the beach, at no great distance, were indistinctly visible, and had, like everything seen on continental Greece, a wretched appearance.

The island of Sphacteria extends from near Navarino Vecchio, I should think, three or four miles southward. It is a moderately elevated ridge of land, quite overlooked by the mountains on the main-land, between which and the island lies the bay of Navarino, where the Turkish fleet was destroyed by the allies.

The entrance into the bay is around the south end of the island, between some high rocks rising abruptly out of the sea.

The citadel of Navarino is upon the main-land, overlooking and apparently capable of commanding perfectly this inlet into the harbor. The depth of water is so great, that large fleets of ships of the line passed the strait without difficulty, and made this fine bay, which is six miles in circumference, the bloody theatre upon which the long-protracted struggle for the independence of Greece was finally decided. Whether the great powers who interfered so unceremoniously in the affairs of the Ottoman Empire *now* approve of the policy pursued, is at least questionable. That it was unjust towards Turkey—a flagrant violation of international law—few of the writers of the present day hesitate to declare. It violated the sovereignty and broke the spirit of a nation which is now regarded as a great bulwark against the ambition of Russia. It remains to be seen whether the degenerate race in whose behalf this sacrifice of blood, and still more deplorable sacrifice of principle, was made, is destined to make some atonement to humanity for the crime upon which its independence was built, by assuming a worthy and honorable place amongst civilized and Christian nations.

The next object of interest on this coast, and about six miles distant from Navarino, is Modon,—a fortress built upon a point of land projecting into the sea. This is regarded as the strongest place in Greece, and is kept in repair, and garrisoned by a considerable body of Greek troops. The town, as usual, consists of some ten or twelve hovels, at no great distance from the walls. Opposite Modon is the bare and rocky island of Sapienza, which extends several miles south ward,—forming a sound, one or two miles broad Near this is the smaller isle of St. Marie, and at a little distance farther south is Cabrera,—more forbidding and desolate in its appearance than the other two, and apparently nearly as extensive as Sapienza. The channel between these islands and the main-land is sheltered from most winds, and may be, I should think, good anchorage. It is exposed, however, to the Sirocco. These islands are bare mountains, with only here and there a thin soil. The mountains upon the opposite coast are of the same description,—bare of trees—of the color of ashes—more precipitous and much more lofty. The whole region bids defiance to culture.

Our passage by Cape Gallo, and across the bay of Coron—the ancient bay of Messenia—was rough and uncomfortable. The bay, measured from Cape Gallo to Cape Matapan, may be twenty-five miles wide. It is quite unsheltered, and the wind and the waves filled it with agitation. Cape Matapan as the most southern land of the continent of Europe, is a point of intense interest, though it presents nothing remarkable to the voyager. The coast maintains its character of cheerless sterility. It is here, as along the rest of our voyage, composed of high and bare rocks, without vegetation or a single tree. We passed in the night from Cape Matapan to Cape St. Angelo,—more than thirty miles across the bay of Kolokythia, the ancient bay of Laconia; so that I missed what I much desired to see, Cerigo, the last of the Ionian islands. We passed it about 1 A. M.; and at daybreak, when I went upon deck, we had doubled Cape St, Angelo, and were steaming northward, with a fair wind and a smooth sea.

Nov. 26th. I have seldom seen a more lovely day than this. All the angry clouds which had covered the sky since our departure from Corfu, and even after the return of sunshine had lingered in the horizon in a very suspicious manner, had disappeared. The atmosphere was mild and soft—balmy would not be an inapt epithet,—and the sky was bright and clear beyond anything I had seen in Europe, out of Italy. We sailed along the bay of Nauplia, the ancient Argos, at the rate of eight miles the hour—wonderful speed for an Austrian steam-boat. All the passengers were now, for the first time, able to keep the deck, and the whole scene was one of unmingled pleasure. The satisfaction of the present was heightened by contrast with previous discomfort and peril, and by a lively anticipation of what was before us. We were now approaching the end of our voyage, and the most interesting portion of Greece was near us. Argos and Mycenæ were at the head of the bay; and just beyond it, in full view, was Hydra, which has earned a reputation worthy of the best days of Athens, by its devotion and sacrifices in the cause of Grecian liberty. We passed within four or five miles of Spezzia, but saw nothing but sterile rocks. The town, which contains four thousand inhabitants, and has some maritime prosperity, was hidden from us by an interesting height.

We passed near Hydra, and had a good view of the island and the town. Nothing can be more cheerless and absolutely forbidding than the whole aspect of this place. It consists of a high mountain, absolutely a bare rock, without a tree or shrub. Not a field nor a garden cheers this desolate waste. It is said that there is not upon the whole island enough earth to form a grave. The harbor even, the only boon which nature has conferred upon this doomed spot, is insecure, and, to a great extent, artificial; and in the days of their commercial and maritime greatness, the Hydriots were compelled, when certain winds prevailed, to find a shelter for their ships behind some rocky islands in the neighborhood.

The only thing that recommended this spot was the security it afforded against Turkish oppression. Animated by a noble love of liberty, these brave men built a city upon its rocky shore, that soon rose to great commercial importance. They were all merchants and mariners, and grew rich by the carrying trade. They had, before the Revolution, a city built of granite and marble—a population of four thousand—and four hundred ships. These, with all their wealth, were consumed in the struggle, though the town was never sacked,—secured by its position from the common fate of Greece. The houses are now mostly empty. Five thousand are all that remain of this gallant people. They are no longer rich; they subsist barely by maritime enterprise, but their trade has mostly disappeared. The Hydriot was the chief instrument in securing Grecian independence. They furnished the most distinguished naval commanders. Their fire-ships were the terror of the Turkish fleet, and their successes revived the spirit and hopes of the people when depressed by disasters.

The remnant of the people deserve well of the nation. Their city, with so few natural advantages, and in the absence of the adventitious circumstances that raised it to such a height of prosperity, is probably destined to still further decline. The towns of continental Greece, with the advantages of better harbors and of a back country susceptible of agricultural improvement, present superior attractions to emigrants from abroad, and have even drawn a large majority of the Hydriots from their barren rocks, to become inhabitants of more favored regions. Many of them are said to have taken up their residence in Syra, which possesses great commercial advantages.

CHAPTER III.

BAY OF EGINA.

HAVING passed Hydra and Cape Skyllo, which is nearly opposite to it upon the coast of the Morea, we had a fine view of the bay of Egina, its islands, and the surrounding coast. I was quite unprepared to see so noble a sheet of water. It is much more extensive than the bay of Naples, being, I should think, not less than sixty or seventy miles in compass. It wants, too, the noble city, as well as the smaller towns that rise on all sides of the latter, and make it the most enchanting and magnificent locality in Europe, or probably in the world. Yet if any part of the world is worthy to be compared with this, it is the gulf of Egina, and I cannot but think there are some features of striking resemblance, though my companions, to whom I pointed out this likeness, could not discern it, or at least did not feel it as vividly as I did.

To my view the promontory of Sunium and of Cape Skyllo answered well to Sorento and the opposite headland that form the entrance to the bay of Naples, while the islands of St. George, Zea, and Hydra, are similar enough in their situation and appearance to Capri d'Ischia to constitute a very decided likeness to the entrance of the bay of Naples, when seen from within; and then the lofty ridges of Hymettus, and the other mountains which reach from Cape Sunium to Athens, and those again that constitute the island of Salamis and its magnificent background, as seen by one approaching the Piræus, form a scene of beauty and even of impressive grandeur which lacks nothing but Vesuvius, with its eternal cloud of smoke, to make it equal to any other scene of loveliness and sublimity upon which my eye has rested.

The Acropolis was in full view at least twenty-five miles from the shore, and by the aid of telescopes we were able, in this transparent atmosphere, to discern the splendid temples and ruins that crown this classic mount, and even to distinguish and determine accurately the different objects, from their resemblance to the engravings with which we were familiar. The city, rising from its ruins, soon becomes visible, as did the beautiful plain of Attica, which extends from the sea to the city, and stretches away for many miles to the north and the north-east, till it meets the lofty mountains by which it is bounded. It was a glorious view, and I have seldom been able to look upon a scene so famous in the history of the world, with a feeling so unmingled with disappointment—with a satisfaction so perfectly sustained.

Nature, I could not but feel, has here prepared a worthy theatre for the creations of genius and the achievements of heroic patriotism. A more intimate acquaintance with Athens, and a careful observation of its topography, have fully sustained these first impressions. There is nowhere else such a multitude of commanding positions. Every important edifice commanded some large, magnificent prospect. The site of the greater part of the ancient as well as the modern towns is sufficiently level, yet it comprehends several lofty hills, rising abruptly or more gradually into heights of various but considerable altitudes, overlooking each other, the city and the plain of Attica, and commanding all of them the most enchanting view of the mountains, the gulf, and the archipelago, with several of its islands.

The Acropolis rises precipitously near the centre of the old city, to the height of, I should think, two hundred feet. It of course overlooks all the other parts of the town; and the glorious structures with which it is crowned are visible at great distances to those who approach the city by sea or land. Mars Hill is only a little less elevated, and commands on all sides, except that towards the citadel, a view hardly less extensive and delightful. The Pnyx, the hill upon which the assemblies of the people met and consulted in the open air, is nearly of the same height. The eye of the orator who spoke from the tribune looked down upon the city which was spread out before him like a map. The Acropolis, with all its splendid structures, was in full view to the right. A little to the left, also in full view, rose upon lower ground the temple of Theseus the founder of the city, which, after a lapse of two thousand four hundred years, is the most perfect and complete structure that bears testimony to the genius of the ancients.

It is obvious that the position of the Athenian forum was chosen for effect, and not accidentally. The tribune from which the orator spoke, is said formerly to have commanded a view of the ports of Salamis and the whole gulf of Egina, as well as the range of magnificent objects above enumerated. Themistocles was wont to point to the fleets, and to the theatre of the naval glory of his countrymen, in order to inspire them with additional attachment for the maritime service, which he regarded as the means of warfare best suited to the Athenians.

The Thirty Tyrants, by removing the Bema nearer to the Agora, and a little farther down the hill, effectually concealed those inspiring objects from the view both of the speaker and the people. This was done in order to repress the ardor of the people for high enterprises, and with this for freedom. About twenty or thirty yards in the rear of the pulpit of Demosthenes there are steps cut in the rock, and other appearances to justify the opinion that *that* was the post of the orator before the days of the Tyrants.

From that spot, all the objects above enumerated—maritime and inland—as well as the more distant mountains which nature had reared up like walls for the ornament and security of Attica, were in view of the orator when he harangued the Athenians to resistance and to daring enterprises. A situation more favorable to high displays of oratory and to powerful effects, certainly never existed; and one is less surprised at the superior efficiency of Athenian eloquence after standing upon the platform where Demosthenes pronounced his masterly harangues, and viewing the inspiring objects that offered their powerful aid in exciting and controlling the passions of the most intelligent and mercurial people who ever listened to the voice of an orator.

The sites of all the public buildings, theatres, temples, and schools, were chosen with the same good taste and philosophical view to effect. It should be stated that the pulpit of Demosthenes was not one of those boxes bearing the name in our days, but a broad platform of solid rock, ascended by three or four steps. It was nearly thirty feet long and twenty wide, with nothing before the speaker, who was fully exposed to the audience, and had ample room to walk to and fro, and indulge in the vehement action which we know characterized Grecian eloquence.

The Apostle Paul seems to have availed himself of the favorable local circumstances that the elevated position of the Areopagus supplied, in his discourse to the curious Athenians. I have already said that this hill was nearly as high as the Acropolis—not less, I should think, than two hundred feet above the bed of the Ilissus. It, too, is a rock, rising abruptly on all sides but the western. It is ascended by a flight of steps cut out of the solid stone. The top, too, has been levelled by the chisel, and presents an extensive surface, capable of accommodating a large assembly. There are seats also on a part of the rock, which are supposed, no doubt correctly, to have been occupied by the judges.

It was in the middle of this noble area that the

PAUL PREACHING AT ATHENS.

Apostle stood, when he, with so much courage and skill, reproved the Athenians for their idolatry, and preached to them the Unknown God, who made the world and all things, and dwelleth not in temples made by hands. From the position where the Apostle then stood, he had all the principal temples of Athens in full view before him, including certainly the most perfect and sumptuous structures ever reared for religious worship. The evidence of their superstition was clear and conclusive, and not to be contradicted by those whose eyes rested upon the Partheon, the Theseion, and all the minor temples of the Acropolis and the Agora.

The Academy of Plato, about two miles north of the city, upon the plain of Attica, combined with the seclusion and stillness most congenial to study and meditation, an enchanting view of the most beautiful and sublime scenery. It is within a quarter of a mile of two little hills of similar shape and elevation. It was by these hills, compared by an ancient writer to the breasts of a woman, that the site of the academy was ascertained, as no monument or ruins remained to attest it. Many fragments of sculpture, and, I believe, some inscriptions, have since been found in excavating for building and in agriculture. The ground is now occupied by a vineyard and a country seat.

CHAPTER IV.

ANTIQUITIES OF ATHENS.

THE Theseion, a temple dedicated to Theseus, built in the age of Cimon, is the best preserved of all the ancient edifices of Athens. It is certainly the finest specimen of architecture that I have seen. This edifice has suffered little from the lapse of centuries. All its columns are standing. The *cella* has apparently undergone some repairs, and a portion of it near the eastern front is covered with stucco. The ornaments of the frieze are mostly gone, though some very fine sculptured figures, having reference to the achievements of Hercules, still remain. They increase our regret for what is irrevocably lost.

This temple has fourteen beautiful Ionic columns on each side, and six on each front. Two also stand at each of the doors or entrances into the interior of the temple, of which the eastern front had one, and the western another. The whole number of columns is forty-two. The present roof of the temple is modern. There was none originally, though it is believed an awning was sometimes used as a substitute. The site is upon a hill which quite overlooks the city, though of less elevation than the Areopagus and the Pnyx.

The materials are the fine white marble of Mount Pentilecus, of which all the public buildings of Athens were composed. The quarry, which is still worked, is about ten miles from the city. The columns of this temple no longer shine with their original snowy whiteness. Twenty-two centuries have imparted to them a rich autumnal hue, inimitable by the painter, in harmony with the serious but agreeable reflections which this venerable historical monument is so well calculated to excite. The Theseion is now a Greek church, though not used for the ordinary purposes of worship.

At no great distance from this edifice, to the east, and in the heart of the modern city, stand several pillars in good preservation, surmounted by a portion of the ancient architrave. This is presumed to be the remains of an ancient temple, but to whom dedicated is not well ascertained. It has been thought to have been erected under the Roman sway, in honor perhaps of one of the emperors.

A little farther in the same direction, enclosing in part the present bazar, is a massive ancient wall, evidently a part of a quadrangle. The northern side is nearly perfect. It is, I should conjecture, for I had not an opportunity of measuring it, at least a thousand feet in length and from twenty to thirty feet in height. A part of the western front also remains, which seems to have been the principal one, and to have contained the principal entrance. It is still adorned with eleven

Doric columns, several of them in good preservation. The whole is built in the most substantial manner, of large blocks of hewn stone, and if it shall not be demolished by man, may exist for thousands of years to come. It is thought to have formed a part of the ancient Agora, or market-place, for which it is still used. It reminded me strongly of the massive wall in Rome, known as the forum of Nerva.

TOWER OF THE WINDS.

Still farther east is a small octagonal building in good preservation, called the Tower of the Winds. Upon its eight faces are so many emblematical figures, representing the various winds which are most frequent in Attica. Those figures flying through the air —horizontal nearly in their position—express both by their visages and habiliments, the peculiar character of their several winds. Those which represent warm and genial breezes, are unclad, and have a mild expression of countenance. The embodied representations of damp and chilling blasts are robed in winter vestments, and have a stern and ferocious expression. The conception of the whole, as well as the execution, is exquisitely beautiful. This fabric was surmounted by a Triton, moveable upon a pivot to indicate the direction of the wind. It served also as a sun-dial. By it many persons still regulate their time-pieces.

Finally, there are some remains of a Clepsydra, or water-clock, which kept the time in cloudy weather. A part of the aqueduct which conducted a stream of water to move this machine, is still entire. It approaches to within a few feet of the town. The construction of this curious chronometer is not known, but the most able antiquaries agree in believing that the remains under consideration belong to such a machine. Altogether, this structure is one of the most curious and interesting remains of ancient art.

THE LANTERN OF DEMOSTHENES.

The Lantern of Demosthenes is near the north-east part of the Acropolis. This is a beautiful structure in marble, with finely sculptured ornaments in the frieze. Its figure is, I think, hexagonal, with a graceful Ionic pillar at each angle, projecting in high relief from the *cella*. It is hardly more than ten feet in diameter, and it is now generally admitted that it was formerly surmounted with a tripod in honor of those who had excelled in the performances of the theatre.

An ancient street, called the Street of the Tripods, extended from this beautiful edifice over very precipitous ground, along the base, or rather upon the eastern side of the Acropolis, to the theatre of Bacchus. This whole street was occupied by splendid trophies of their theatrical victories, which gave it the name. Two only remain beside the Lantern of Demosthenes. These are two simple marble pillars, which stand upon a high cliff that overhangs the theatre.

They were formerly surmounted by tripods, as is known by an inscription found upon the spot. Upon the same cliff, by the side of these columns, stands a curious sun-dial, made of a large block of marble—its southern surface concave—upon which are drawn the lines that mark the hours of the day. This was visible to the people in the theatre, and was doubtless for their accommodation.

The theatre of Bacchus is excavated in this side of the Acropolis, almost immediately below the Parthenon. It is semi-circular, of immense extent—the arc toward the Acropolis, and hewn out of the solid rock—the chord upon the declivity of the hill toward the Ilissus. This lower side was supported by an immense wall of large blocks of hewn stone, many of which are still in their places. The seats rose amphitheatrically upon the side of the hill, one above another to a great elevation. The greater part of these is covered with a mass of rubbish. Some of the highest seats have been disinterred. These are cut in the solid rock.

This, as well as the other Grecian theatres, was without a roof, the exhibitions being in the open air. It commands a grand view of Hymettus, the sea, and several of the interesting localities, calculated to have an inspiring influence upon the audience as well as the performers, an object of which these people never lost sight in choosing the sites of their public assemblies. The theatre of Bacchus was capable of seating at least from ten to twenty thousand people. It is difficult to conceive how a speaker in the open air could make himself heard by the vast multitudes who assembled here, and in the place of public meetings upon the Pnyx. The climate is certainly very favorable. This pure atmosphere transmits sound admirably, and I am sure that a man may be heard, as well as seen, distinctly much farther than under more troubled skies.

The Odeium of Regilla is a Roman theatre, also high up the side of the Acropolis, and commanding, like that of Bacchus, a magnificent view of land and sea. It is very large, though of less extent than the other. Very large remains of the walls are extant. The entrance looks to the north-east, where the arches rising upon arches remind one of the Flavian amphitheatre at Rome. This structure is of a comparatively modern era, and it never was, like the theatre of Bacchus, associated with the public business as well as the amusements of the Athenians. Many of the marble seats of this theatre are still in their place, and the workmanship is substantial. It was built by Herodes Atticus, and named in honor of his wife.

THE TEMPLE OF JUPITER OLYMPIUS.

This temple is east of the city, near the Ilissus. This was unquestionably the largest and most sumptuous of Greek temples,—it was perhaps the largest in the world. Begun in the early ages of Greece, it was several centuries in building. The emperor Adrian completed it. Nothing remains but the immense platform upon which the vast edifice was reared, and sixteen splendid Corinthian columns, which still bear testimony to its grandeur. They are about sixty feet in height and twenty in circumference, all of Pentelic marble.* A portion of the architrave still rests upon these pillars. It consists of massive blocks of marble, which lead us to admire the skill that raised them so high, when, if the conjectures of many learned men are correct, little was known of those contrivances by which human strength is now aided in accomplishing such works. Upon a portion of this architrave is a cell, built of brick, in which it is said a hermit spent many years of his life, having his food brought to him by means of a ladder of ropes. He remained for six years in this aërial habitation without descending. The foundation of this temple covers several acres.

* Thomas Bellot, F.R.C.S.E., Surgeon of the Royal Navy, gives the following account of the fall of one of these pillars, a catastrophe of which he was an eye witness:—"On the night of the 26th of October, 1852, the centre pillar of the three, which formed a part of the inner south peristyle of the Temple of Jupiter Olympius, was thrown down by the gale from the south-east. The column fell due north, and lies prostrate, the drums (the sections of the shaft) preserving nearly their relative positions, though separated. The fallen pieces lie horizontally, and nearly touch each other, like bricks arranged to knock each other down in their fall. The upper half of the capital, with its Corinthian volutes, is completely capsized. The square marble base of the column rested upon two square courses of coarse limestone, two feet thick each course. The soil or earth giving way under the north side of the pillar, the course broke across from east to west, and when the column was inclined at a certain angle, the second drum or section slipped off the first or lowest, carrying with it all the upper column in one piece. The column fell at a right angle to the long diameter of the temple, which lies east and west. The drums were each connected by two small iron bars, five inches long and an inch and a half square, fitted with lead into the marble, so as to prevent the oxidation of the iron discoloring the marble. These bars are either drawn from their sockets or broken across. The pillar is capable of being re-erected."

It must have been the most expensive of ancient temples.

The columns are the most magnificent I have seen. It is believed that there were at least one hundred and sixty, — many more according to some antiquaries. Enough does not remain to furnish a full plan of the original edifice, though no doubt is left that it was the principal work of the kind in Greece. Some very large remains of the terrace which supported the foundation of this temple upon the south, are still to be seen. This wall is constructed of large blocks of hewn stone, and has an elevation of nearly twenty feet in the highest part. This was demanded by the nature of the ground, which here declines very rapidly towards the Ilissus.

This ancient river is now dry. Its bed lies along the base of Mount Hymettus—is rocky, and in some places precipitous. During my stay in Greece it had no water. It makes some figure in the Greek writers, though it was only an inconsiderable rivulet, serving the ancient city for a variety of useful purposes. It flowed close to the walls of the city. It was probably a perennial stream, though it is said to have forsaken its channel at times to pursue a subterranean course. Now it is dry for eight months in the year.

THE STADIUM.

The stadium, the place for gymnastic exercises, was situated less than half a mile from the temple of Jupiter Olympius, higher up the Ilissus, and on the oppo-

3

site side. A stone bridge, of which there are ample remains, gave access to it from the city. This stadium is excavated from the lower declivity of Mount Hymettus. It is of an oblong form, and of great extent, capable of holding all the citizens of Athens when its population was greatest. Nothing remains but the excavated area,—the seats and other apartments having long since disappeared. It was an amphitheatre; and rising from the centre, which was the arena devoted to the wrestlers, were the seats for the spectators, one above another for a great distance up the inclined sides which were formed by excavating the hill.

By a careless observer this area might be mistaken for a small valley formed by the hand of nature. Its perfect regularity of form, however, demonstrates that it was wrought by human skill. The notices of ancient writers leave no doubt that it is the Stadium. Under the Roman dominion, it was devoted to the contests of gladiators. The Greeks, it is believed, never encouraged this species of amusement, and none of their public places seem to have been constructed for this purpose. Nothing gives us so unfavorable an opinion of the Roman character as their fondness for these bloody exhibitions. A people who could relish such amusements must, no doubt, have been essentially defective in the finer sensibilities of our nature, or grievously demoralized by long familiarity with scenes of violence and crime.

The Lyceum was situated about half a mile farther up the Ilissus, in a retired and quiet spot near the city, and yet sufficiently remote from its tumults to favor study and contemplation. There the ingenuous youth of Athens resorted, to imbibe the lessons of wisdom and virtue to which this classic spot was consecrated. Some gardens and a field of wheat now occupy the level spot, which antiquarians agree in assigning to the groves of the Lyceum. Not a tree remains. No vestige of the structures which adorned this haunt of the Athenian philosophers—none of the splendid fountains and statuary which lent their attractions to the scene—have escaped the ravages of time and the cupidity of collectors.

The Lyceum is nearly east of the city, much nearer than the Academy; but its situation is less conspicuous and commanding, and not less favorable to contemplative retirement. None of the interesting localities of Athens have at present less to distinguish them from the surrounding region in which they are nearly lost, than these two celebrated spots. Probably they never contained any considerable structures. The groves, under whose shades the lessons of wisdom were uttered—some seats, to diminish the fatigues of study, with the fountains and statues, always to be found in the gardens and promenades of the Greeks as well as the Romans,—were composed of such materials as could easily be removed and converted to other purposes. This may account for the want of all such remains as might have been expected to fix their localities with a degree of certainty that should be entirely satisfactory to the curious inquirer.

Fortunately, these sites are surrounded by some of those permanent natural objects which remain when the works of man are obliterated. By them we are guided to the interesting places where Socrates and Plato instructed the youth of Athens in the lessons of an enlarged and humanizing philosophy. It is in the midst of associations like these that the calmest mind is allowed to become imaginative, and finds it easy to recall and re-people scenes that have been consecrated by the highest examples of wisdom and virtue.

THE PARTHENON.

CHAPTER V.

ANTIQUITIES OF ATHENS.

THE Acropolis contains upon its summit some of the finest antiquities of Athens and the world.

The Propylæ stands at the only entrance of this fortress. It is, as its name indicates, the gateway through which access is had to the interior. This beautiful structure stands upon the upper part of the steep declivity on the western side of the mount. It is composed of magnificent Doric columns of Pentelic marble. Twenty-one are now standing. This colonnade has two fronts,—one towards the Pnyx and the Areopagus, which was seen by those who ascended to the citadel,—the other towards the interior. They are similar in appearance—each consisting of six columns, surmounted by an architrave and frieze, which was formerly richly ornamented with sculpture. Another row of six columns stands between the eastern and western fronts. The whole number of columns was sixty. Of these, thirty-nine are now standing, surmounted for the most part by the architrave.

The splendid sculptured ornaments of the frieze—

the *chef d'œuvre* of Phidias, and the peculiar glory of this temple,—have been for the most part removed. Some of the figures are lying mutilated upon the ground, but a large part of them were carried by Lord Elgin to England, where, under the name of the Elgin marbles, they constitute the most precious treasure of the British Museum. Lord Elgin was for a while regarded as a patron of the arts, and a public benefactor. This opinion has been reversed, and perhaps no man has been the object of more frequent and bitter reproaches. It is difficult not to confirm the sentence of condemnation.

Every one who looks upon the mutilated façade of the Parthenon must desire strongly to see these dilapidations restored so far as may yet be possible. The feeling may not have been so strong while the Turkish power continued; but now that Greece has become an independent Christian state, and increasing numbers of scholars are annually visiting its classic remains, a more deep and pervading indignation will be felt towards the spoiler of this noblest monument of genius; and the British nation, by retaining what was so unjustly and sacrilegiously taken from its rightful possessors, will be regarded as participators in the crime.

The sculpture of the frieze that rests upon the interior range of pillars belonging to the western front, is nearly entire, and most admirable. Nothing can exceed the truth and spirit of the figures; and the finish is exquisite. How careful must this great artist have been of his reputation! These ornaments were made to be elevated more than forty feet from the earth, where the perfection of their finish cannot be appreciated, and where small defects must be concealed. Still, every part is finished with the most laborious and accurate attention. The utmost care was bestowed upon beauties which, in their original situation, must have remained wholly undiscovered. Nothing which has since been produced by the chisel gives us so high an idea of the power of sculpture as these fragments of Phidias.

The light and chaste proportions of this temple, which can yet be fully appreciated, though a part has fallen, fill the mind with lively admiration. One becomes dissatisfied with all inferior creations of the architect. The choicest remains of Rome are heavy and lifeless. The beautiful Madelaine of Paris, an avowed copy, is felt to be a bungling imitation of what human genius seems destined never to equal. In this department of art, Athens, to the present day, stands unrivalled. The Parthenon is the crown of the Acropolis. It is the first object seen in approaching Athens, whether by land or sea, and the view to be had from its summit is one of the most beautiful and interesting in the world.

There are two other temples upon the Acropolis. Anciently there were several more, of which no vestige now remains. The Erechtheium is an unique edifice, having three fronts, through which entrance was had into as many separate parts of this edifice, each dedicated to a separate divinity, and constituting in effect three temples. This structure is in the Ionic style, of which fourteen beautiful columns are standing.* They perfectly satisfy all that the mind is able to conceive of chasteness and beautiful proportion. Their slender, inimitable form, contrasts admirably with the massive Doric pillars of the Parthenon, which we have just left.

The main body of this edifice is about ninety feet in length. One of the fronts, south, is adorned with beautiful caryatides instead of columns, which have been the admiration of all visitors. One of these, too, has been rifled to adorn a British collection.

Another small temple stands to the right of the front of the Propylæ in entering the Acropolis. It was dedicated to the wingless Victory, a beautiful conception of the Athenian mythology, according to which the favors of the fickle goddess were to remain forever with the favorites of Minerva. This temple was for several ages entirely lost, but the present intelligent antiquary, who is fortunately intrusted with the care of the precious monuments of art in Athens and the vicinity, has succeeded in discovering its scattered parts, and is reconstructing one of the most agreeable and delicate of the ancient edifices of this wonderful place. It is of the Ionic order, and has

* Two of these columns were blown down and broken in pieces by the violent hurricane which devastated Athens on the night of the 26th of October, 1852. The two beautiful cypresses, one by the Tower of the Winds, the other by the mosque in the Agora, also fell; one of them snapped in two, ten feet from the ground. There was also immense damage done to the Palace-garden, where all the large trees were blown down, and the interior of the Palace greatly injured on the south side.

seven of the eight original columns standing. The *cella* is hardly more than fifteen or twenty feet in length. The site is commanding. It was placed in front of the Parthenon, but from its inferior size, does not hide or obstruct the view of that magnificent edifice.

The other ancient structures, of which remains more or less perfect have come down to us, are less important and striking than those above enumerated. Northwest of the Acropolis, and distant about half a mile, is a high hill called Museium. This is surmounted by a monument in honor of Philopappus. It is of white marble, and there are yet some remains of the statues of which a considerable number once adorned it. This structure faces the Acropolis, and is about forty feet in height.

The large arena of the Pnyx, designed for the public assemblies of the Athenians, rests at its lower side upon a remarkable terrace. It is of Cyclopian architecture, constructed of enormous polygonal stones, laid without cement. It is certainly a work of the earliest days of the republic. This vast area is excavated upon its upper side out of the rock, to the depth of nearly twenty feet.

The Pulpit of Demosthenes is excavated in the same rock, as well as the steps by which it is approached on the side of the area, and those also which form the ascent from this platform to the higher parts of the hill, rising immediately behind the orator, where it is believed stood the old tribune which commanded a view of the sea and the ports. The circular area of the Pnyx which was thus prepared by this huge Cyclopian wall, and by excavations for the meetings of the people, is of great extent, capable of holding at least a thousand. There is no appearance of seats, nor is it likely that any such conveniences were provided for the multitude.

CHAPTER VI.

THE ACROPOLIS.

THE walls of the Acropolis, which enclose so many precious monuments of antiquity, are themselves well worthy of attention. Parts of them are very ancient, and of great historical interest. They are the work of different ages and races. The most ancient portion is the Pelasgic wall on the northern side of the citadel. It is thought to have an antiquity corresponding with the residence of those people in Greece—an era if not strictly fabulous, remote and obscure. This wall is of the Cyclopian style, and is the only specimen of this massive species of architecture in Athens. Farther east upon the same side of the citadel, is a portion of the wall built immediately after the retreat of the army of Xerxes. It bears evidence of the haste with which the Athenians reconstructed their fortifications, and affords a very interesting confirmation of a passage of Grecian history, which reflects the deepest disgrace upon Sparta. The jealousy with which that selfish and ambitious State always regarded Athens, was strikingly manifested at this time, when, under pretext that the citadel of the rival city, which was now only a heap of ruins, might afford a dangerous shelter for the enemy, in case of another invasion, and become a stronghold from which the Persian forces might sally forth for the conquest of Greece, it was secretly resolved to prevent the Athenians from rebuilding their ruined walls. Themistocles penetrated this base and wicked conspiracy against the liberty and independence of his country. He was ambassador to Sparta, and warned his country of the design of their jealous rival, at the same time urging them to labor day and night in rebuilding their fortress, whilst he with consummate address prevented the Spartans from taking any decisive measure till he had upon various pretences gained time enough for the completion of the new walls. He then boldly reproached them with their cowardly designs, and defied their power.

A portion of the wall which was built under these interesting circumstances, remains. Though solid and massive, the material is heterogeneous, and was manifestly taken from other buildings. Amongst them are many *frusta* of fluted marble columns, the remains, no doubt, of those superb temples which had been demolished by the barbarian enemy. These splendid fragments are apparently, for they are at a great height above the spectators, not less than four feet in diameter. One account says that Themistocles caused these fragments of the temples of the gods to be built into the wall, in order to inspire posterity with a lasting hatred against their sacrilegious invaders. The former seems to be the true history of this interesting section of the Acropolis.

Considerable portions of the present wall are ascribed

to Cimon. Finally, the Venetians and the Turks, and the modern Greeks, have each constructed a part,—exhibiting, as these successive masters of Greece do, whenever their works are seen in juxta-position, a lamentable proof of the progress in degradation and decline of the arts from the days of Themistocles to the present time. The havoc made of the splendid structures of the Acropolis by successive wars—the shells and fragments of shells which are dug up by the excavations, and left in all parts of this fortress,—are affecting proofs of the bloody vicissitudes of which this interesting spot has long been the theatre.*

* During the past year, most interesting excavations have been made at the Acropolis by M. Beulé, member of the School of Athens, at the expense of the French Government. An enormous breach was made in a wall built by the Turks, which hid the Propylæ. The earth which covered the bastions was also removed, and now, instead of a low door badly built, and placed in the side walls, a majestic entrance to the Acropolis is revealed, fronting on the Piræus and Salamis. The newly-discovered wall is of white marble, decorated with friezes and cornices, and complete, although the materials are defaced by time. Two towers defend the entrance, at the right and at the left; and in the middle is a Doric gateway, corresponding with the grand gateway of the Propylæ. It is from these that one can behold the grand plan of the monument of Mnesicles. The immense stair-case, which ascends to the summit of the Acropolis, and of which the last steps have been discovered, is seventy feet in height. The king of Greece has expressed the most lively satisfaction at the brilliant results of these efforts to reveal the glory of the ancient citadel of Athens. Before leaving Athens, M. Beulé had placed near the gate of the Acropolis a large slab of marble, on which is engraved a Greek inscription, of which the following is a translation:—"France has discovered the gate of the Acropolis, the walls, the tower, and the stair-case. 1853. Beulé."

The temple of the Eumenides is rather a work of nature than of art, though of great interest to the curious and intelligent traveller. It is under the south-eastern angle of the Areopagus. A fissure has been made in the lofty rock, apparently by some convulsion of nature. An immense mass is severed from the mount, from which it is removed fifteen or twenty feet at the base, while at the summit the distance is much less. This deep and gloomy chasm, sheltered by the overhanging rock, was the temple of the Eumenides. There is a fountain in the most interior part of this cavern, dry, it is said, in summer, but full, when I saw it, of a blackish, nearly stagnant water. There are some niches in the rock, designed, no doubt, for statues or votive offerings. It seems highly probable that this cavern, or temple, is nearly the same now as it was when seen by the ancient writers; and certainly no architectural erection could have been better adapted to the rites of a gloomy and terrible superstition. It is immediately below that part of the Areopagus which was occupied by that judicial assembly.

The Grotto of Pan is also a natural cavern in the north side of the hill of the Acropolis. Here, too, are several niches cut out of the living rock. In the eastern side of the Pnyx there are some chambers four or five yards long, by half that width and height. These are excavated from the rock, and are closed with doors. I know not upon what authority they are called the prisons of Socrates. It is currently said, that the philosopher was confined there by his capricious and ungrateful country. These cells would certainly be very secure, and not ill adapted otherwise to the purposes of a prison.

I have here enumerated all the antiquities of Athens, with the exception of a multitude of interesting fragments and inscriptions, to be seen in several collections, or in the walls of modern buildings, or finally in various localities, where they have been found in excavations for foundations or for building materials. Almost every house, however mean, has in its wall some fragment of marble, often exquisitely chiselled, and evidently a part of some ancient structure. One sees capitals, and fragments of beautiful pillars, lying half buried beneath heaps of rubbish, or built into the stair-cases or walls of modern houses, which have themselves become ruins by the violence of war, or the action of the elements upon their frail structures.

Nearly all the churches contain columns and other remains of ancient edifices. These precious relics of better days are arranged with an utter disregard to fitness and symmetry, which sufficiently shows that they are not indebted for their present situation in holy places to any lurking remains of taste for the arts, though a certain blind reverence for antiquity may have exerted some influence on the architects of these grotesque buildings. There are, it is said, three hundred churches in Athens. Not one has the slightest architectural pretensions. Most of them are without roofs,—many never had any, but are mere enclosures of loose stones with a kind of rude altar consecrated to the honor of some saint. Twelve or fifteen churches would be an ample supply for the population of Athens.

There is, however, no reference to utility in these constructions. It is deemed an act of piety to build a church or chapel. This is sometimes prescribed as a penance. They are often built upon the summits of hills and mountains, remote from the population and nearly inaccessible. Hundreds of these commonly wretched structures are seen in a journey through Greece, where public service is never celebrated, or at least only upon the fête-day of the saint to whom they are devoted. I was informed that the priests often direct persons, for particular delinquencies, to procure a certain number of masses, by way of expiation, to be performed in these solitary fanes. These chapels abound where the ruins of ancient edifices afford abundance of materials, without any other labor than that of piling them up in some rude way. At Lewctra, and some other places, nearly all the old materials have been in this way consecrated, though nothing appears but walls laid up in the clumsiest manner, having at one end of the enclosure two upright stones, often the fragments of pillars, surmounted by a slab of marble, by way of an altar. The peasants cross themselves as they pass, and as to the rest, sheep and goats enjoy free ingress and egress.

Of the celebrated Long Walls, sixty feet in height, connecting Athens with the sea, there are inconsiderable remains near the Piræus. They consist of large blocks of square stone, partly in their original positions and partly removed. These stupendous monuments of the enterprise and wealth of the Athenians seem to have been of the most solid construction, and we should be surprised at their disappearance but for the great facility afforded for removing the materials by the proximity of the sea.

CHAPTER VII.

MODERN ATHENS.

By a census which was completed just before I arrived in Athens, its population was found to be seventeen thousand. A number of these, perhaps a majority, are foreigners,—that is, not natives of the kingdom, but Greeks from Turkey and Asia Minor, and a good many Europeans. A large part of the scanty capital which is employed in building and trade, was brought in by these foreigners. The city has probably a larger population at present than at any period since the Turkish domination commenced. It has little regularity, convenience, or elegance in its plan, though in these respects it seems, judging from the ruins that remain, not to be inferior to the town which was destroyed in the late war. It is even said that ancient Athens, with all its splendor and wealth, was no better in this respect, the houses of private individuals being mean and the streets narrow and irregular. Those of the present city are excessively contracted, being hardly six or eight feet wide. They are not paved, and are extremely filthy. Still, there are several thoroughfares of better dimensions. More time will doubtless produce further improvements. Pavements will be made and rubbish removed.

Nine years since, there was not one habitable house in Athens. All had fallen a sacrifice to the violence of war. The people returned with the return of peace, poor and unsheltered, and it was out of the question to impose upon them an obligation to widen the streets and build eligible houses. That necessity which acknowledges no law pressed upon them with a severity hardly ever known. Beside, they were quite unaccustomed to the style of building which pervades in more wealthy and civilized countries. I apprehend the present town is more elegantly built than anything even in Greece, since the fall of the Byzantine empire. I thought Athens a very poor and unsightly collection of shabby habitations, but after I had made the tour of Greece it had the aspect of a well-built town. What is most to be regretted is, that the most populous part of the town covers a portion of the ancient city, which has never been excavated. It stands upon a bed of accumulated ruins from ten to fifteen or twenty feet thick, which is no doubt a rich mine of antiquities, which must forever be lost to the world, unless some terrible revolution shall again overspread this fatal land with new desolation.

The government has been much blamed for making Athens its capital, chiefly because it has rendered impossible those excavations which could hardly fail to enrich the world with many highly valuable discoveries. Some think that Nauplia, others that Corinth, Patras, or the Piræus, should have had the preference, as better suited to commerce, and as free from the strong objection I have just mentioned. Athens should have been left in its venerable ruins—a place of pilgrimage for the antiquary and the scholar. I do not think so unfavorably of the choice made by the government. I know not how far a government is at liberty to allow sentiment and classical enthusiasm to influence the decision of economical questions. The ground which it would have been most desirable to reserve for excavations is precisely that upon which the town destroyed by the war was built. Of course, it was private property which the government was not able to buy, and could not interfere with on other terms. The people here, as in other parts of the country, returned to their former homes, with affection for the sacred spot, hallowed by its having been the home of their fathers for thousands of years, and but the more dear to them for its calamities. Would it have been wise in the government to disregard this natural attachment, and to renew the attempt made two thousand years ago, to transplant the Athenians and lay the foundations of a new city? Corinth and Nauplia are decidedly unhealthy, whilst Athens is famed for the salubrity of its situation.

The rapid growth of this city I consider as sanctioning the choice made by the government. Multitudes have no doubt been attracted by its name and ancient renown, and the affluence of intelligent strangers will ensure a degree of wealth and a rapid advance in civilization and refinement much wanted by the country, which could not have been realized in any other locality.

A good road has been constructed to the Piræus, and a railway, which, as the ground is very favorable, could be made with little expense, would go far to remove the commercial objection. No one would ever wish that Edinburgh with its schools were removed from its present beautiful site, of which Athens strongly reminded me, to the more commodious trading position of Leith. Athens is now the only spot in Greece which exhibits any appearance of active prosperity. The residence of the court has much influence in producing this result, but its lovely, healthful situation, and its classical wealth and association, I think, have done much more, by the strong inducements they hold out to wealthy travellers and emigrants.

A stranger, in walking through some of the streets of this renovated capital, is struck with the great appearance of activity and business. The number of shops is very great in proportion to the size of the town. Several of the streets are much thronged, and a multitude of people are seen engaged in mechanical employments. More careful observation and more familiar acquaintance, however, show that this activity and bustle are greatly out of all proportion to the business done. Everything is done in the smallest way. There are no large stores, and very few considerable ones. Business that ought not to employ more than one or two persons, and that might be confined to a single shop, is subdivided amongst a dozen. Capitals are excessively small. Men being strangers to each other without mutual confidence, combinations in trade are impossible. Hence a multitude of small traders with little business upon the whole.

There is much of the parade and ostentation of business, with only the most trivial results. Two or three Pearl street merchants sell more than the whole of the craft in Athens. The stores and shops are all open in front, the whole being formed of moveable planks, and closed only at night. The goods of the merchant, as well as the work of the mechanic, are all exposed to view. The number of shoemakers and tailors is so large, that I presume they not only supply the demand of the town, but of the country where mechanics are scarce. Bakers are also numerous, but one sees very little manufactures of any sort beyond these three classes, who labor to supply immediate wants. Paper, leather, and other articles, the first with which a civilized and industrious country supplies itself, are imported.

I was struck with the number of coffee-houses and drinking and smoking establishments in this city. I know not how many there may be in the city, but I am sure that I have seen several hundreds of persons in these places of idle resort, in a walk of ten minutes after dark. They are seated around low tables, with a cup of coffee or a glass of spirits or wine before them, and the largest portion of them engaged in playing cards. They seemed to play for money—small sums, no doubt, as the coin upon the table was always copper. I could but fear that a very low state of morals prevailed. The common people are loud and quarrelsome. Their tones are angry and their gesticulations violent and alarming, but I never saw them strike, though I often expected serious results. In this they reminded me of the French populace, who storm and beat the air furiously, but always keep the fear of the police before their eyes. The industry of the country is greatly injured by the holy days of the church, which are, I believe, more numerous than they are amongst the Catholics. They agree, too, with the Catholics in paying more respect to their saints' days than to the Sabbath. The shops are open, and business proceeds as usual after the morning service in the churches, whilst upon a fête day a Greek cannot be induced to work. All the circumstances of intemperance which have fallen under my observation, have occurred on such occasions. I arrived in Athens the night before the commencement of Lent, when, during a period of forty days, the Greeks are prohibited the use of animal food—not of flesh merely, as the Catholics are, but also of butter, cheese, and eggs. The streets were thronged by riotous Bacchanalians, who were indemnifying themselves in advance for the privations of this holy season. Their songs and outcries resounded from street to street, and, though much fatigued, I was quite unable to sleep during the whole night.

CHAPTER VIII.

THE GREEK CHURCH.

I MADE many inquiries with regard to the Greek church and its influence over the people. The clergy derive their support from marriage, christening, burial, and other fees, and from the contributions of the people when these fees prove inadequate to their maintenance. Their whole income, from whatever source derived, is very inconsiderable. The management of ecclesiastical matters belongs chiefly to a synod composed of the principal clergy. The bishops, who belong to this body, have a stipend from the State. Others, as well as the inferior priesthood, receive nothing from the government, though this church is the established one. All religions are tolerated by the fundamental laws. The Greek clergy are said to possess little influence over the people, though there is a bigoted attachment to the church. The priesthood is chiefly of the lower orders, and badly educated. I heard anecdotes of them that went to show the prevalence of the most gross and shameful ignorance.

This sufficiently accounts for their want of influence. The people of all ranks, it is said, regard them in the discharge of their sacred functions at the altar, with the highest veneration, but personally and in the intercourse of life, they enjoy little consideration. They are not often seen in conversation with gentlemen in public places, but are manifestly left to associate with the lowest of the people. This one observes of the Catholic clergy in several countries in Europe devoted to that faith. The Catholic clergy, however, differ from the Greek in maintaining everywhere a decided influence over their flocks. It is not at the altar only that their power is felt. It is pre-eminent in political and other questions, and those who seek to act upon public opinion, are studious to secure the co-operation of this powerful body. In Greece, I could not perceive that the influence of the clergy was taken into the account in political questions. The liberals speak of it as insignificant, though, in general, unfriendly to their designs. Perhaps they undervalue it, and are too little solicitous to secure the aid of a numerous body of men, who, it seems to me, must always possess considerable weight in all questions in which they please to enlist, so long as they are regarded by the multitude as true ministers of Christ. The king has not, it seems, been inattentive to the clergy, whose favor he has, to a considerable extent, secured.

The doctrines of the Greek church find much more favor in the eyes of the Protestants than do the dogmas of the Catholics. No opposition has hitherto been raised in Greece against the circulation of the Scriptures, though the reading of them is not urged as a duty; nor is it deemed very essential to those who enjoy the privilege of attending on public worship, and

4

of learning their Christian duty from the mouth of the priesthood. From all I could learn, these instructions are at best of doubtful tendency. A gentleman who is well acquainted with this subject, and who takes a lively interest in all that is connected with the spread of piety, assured me that the preaching of the Greek clergy is little calculated to produce high moral results. It is almost wholly employed in the inculcation of the mere ceremonial of the church. It dwells upon the enormity of indulging in the use of flesh or eggs during the Fasts, when they are prohibited,—upon the efficacy of confession or of penance,—and a tedious *et cetera*,—which, to Protestants at least, must appear pitiful trifles. The clerical costume is a black cap and gown. The beard is worn long. As far as I had opportunity to observe, the priests are men of vulgar manners,—many of them are filthy in their dress and persons, and would be taken for men without much intelligence or education.

It would not be very hazardous to infer, from what I have said of the character of the teachers of religion, and of the dogmas upon which they lay the greatest stress, that public morals are deficient in elevation and purity. I, however, saw nothing to induce me to believe that the Greeks are essentially worse than their western neighbors. From certain vices, which flourish only in connection with luxury and great wealth, they are, of course, nearly exempt. Their females lead quiet and retired, and may we not hope exemplary lives?

The only theatre in Greece is still in an unfinished

state. Thus far, therefore, the country has been exempted from a most potent corrupting influence. The Greeks are commonly charged with dishonesty in their dealings, and with being, almost universally, liars. I am sorry to say that I saw nothing which induced me to question the correctness of this statement; and I much fear that this people are more deplorably deficient in integrity and veracity than any of the nations of western Europe. These are vices that are nurtured by oppression and servitude. The Greeks have been trained in this school for many generations. An age of liberty, if Providence shall deign to admit them to such a privilege, or even of a regular administration of tyranny,—of which they have some tolerable prospect, —may work a great change for the better in this respect. I saw more instances of drunkenness in Greece than I saw in France and Italy during a much longer residence. Compared with Americans, however, they must not be called intemperate. This is a vice that does not legitimately belong to their soft and genial climate. Robberies are still very common, and seem hardly to be regarded as crimes here. A Greek speaks of having followed this profession with perfect unconcern, and he finds employment as a laborer or a servant as readily as if he had been bred to peaceful avocations. This is one of the fruits of civil wars, which so long desolated the country. A generation must pass away before rapine and bloodshed will be viewed with merited detestation and horror.

Education receives the encouragement of the government, and the people manifest great eagerness to secure to their children the benefit of schools. The University of Otho, at Athens, has two hundred students in the several departments of study. Twenty-seven professors give lectures in the modern Greek language. A library of considerable extent has been secured, chiefly by donations from Europe; and collections in natural history are commenced. Six or seven of these professors are Germans—the rest are Greeks, who have had a European, mostly an Italian education. To diminish the expenses of the establishment, many of the professors hold other offices under the Government. Students are here from Macedonia, Asia Minor, and Constantinople.

More than two hundred attend the lectures, which are in modern Greek. I have heard several anecdotes of the sacrifices and poverty of the students, which indicate a degree of enterprise and stubborn purpose that would do honor to New-England. As yet, no suitable building has been provided to accommodate the University. The foundations of such an edifice have been laid, and an appeal made to the friends of Greece in Europe and the United States, for the means of completing it. Very liberal subscriptions have been obtained in Greece for the same purpose. The funds of the State are too much embarrassed to accomplish this important object. The University has a department for the instruction of teachers.

There are three hundred schools, of various grades, in different parts of Greece,—many, perhaps most of them, are on the Lancastrian plan. The school in Patras has three hundred scholars, and one in Argos has about that number. Every town and village is required to have a school. The Government aids in their support only when there exists an inability on the part of the people to provide for the necessary expense. The plan, though designed to be uniformly adopted, is, as yet, but partially carried out, as is obvious from the number of schools,—three hundred, in a population of eight hundred thousand, being a very inadequate supply.

A number of schools are sustained by contributions from abroad. That of the Rev. Mr. and Mrs. Hill, in Athens, is the most important. It has six hundred pupils of all ages, and of both sexes. Mrs. Hill has three or four assistants besides Greeks. She has pupils from Asia Minor and Constantinople. The school established by the Rev. Mr. Robertson in Syra, is now conducted by a missionary in the employment of the Church of England, and is said to be flourishing. Finally, the missionaries of the American Board of Commissioners for Foreign Missions have a prosperous school in Sparta—one of the most savage parts of Greece, where such an enterprise falls strictly within the proper sphere and character of missionary work. Many other schools are supported by the Greeks themselves, by voluntary contributions.

Upon the whole, the interests of education are highly appreciated, and have made a gratifying progress.*

* There are in Greece at this time (1854) three hundred and thirty-eight primary schools for boys, and forty-nine for girls, attended, the former by thirty-three thousand eight hundred and sixty-four boys, and the latter by six thousand three hundred and twenty-three

It is a circumstance of no small moment that the New Testament is the most common book in all the schools, native and foreign. The want of suitable books was a serious obstacle to the success of the first attempt in behalf of education. The liberality of individuals, but chiefly of the Bible Societies of England and America, has supplied this want in the best possible manner. The children of Greece are imbibing the pure truths of the gospel from the uncorrupt and living fountain. The blessing of God may make this the means of purifying the Church, and of introducing a pure and saving Christianity. The American Board of Foreign Missions has four missionaries here, laboring with a zeal and fidelity for which the agents of that society are everywhere proverbial. Two are stationed at Athens, whose chief business is the publication and distribution, by sale and donation, of Bibles and religious books. From this source the schools of Greece receive a large supply of valuable publications. This is, perhaps, the most hopeful of the influences that are now active for the regeneration of Greece. Dr. King, the pious and veteran missionary, also preaches to a

girls. There are eighty-six secondary ancient Greek schools, with one hundred and fifty-eight teachers, and four thousand three hundred and eighty-three pupils ; seven gymnasiums or superior schools, with forty professors, and one thousand and seventy-seven pupils ; and a university, with thirty-nine professors, and five hundred and ninety students. Besides these, there is a Normal school for the formation of schoolmasters, an ecclesiastical seminary, besides the faculty of theology, a polytechnic school, a school of agriculture, and other establishments necessary for instruction, such as the National Library, the Botanic Garden, the Astronomical Observatory, and the museums. The State expends yearly for public instruction, $701,573.

small Greek congregation. His excellent colleague, the Rev. Mr. Benjamin, is wholly employed in producing good books. No particular encouragement has as yet attended the preaching of the gospel to this people. Still, as the appointed and honored means established by Christ, it is entitled always to the first place amongst the agencies to be employed for the salvation of the heathen as well as Christian world. As yet, the circulation of books, including the Holy Scriptures, must be regarded only in the character of an experiment—an experiment indeed of high and sacred interest—yet but an experiment, which God may honor by imparting an efficiency commensurate with the vast extent to which it has been adopted by His people;—or he may dishonor and reject it, to manifest more fully the superior dignity and importance of the living ministry, which Christ has himself ordained. For this, the Church, nothing slothful in the great work which it has prayerfully begun, should yet be prepared.

I am not aware of the mode of action adopted by the missionary from the Baptist Board in the United States, stationed in Patras. I did not see him when in that city, not having been informed of his residence till at a subsequent period.

CHAPTER IX.

OTHO.

THE success of the means used for the moral elevation of this kingdom, is so dependent upon the government of the country, as to make the unpromising tendencies of King Otho's rule a subject of lively regret to those, who usually abstain from all participation in politics. There is in Greece a government and a liberal party,—the latter is almost universally favorable to the efforts made by American and English Christians to enlighten the people; the former is believed to be decidedly hostile to all such foreign interference.

The king, though absolute, is not sufficiently firm in his position to manifest active or open enmity. Perhaps he is unjustly suspected, and may yet prove a friend to measures, connected certainly with the best interests of his people.

It is well known that Otho was selected, when yet a boy, to be king of Greece, ostensibly that he might receive an education suited to his future position. A regency administered the government during his minority. Its blunders were gross—its oppressive measures bore hard upon the prosperity as well as the spirit of Greece. Still there was hope in the early assumption of the reins of government by the king. The people had been taught to expect the promulgation of a liberal constitution, and the establishment of a representative body by which their wishes might be heard and their wrongs redressed.

In the meantime, the young Otho, whose crown was held in abeyance till he should learn how to rule, drank in the principles of absolutism. His accession to power brought to the expectant Greeks no guaranties for liberty, nor even for security. They have clamored for representation to the present moment, but without success, and with some faltering of hope. They have succeeded in getting rid of the largest part of the mercenary Bavarian army, which the king, with an incredible fatuity, had brought for the security of his throne against the brave people, who had invited him to rule over them. But one Bavarian minister is left, though many are still engaged in the subordinate offices. These sacrifices have been made to allay the popular feeling, which was greatly excited by a policy that regarded the Greeks, who had just shaken off the Turkish yoke by prodigies of valor and incredible sacrifices, as a conquered race, and sought to make them an appendage to a third-rate German State.

The army of mercenaries has, however, been replaced by one of natives, ten thousand strong, the largest, in proportion to the population which supports it, known in the civilized world.

The taxes imposed under the Turkish rule have been variously and greatly increased, whilst the annoying and ruinous mode of collection remains unchanged. A revenue of fourteen millions of Drachmas, nearly two and a half millions of dollars, is paid by eight hundred thousand people, the poorest perhaps on the face of the earth, and inhabiting one of the most sterile regions of the globe—a people without manufactures, without trade, and nearly without agriculture. Two millions only result from duties levied on commerce. Twelve millions press upon the agriculture of the country. The tax is collected in kind, and amounts to a tythe of the products of the land. The produce of the worst land, of which a large part or the whole of the value has been expended in the culture, pays in the same proportion with that of the best, which has yielded the most abundant profits. The taxes are farmed, and the purchaser, who is his own collector, has a discretionary power, which he does not fail to abuse to the oppression of the poor peasant.

The grain is carried, before threshing, to a public floor, to prevent concealment or fraud. The farmer's tenth is then carried to the market, if not more than six leagues, by the peasant, who has also to carry home his own part of the wheat—his straw and chaff. Count also the loss in carrying wheat in the bundle on the backs of mules, for there are no roads, and some estimate may be formed of the oppression of this most barbarous and wicked system. It is from a treasure thus obtained, that the King takes a hundred and twenty millions of drachmas for his own expenses, and to build a splendid marble palace, expected to cost five millions of dollars. Since his accession, a tolerable road of about twenty-five or thirty miles has been made. Besides this, there is none in Greece upon which a cart can pass. There are no carriages except in Athens, Nauplia, and Argos. It was well said to me by an intelligent Greek gentleman, "The Bavarians have placed the huge saddle of a camel upon the back of a poor donkey." The people bear a system so intolerably oppressive, partly from fear of foreign interference should they resist—partly from a dread of anarchy, from which they have suffered evils even worse than those of tyranny—and partly from the hope of melioration, by the final introduction of representation, which they believe a press yet partially free, and the growing intelligence of the country, will finally extort from the ruling power without bloodshed.

In the meantime the king uses, and will use the means, which are always at hand, to fortify his power and silence opposition. He has offices to bestow; and the Greeks—the best of them—are too poor to resist such attacks upon their independence. The attractions of Court, few and poverty-stricken though they must be—have yet a seductive power over persons of a certain class, and are not without their influence upon the public mind. The progress, too, of time and events, along with a growing despair of realizing the bright anticipations of freedom which cheered the Greeks in the field of battle, will produce its sedative influences,—in some, a sullen indifference,—in others, an oblivious contentment,—in all, a growing indisposition to distrust a system of government which has the advantage of being established, and which gives a sort of security to person and property, without being utterly inconsistent with some degree of social and domestic enjoyment.

Some facts have come to my knowledge, which show that security for property is at best imperfect. When King Otho laid out the grounds preparatory to the erection of his palace, he paid no attention to private property. Amongst others, he appropriated the land of Mr. F——, an Englishman, and that of Mr. ——, a citizen of the United States; and this without consulting them—without having made them any compensation, though several years have since elapsed, and this act of justice has been repeatedly solicited at his hands. Such an act of lawless oppression would shake the throne of the sternest despot in civilized Europe. In Greece, where first principles are still to be settled, it only excites some complaints.

It must not be forgotten that the king of Greece has a most difficult part to perform. It is no easy thing to adapt a system of laws and administration to a people, degraded and demoralized by centuries of such oppression as Turkey has exercised over Greece. Men, long habituated to a government of caprice, violence and injustice, learn servility, disloyalty, treachery and cunning; and they should not be expected to adopt suddenly the practice, or even the semblance of the opposite virtues. Greece is essentially barbarized. She has not—she could not by any possibility possess the qualifications which fit a people for republican institutions. Great, and, in many instances, insuperable difficulties have been met with in attempting to replace the half-feudal, half-robber municipal regulations which prevailed under the Turkish rule, by a system borrowed chiefly from the French code.

The press is not legally free, but it is so in fact. The French system is adopted. A publisher must deposit a large sum of money to pay fines, if he shall incur such a penalty, and a responsible editor is answerable to the tribunals for all that appears in his paper. The affair is managed thus: a company having raised the money requisite for the deposit, some person who will endure imprisonment for moderate pay, commonly an indigent student, is announced as editor. The paper is conducted in a free and fearless spirit, canvassing public measures without restraint, only avoiding what may be personally offensive to the king. If trouble arises, the vicarious editor is ready to go to jail, where he can still pursue his studies, make some money, and fare better than he does elsewhere. It is said the office is rather coveted. An untrammelled press is a check upon an arbitrary government, and no doubt the best substitute for a representative assembly, to which I think it must ultimately lead, if its freedom be not stifled.

The people have been unfit to exercise the elective franchise, even in the humble sphere of village appointments; and the petty functionaries, upon whom they confer the power, seldom fail to practise the lessons of tyranny, peculation and bribery, which they learned from their old masters. I had these facts from a gentleman of great intelligence, familiar with the internal condition of Greece, and withal a liberal, who wishes the establishment of representative government. He deems it, however, as many of the best friends of the nation do, an evil only of less magnitude than the unenlightened despotism, which now presses like an incubus upon the country. Doubtless, many allowances are to be made for the young king, who has to choose between such evils. Birth and education have prepared him to lean towards absolutism. With all the good intentions which his friends claim for him, and which even his enemies concede, it is morally impossible that he should possess the requisite knowledge of the people, and of the condition of the country, to govern wisely. He has no means of becoming acquainted with the public wants—no experience which would enable him to adapt the measures of his government to the exigencies of a people, where everything is to be created *de novo*,—habits and character, as well as intentions.

Compelled to dismiss those counsellors upon whom he naturally relied, and who did not fail to demonstrate that, however hacknied in the state dogmas of European absolutism, they were unfit to make laws for Greece, he has selected others, who probably lack his confidence no less than that of the nation. This has thrown him upon his own very scanty resources. He is believed to originate all the measures of government himself, not because he is competent to legislate, but because his ministers are even less so. The odium of unpopular measures must hereafter rest upon the sovereign. He has lost one advantage by the dismissal of the Bavarians. Yet this act, which was certainly one of necessity, ought also to be regarded in the more favorable light of a sacrifice to the wishes or to the prejudices of his people.

The favor extended by the king to public education, is another bright feature in his policy. In some minor things, he seems not disinclined to conciliate the regards of his subjects. He has adopted their national costume. Though a Catholic, and of the most bigoted Catholic stock in Europe, he assists at the religious ceremonies of the Greek church on certain occasions. In more favorable circumstances, he would probably be neither worse nor better than his father, and other more absolute kings. He but follows their example in taxing the people to the full extent of their ability to pay, in improving the capital and neglecting the rest of his kingdom, and in providing for the gratification of his luxury and vanity, by the erection of a sumptuous palace, such as might have suited Louis XIV. or Catherine of Russia, together with several other edifices of great utility, but beyond the resources of the country.

CHAPTER X.

NATIONAL EXPENSES.

Of all the improvements desirable and possible in the system of government which now presses upon this unhappy country, the diminution of the taxes seems to me the most indispensable. How it can be effected it is difficult to conjecture. The public debt is considerable, and neither principal nor interest is paid. Yet the annual receipts of the treasury fall short of the expenditure by two millions of drachmas. The army is the most expensive part of the public establishment. The amount of the civil list, though much less considerable, is so disproportioned to the resources of the kingdom, that the grievance is even greater than the oppression. No retrenchment can be expected in this quarter. The maintenance of royal dignity and splendor is deemed doubly important when it has no basis of public affection and confidence. The same considerations will probably prevent any reduction of the army—the most enormous abuse under which Greece at present suffers. This army of a thousand men is equal, taking the population at eighty thousand, to one soldier to eighty inhabitants.

This army is independent of a considerable police force, which is indispensable, and of the national guards. The revenue at fourteen million drachmas, equals about three dollars per head, or fifteen dollars to each family. This is less than is paid in Great Britain and France, but taking into view the extreme poverty of Greece, it is a higher rate of taxation by far than is known in civilized Europe, and sufficient, I am confident, to prevent any considerable progress in wealth and civilization. It is in this view that I consider heavy taxes the worst part of the system of King Otho.

I have been disappointed in Greece. With regard to its historical and classic interest, and its ancient remains, my expectations have been more than realized. It is on these grounds, the precise region which an educated man would desire to see above any part of the world. It is with regard to its resources and present condition, that I had been misled by the numerous accounts of the country, which have been read with so much avidity in America since the revolt from Turkey. I think these accounts have generally been colored by a certain enthusiasm, natural enough, and perhaps allowable in the writers, but not very favorable to the purposes of such readers as seek for accurate information.

It would not be easy to give a stranger an adequate idea of the poverty of the country. In the first place, the whole kingdom contains only a little more than thirty thousand square miles, about as much as Virginia or Missouri. Of this area, three-fourths at least are composed of barren rocks, which are incapable of tillage. From Albania to Negropont, the whole sea-coast of Greece is encumbered with a continuous chain of rugged, bare mountains—literally naked rocks without trees or verdure, and perfectly destitute of soil. Within this mountain wall, which encompasses the whole kingdom, there are many fertile valleys and a few plains of a large extent. In several instances, the hills and the declivities of the mountains are susceptible of a laborious and expensive tillage by means of terraces.

The plain of Argos contains, it may be, fifty square miles of good land. The arable part of that of Lavidia is less extensive, but very productive in wheat, cotton, tobacco, and rice. Bœotia has a large region of excellent land—now, as it was anciently, the best part of Greece. The tracts of good land here enumerated, are always spoken of as the best as well as the most considerable in Greece. I travelled about three hundred miles in the interior, and, judging from what I saw, as well as from all I could learn from many intelligent residents in the country, I am persuaded that the arable land in the whole kingdom is not equal to half a dozen counties in the United States. More than that is under cultivation, but I speak of land suited to the plough, and of fertility to reward its labor. A multitude of little patches, tilled with the spade or hoe, are found in various situations. Corn or vines or olives are grown on terraces. Considerable portions of the interior mountain districts afford a scanty herbage, upon which flocks of sheep and goats are subsisted.

One-fourth part of the whole country—possibly a third, though I think not—possesses a measure of those facilities out of which a hardy and abstemious race of men, impelled by dire necessity, learn to force a meagre and barbarous subsistence. Greece, as is well known, imports a large part of its corn, as well as all the manufactures which it consumes. The exports, chiefly of currants, amount to two million drachmas. Whilst many parts of the country, little fitted for agriculture, are laboriously tilled for very scanty returns, scarcely one-half of the arable land is occupied. Two-thirds of the good land belong to the State. It was public property under the Turks, and was greatly increased by confiscations upon their exports from Greece.

A small part of this government land is tilled by tenants, who rent from the king; but for the most part it lies waste, overrun with thorns and brambles. The shepherds bring their flocks hither, when the exhaustion of the mountain ranges drives them to winter in the valleys. Cultivators prefer to rent the lands of private persons, who make advances of capital in the shape of seed-corn, implements, and stock. This the government does not do, and the lower rent at which its lands are offered do not compensate for the want of these facilities, in a country where the tenants are extremely poor.

A system has been adopted for the sale of the public lands, but hitherto it has had little success. The lands are offered at public auction to the highest bidder. The sum thus offered is payable in instalments of nine per cent. per annum for thirty years, when the land is granted in fee to the purchaser. Thus thirty years are necessary to perfect a title, which in most instances must devolve upon another generation. Few sales would be effected on such terms even in countries, where the credit and stability of the government are above suspicion.

One of the most striking features of Greece is its want of wood. I travelled twelve days in the Morea and Northern Greece, without seeing a single forest-tree, with the exception of half a dozen stunted ones from ten to twenty feet high in the island of Egina, and an old plane-tree at Delphos. On the thirteenth day I saw a few pines and planes near the Straits of Negropont. On the road thence to Athens, one every now and then sees a few bushes, and here and there a stunted tree. I was cheered with the sight of a score of venerable oaks on the northern declivity of Mount Pentelicus.

I was told that some parts of the North of Greece and the island of Negropont have a better supply of timber. With the exception of the oaks I have just mentioned, I did not see a single tree fit for the purposes of architecture and ship-building. Timber for these purposes is imported from Trieste. Much of the timber, it is said, as well as everything else of any value, was destroyed by the Turks. I presume it was very scarce before. A plentiful supply of fuel is obtained from the uncultivated lands, where there is a low growth of knotty, crooked bushes, which seem, however, to have no tendency to become trees. These are cut up, or rather dug up, by the peasants, and carried upon donkeys, often a great distance, to the villages and towns.

There is reason to believe that the mountains of Greece were once clothed with wood and verdure, at least to a much greater extent than now. The soil has been gradually borne away by rains and torrents into the valleys beneath, till nothing is left to afford nutriment to vegetation. This is no doubt partly the result and partly the cause of the disappearance of forest-trees. Another result has been the drying up of rivers and streams of water. One is perpetually passing over these dry beds, which are never full except after long rains. Many rivers and streams of classical and historical celebrity, and of great utility for economical purposes, no longer exist. Their dry and rocky channels alone remain, to bear testimony to the veracity of ancient geographers, and to the important physical changes which have no doubt largely contributed to increase the sterility of a country, which, however, could never have been extensively adapted to agricultural purposes.

I have spoken elsewhere of the scarcity of domestic animals, with the exception of sheep. When, in addition to the physical and actual condition of Greece, it is recollected that almost every species of moveable and visible property—houses, money, stock in trade, ships, and implements—were annihilated by the most desolating war which history records, some adequate notion may be formed of the extreme poverty of the kingdom, and of its inability to bear a rate of taxation which would be burthensome to a rich and advanced people. It seems absolutely incredible that the Greeks should be able, by any sacrifices, to satisfy the exorbitant demands of the tax-gatherer.

We may better understand this subject by a consideration of the domestic and economic habits of the people. If they lived as expensively as Americans, or even Europeans, not only could they not pay their taxes, but their sterile country could by no possibility support them. As it is, there is room for a considerable increase of population. I think the daily expense of one American would support five Greeks. They eat no meat, and, with few exceptions, neither butter, cheese, nor milk. A piece of black bread of the coarsest and cheapest sort, and a few garlics or olives, constitute their food—the whole cost of which for a day may be four cents.

What I say on this subject is the conclusion derived from careful observation and many inquiries. Our servant and muleteers often ate nothing till after noon, and said they were accustomed to such abstinence and found no inconvenience from it. Other expenses are on much the same scale. The common Greek has no costly furniture, neither table, chairs, nor beds, neither floor, chimney, nor windows to his house. He has no carriages nor carts, no barns nor outhouses. A hovel, which demands no skill above his own for its construction, contains him and his family, his oxen, donkey, &c. He is inured to filth and vermin, and to all the privations implied in the destitution I have described. His clothes are of the coarsest, cheapest sort. There are no highways to whose construction and repair he must contribute—no contributions, or next to none, to build churches and school-houses, which are of the same style with his dwelling. A benignant climate renders this primitive, barbarous style of living, consistent with the preservation of life and health. The Greek, therefore, having no expensive wants of his own, is able to contribute so largely of the meagre product of his industry to satisfy the exorbitant demands of his government, which, with the habits of civilized life, he could not possibly do. In this view, it is the interest of the government to keep him what he is, a stark barbarian,—an object which, whether designed or not, will be pretty effectually secured, by means as simple as the annual collection of the revenue.

The standard of taste and comfort is degraded. No wonder that centuries of oppression should have produced such results. Still, the flattering accounts which had fallen under my notice had not prepared me for so general a prevalence of degradation and barbarism. Those who look and labor for the regeneration of Greece, and her elevation to the dignity of a civilized country, must have patience. Great changes cannot be wrought hastily. It savors of a school-boy enthusiasm to expect that, because in the days of Pericles and Epaminondas, the Greeks were polished, and highly civilized, the present occupants of the country, who are perhaps as nearly allied to many tribes of barbarians, who have at different periods overrun and occupied the classic land, as to the heroes of

Marathon and Platea, are to be suddenly invested with the high attributes of moral, social, and intellectual excellence, which are always of slow growth, and the results of favorable circumstances, accompanied with careful and long culture. In Athens, and some other places, the intercourse of trade and commerce, and still more, the settlement of a large number of foreigners, may be expected to work a speedy and considerable improvement; but many years, probably generations, will pass away before an effective civilization, such as pervades the masses in the United States, and in one or two of the nations of Europe, can reach the interior and remote parts of Greece.

I do not distrust the power of moral influences. In proportion as these are multiplied and judiciously directed, may we hope for the regeneration of the people. Should it please God to revive Christianity in the Greek church, all that I have said of obstacles and delay should be greatly modified, or wholly rejected. Unfortunately, there is not, as far as I can learn, any very decisive indication of such a revival. With a creed not very remote from the truth as it is in Jesus, this church, to which the people are blindly devoted, has neither intellectual nor spiritual power for great moral achievements. The foreign agencies are decidedly unequal to the wants of the country, nor have they, as far as I can learn, been signalized by any very marked token of the divine approbation.

Agriculture, and other branches of industry, have been retarded by the want of capital. Money has been scarce since the peace, though the disbursements of Europeans have no doubt brought considerable alleviation. Capital has also been imported into Greece by the foreigners, chiefly Asiatic Greeks, and others, who have invested it in building in Athens. Some Europeans also have made purchases of property, but I think chiefly of the Turks, who left the country, and were allowed, in northern Greece, to sell their land, which in the Morea was confiscated. Still, great inconvenience has been felt for want of funds, which has been aggravated by the course of trade,—the imports having exceeded the exports from two to three or four-fold. The payment of interest on the foreign loans, if that shall ever occur, will produce another exhausting drain. No uniform rate of interest has been adopted, or indeed could be, under such circumstances. It has ranged from 15 to 30 per cent., according to the demand for money, and to the security which the borrower was able to give.

The agent of a rich English house has arrived in Athens, within the last two or three months, to obtain permission from the government to establish a bank on English capital. A charter was granted, during my stay in Greece, for a bank and a loaning institution. The proprietors were allowed to take 8 per cent. on loans secured by real estate, and 10 on ordinary discounts. Sanguine expectations are entertained of the good to be derived from this institution; and, if properly and liberally conducted, it may tend greatly to the encouragement of industry and enterprise. Many land-owners are now obliged to permit their estates to remain totally waste, for want of capital to put them in a state of cultivation. This class of persons, especially, is expected to derive great advantages from the loans, which it will form a part of the business of the new bank to advance upon mortgages.

Those who have observed the effect of these institutions in other countries, in stimulating speculation and producing ultimate embarrassments and bankruptcies, will hardly expect that Greece will realize all the advantages so confidently anticipated from an institution which is hailed by them as the harbinger of unexampled prosperity, and even of the establishment of a liberal legislation. This effect, it is thought, the bank will indirectly produce, by giving rise to an independent class of agricultural proprietors and cultivators, which can hardly be said at this time to exist.

The government has shown much doubt and indecision as to the course it should adopt with regard to the introduction of this monied interest into Greece. After receiving the proposals of the English agent favorably, and making considerable progress in the arrangement of terms, unexpected obstacles arose, and objections were multiplied. The removal of these only tended to produce new ones, till at last the agent became convinced that the government had no other design but to defeat, by delay and management, an enterprise which, in the state of the country, and especially with the exaggerated expectations of the public, they were unwilling formally to reject. Under this impression, he gave notice that, if the charter should not be granted by a certain early day, which was fixed, he would break off the negociation, and embark for England. The day arrived without any news from the ultimatum. He sent his baggage to the steamboat, and his family followed. The gentleman was accidentally delayed in his departure for a short time, after he was expected to leave. At this moment the permission so long sought for in vain was sent to his hotel. Under all the circumstances, it was universally believed that it was the intention of the government to defeat the enterprise by withholding the communication until after his departure, and to escape the odium of rejecting a public advantage by this poor artifice.

CHAPTER XI.

EGINA.

NOVEMBER 3d. We left Athens at 8 in the morning, having engaged a boatman to take us from the Piræus to Egina, and thence to Epidaurus, for which we are to pay forty-three drachmas—about seven dollars. Upon our arrival at the wharf, we met with a vexatious delay of nearly two hours, and finally got off at 11 o'clock. Our dragoman, Demetrius, bore it more patiently than we. He is hired by the day, and it is his interest to prolong our journey by all practicable means. He alleged some difficulty in procuring the necessary papers at the health office, for these profitable manœuvres are practiced in young Greece with a dexterity that would do credit to the hungry employés of older governments. We had given the man special orders to prevent delay by making due provision the previous night, and as this was rather an inauspicious commencement of operations, we gave him a lecture upon his carelessness or bad faith, which I hope may prove useful hereafter. Our boatmen steered directly for an ancient temple upon Egina, which was the chief object of our visit, but after we had approached within three or four miles of the landing-place, they sheered off to the right for the harbor of Egina, which was at the distance of ten miles, alleging that there was no good anchorage nearer, and in spite of all our remonstrances, refused to attempt a landing. This adds one day at least to our voyage, since we must visit the temple on horseback to-morrow, and then proceed to Epidaurus, instead of reaching that place to-night, according to our original plan. We thought this change unnecessary, and did not fail to remonstrate against it earnestly. It, however, turned out for the best.

The light, changeful breezes, by which we had been baffled and delayed, became after an hour a heavy gale, which tossed our frail bark to and fro at its will. We secured ourselves as well as we might from the cold, suddenly become very piercing, by creeping under the deck and covering ourselves with our quilts. We were soon intolerably sick from the motion of the boat, and, I apprehend, in no little danger. The boat was small, though of the usual size of Greek craft employed upon these coasts. With little ballast,—of sand covered with gravel, upon which we spread our quilts under a deck raised about three feet above the primitive floor, the sails were of enormous dimensions, and either from want of force or skill, our *padrone* and his three assistants, two of whom were boys, managed them with great difficulty, which was of course greatly increased, as it became necessary to tack frequently, and the sea was greatly agitated by the furious blast. It was eight o'clock in the evening when we landed at Egina, though the distance from the Piræus is estimated at only eighteen miles, and we had embarked at 9½, and sailed at 10¾ A. M. We sent Demetrius on shore to engage a place to sleep upon the floor of the only inn in the place—the only accommodation of the kind in Greece, with the exception of Athens, where we found tolerable hotels, and as we have been informed, Patras and Napoli di Roma. Our messenger soon returned with the unpleasant tidings that the tavern was occupied by revellers and dancers, and could not afford even this poor accommodation.

We at length found shelter in what passes for a coffee-house—a wretched place without a floor or any other comfort, except a roof and a few rough chairs. The front room, the best in the house, is partly paved with pebbles. The family and the lodgers were already gone to rest upon a bench of convenient width and height, that extended around three sides of this apartment. They were stretched one after another upon the bare plank, covered with their garments, and some with their hooded *capotes* of thick hairy cloth, and gaudily trimmed according to the fashion of the country. I observed that they had no pillows, or substitute for them, but laid their heads upon the bench, of course considerably below the horizontal position of the body. They slept soundly, however, and seen by the glimmering light of a small lamp suspended in the middle of the room, the group was picturesque.

We were shown into a back room used for cooking, and occupied by old tubs, barrels, utensils, fuel, lime, piles of vegetables, with nameless kinds of filth, which we had neither time nor inclination to investigate very closely. In one corner of this room was an elevated platform, where Mr. and Mrs. C. spread their bed. In another was a low arch, not unlike an enormous oven, in which an old table had been placed apparently as a receptacle for such unsightly objects as it did not comport with their style of housekeeping to place in more conspicuous positions. Here, after Demetrius had performed some ablutions with an old broom, I contrived to spread a thick cotton quilt, which I had bought in Athens, to answer the purpose of mattress, sheets, and all other appliances of a bed, and with my cloak tightly rolled for a pillow, I soon fell asleep, and enjoyed for several hours a profound repose, such as I had not had for many months. Unfortunately, the customers who were asleep when we came in after eight o'clock, began to rise at three, and I was disturbed by the landlord, who came to kindle a fire and make coffee for his guests. There was no more quiet for the rest of the night.

November 4th. The harbor of Egina, where we landed last night, is fit only for small craft, for which it seems to be safe. A few only were visible, not more than fifteen or twenty, with fishing-boats of still smaller dimensions. There is little appearance of trade, though the town is said to possess more commerce than it formerly did, and to have, as well as the whole island, an increased population. This, however, cannot amount to more than a few hundreds. The houses are several of them well built, at least for Greece, where all that is old, even so old as twenty or thirty years, is in ruins, and what is new is generally of the slightest and cheapest construction. The chief building in the place is a very extensive structure of stone, erected, during the administration of Capo d'Istria, for a seminary of education.

It might from its appearance accommodate several hundred students, but it is now unoccupied, and is likely to be so, as it is superseded by another institution of the same kind—a school of industry which has been established at Athens. Another building, which I took for the town-hall or court-house, is also substantially built and of considerable dimensions.

The region back of the town to the extent of two or three miles, is nearly level, and, possessing the advantage of a fruitful soil, is well cultivated in vegetables, grain, vines, and olives. Considerable quantities of vegetables are sent to the Athenian market. Immediately behind this fruitful plane rise lofty, sterile mountains, like those which constitute all the islands as well as the mainland of Greece, so far as I have seen it. These, however, are interspersed with many valleys of small extent, yet susceptible of tillage. The sides of the mountains, too, when not quite bare of soil, are terraced with much labor, and planted with olives or sown in grain. Upon the whole, Egina is better cultivated and seems to be more productive than Attica.

Some travellers speak of it as a fruitful garden, rich in the products of a genial soil. I saw little in passing through the island to justify these praises. It has the general appearance of sterility, and the larger portion of its surface is incapable of tillage. The rest is nearly all covered with stones, and at the depth of only a few inches in many places where excavation had been made, all is solid rock. The scarcity of water must render irrigation impracticable to any great extent. Considerable industry is exhibited in cultivating what is tillable, and several comfortable cottages and good farms are seen in different parts of the route to the ruins of the temple of Jupiter Panhellinius, which is nearly at the opposite end of the island from the port, the road passing nearly through its centre.

It is not indeed a road, being hardly practicable for foot passengers. It is a steep, narrow, rocky pathway, winding in every direction along gullies and precipices. No labor is employed to keep it in repair, and it was obviously made at first, as it is now maintained, by the feet of the donkey and human beings who travel it.

About half way between the present town and the temple, are the ruins of another Egina, built by the Venetians. It was built near the top and on the almost perpendicular side of a conical mountain. This place could have been chosen only for the security which a citadel occupying the pinnacle of the mountain afforded to the city below, which it overlooks, as indeed every house completely overlooks the one immediately below it. No carriage of course ever ascended this aërial town, and it must have been nearly impossible for loaded donkeys to do so, though it is difficult to say what these hardy, docile animals may not be trained to achieve in the way of climbing. Two or three houses seem still to be occupied. The rest are unroofed, and the most of the walls have fallen in. I observed one church, which seemed to be kept in repair. This town was deserted to build the one upon the shore, which is every way superior in position and commercial advantages. It occupies the site of the ancient Egina, though no ruins are visible, with the exception of a single marble column, a few rods north of the limits of the town, supposed to have belonged to a heathen temple.

The ruins of the temple of Jupiter Panhellenius was the chief object of our visit to Egina. It is situated near the eastern end of the island, here not more than a mile wide, upon the ridge that rises nearly equi-distant between the northern and southern shores. The hill is of considerable elevation, but it is overlooked by those which lie near it, both east and west. It is, and, for aught that appears, always was, remote from human habitations. The ascent is easy, and the view one of the most magnificent that can be conceived. It embraces nearly the whole island of Egina, with its precipitous, rocky mountains and deep valleys. To the north are Athens and the Piræus, together with the splendid ruins of the Acropolis. The mountains of Attica, and the coast as far as Sunium, the island and gulf of Salamis, with its numerous smaller islets, and the coast of the Morea, are seen from the same side. On the south, the view is scarcely less extensive, though certainly the objects are less imposing. They include, however, Hydra and several other islands, the shores of Peloponnesus, and a vast extent of sea.

This temple is represented to be one of the oldest in Greece, and the gray porous stone of which it was constructed give to its remaining columns, corroded as they are by time, the appearance of hoary age beyond any ruins I have elsewhere seen. These columns, originally thirty-six in number, twelve on each side and six at the ends, besides two rows of smaller ones in the interior, of which many pieces remain, though all are fallen, are about nine feet in circumference at the base. They are of the Doric order,—each has twenty flutings, which are therefore a little less than six inches wide. Twenty-three of these columns are yet standing.

The eastern front is unbroken, and, seen at a little distance, the columns appear to be perfect, though, upon a close inspection, they are found to be considerably abraded. Their solidity is unimpaired, and, without some convulsion of nature, they may stand two thousand five hundred years more—a memorial of the taste and genius of the ancient Greeks. Twenty-two of these columns are surmounted by huge blocks of the same species of stone, constituting the architrave of the temple, which is thus far entire, though the cornice and frieze, formed of less massive materials, have all fallen and disappeared. They have probably been carried away by antiquaries and amateurs to adorn the galleries of Europe.

Portions of them are said to have been purchased by the King of Bavaria, and now adorn his museum at

Munich. When this sale took place, I know not. Who, it might be asked, has a right to dispose of these precious remains of antiquity. Is it possible that the government of Greece has increased its revenues by the sale of what should be considered the most valuable resources of this poor and exhausted country? It is a disgrace and a crime to have perpetrated or to have connived at such a transaction, and it is hardly credible that such a lover and patron of the fine arts as the King of Bavaria is known to be, should have been a participator in it. He is understood to have neglected the more important interests of his kingdom in his zeal for the promotion of architecture, sculpture, and painting, and it would be peculiarly unfortunate for his reputation, should he fix upon it the stigma of having robbed the dominion of his son of any of those inimitable works of art which constitute their peculiar attraction, and may, if left to their rightful owners, the Greek nation, have a decided influence in accelerating their return to wealth and civilization.

This temple had its front to the east, where a large part of the ancient pavement remains entire. The ascent to it was by three steps, which are also in good preservation. They are little calculated for the comfort of those who may ascend them, being nearly a foot and a half in height. It is remarkable that in all these public edifices, the Greeks had more regard for symmetry than convenience. The steps leading into the Parthenon, are nearly two feet in height. It is obvious that these must harmonize with the magnitude of such structures far better than such as have more adaptation to convenience. It may be said that these temples were not designed for public assemblies. It seems probable that few besides those immediately engaged in the performance of religious ceremonies, were accustomed to enter them. Those who were mere spectators remained without in the open air. The diminutive size of many Greek as well as Roman temples, renders this conclusion unavoidable. The stones of which the temple of Jupiter Panhellenius was built, are large and massive. I measured one, which must have occupied an elevated position in the building, that was about fourteen feet long by four thick, and it was of still greater width.

We returned from these interesting ruins at 1 P. M., much fatigued but highly gratified. Our voyage to Epidaurus was accomplished in two and a half hours, with a fair wind and a smooth sea.

CHAPTER XII.

ANCIENT EPIDAURUS.

DECEMBER 5th. We spent a little time last night in looking at the very slight remains of ancient Epidaurus, a city which possessed some importance amongst the Grecian republics. It was built on both sides of a promontory of small extent, but of considerable elevation, which rises from a flat back-ground into the bay of Salamis. On either side of this promontory is a small harbor, said to have been occupied by the ships of the ancient city. Only one is now used, in which a few coasting vessels, or rather large boats—I should think not more than five or six, were moored in apparent security from the sea. Several fragments of statuary, evidently antique, are lying in a ploughed field, which was probably near the centre of old Epidaurus.

One is a part of a monument to the dead, and is of good workmanship. In several places are seen, overgrown by a thick and tangled under-brush, massive blocks of stone, which were undoubtedly the foundations of important public buildings. In another locality, I saw a block of fine white marble, which had the appearance of having been recently disinterred. It was chiselled in the manner of an architrave, though not elaborately. Other blocks of the common stone lay partly uncovered in the same place, and all probably belonged to some edifice of which it is not improbable that further excavations may reveal the means of forming some more definite idea. These constitute the sole remains of a city once powerful and opulent.

The modern Epidaurus consists of half a dozen respectable looking buildings, which seemed to be occupied as shops, and of fifty or sixty cottages, mostly of mud walls, and occupied by the cultivation of a small tract of level fertile land, which lies between the beach and the mountains. Several more were engaged in ploughing with oxen, which are mostly used for this purpose in Greece. The plough is here, and, I believe, throughout the kingdom, of the most primitive and clumsy construction. The beam is long, reaching to a yoke, and the cattle are attached to it as to a cart. It has but one handle, which is commonly held in the left hand, and in the right is a pole eight or ten feet in length, armed at one end with iron, to clear the share, and used also to quicken the speed of the oxen, for which purpose it is sometimes pointed with a goad. The share is only a straight piece of iron eight or ten inches long by four wide, which turns the furrow equally on both sides. The ploughing is shallow, and certainly very imperfect. I have often seen the same kind of plough in Italy, where it is in common, if not exclusive use. It is the only plough in Greece, and is probably the same which was used in the days of Homer and Hesiod. I was told that several proprietors had lately imported English ploughs into Attica, with the hope of introducing a more thorough and perfect tillage. They were laid aside, however, by the peasants after a short trial, and there seems little probability that this approved implement of agriculture will soon be supplanted, though certainly it would tend more to the advancement of the country in wealth and civilization than the adoption of the Frank dress, which threatens to become general at least in the towns. The peasantry, it must be allowed, have hitherto resisted this innovation upon their hereditary customs, and perhaps they at least may, for a long time to come, preserve some of the distinctive features of the Grecian character.

Our accommodations at the inn were less disgustingly filthy than at Egina, but they were less comfortable. The weather had become cold. We landed chilled with the east wind, which had wafted us so speedily across the bay of Salamis, and were shown into a room in the upper story, where there was no means of kindling a fire. The wind poured in upon us through a hundred apertures, and I found my thick quilt of cotton an insufficient protection against the cold. We engaged five of the horses to carry us to Napoli—three for Mr. and Mrs. C. and myself, one for Demetrius, and one to carry our baggage. They were all wretched-looking animals, such as no man in America would think of attempting a journey with. For these horses and their guides, of whom three accompanied us, we agreed to pay five and a-half drachmas, about eighty-two cents each. Mrs. C. had brought a side-saddle from Athens. I was complimented with a remnant of an old Turkish saddle, the worst and least convenient certainly in the world. The other horses were surmounted with huge frames of wood, extending almost the whole length of the animals, with cushions, or some other appliances, under them to protect the horse, and blankets and quilts above to protect the rider. I believe there was a single bridle, and that broken in several places, and without a throat-latch. The rest rode with clumsy rope-halters, which, however, the animals obeyed tolerably well. Our beds, bags, trunks, baskets of provisions, and cooking-utensils, were piled upon the pack-horse, till he was quite lost under his huge burthen. The rest was distributed amongst the riders, as they could take charge of it.

Thus prepared and equipped, we set off for Napoli, about thirty miles distant, a little before 8 A. M. The novelty of our situation, and the grotesque appearance of our cortege, were at first a source of amusement, and tended to beguile our journey of its fatigue. Our way at first lay through a valley of a few hundred yards in breadth, bounded by high mountains, not like those we had been accustomed to see in Greece, bare of trees and vegetation. A few stunted bushes and scattered shrubs, which had not yet been discolored with frost, partly covered their nakedness, and relieved them of that aspect of savage and desolate sterility which now impressed me with a feeling that bordered upon positive pain. The valley was naturally fertile, and had formerly been tilled, as the scattered olive-trces bore testimony. It was now overrun with a rank and tangled growth of bushes, briars and shrubs, which overhung our path, and often left no room to pass. To increase the difficulty, it rained with great violence; and the necessity of lowering our umbrellas every moment, and of brushing off the rain-drops from the obtrusive foliage with our heads or shoulders, added materially to the discomfort and toil of the journey.

As we advanced, the mountains on our right and left gradually approached each other; and by the time we had advanced three miles, we were threading our way along the dry bed of a mountain torrent, sometimes on one side, and sometimes on the other of the rocky pathway, always obstructed by the brushwood and the projecting rocks, that scarcely left a place for the careful animals to put down their feet. We soon began to ascend the sides of the mountains, the valley no longer having sufficient width. Our path became more and more precipitous and difficult, till we were clinging to the side of the steep declivity, at the height of several hundred feet,—our path a mere incision in the rock of hardly a foot in breadth, and an absolute precipice above and below us. Our lives evidently depended upon the steadiness and skill of our horses; and for several miles a single trip would have been fatal. These sagacious and experienced animals evidently reconnoitred every step, and warily chose the spot for every movement of the feet. They stepped long or short, as the case might require,—sometimes resting upon the projecting point of a rock, sometimes carefully reaching over a suspicious looking place.

The road was for considerable distances worn into the rock or hard soil, to the depth of a foot or more, occasionally not six inches wide at the bottom, or terminating in a positive acute angle. For nearly two hours we proceeded in this way, without any accident, and about 11 A. M. we came into a more open region. This soon spread into a pleasant valley of considerable extent, which formerly contained the grove of Esculapius, and all the appliances of an ancient watering-place. The ruins which still remain attest the great extent and magnificence of this city of invalids. The foundations of a large town are spread all around over the valley. The sites of several temples are indicated by masses of hewn stones of large dimensions, such as were hardly ever used in building private dwellings. Besides these, there are remains of buildings so perfect as clearly to point out their uses.

There is a large theatre on the south side of the valley, formed by excavating the side of a mountain, so as to form an area capable of containing an immense audience, not less, I should think, taking estimates made of other similar areas which I have seen, than three or five thousand persons. There are fifty-eight rows of seats, rising one above another around this vast semi-circle. These seats are a little more than a foot in height, from which the elevation of the whole structure is readily appreciated. They are, I think, more than two feet wide, and, from the grooves cut in all of them, seem to have had a wooden back, constructed for the greater ease of the spectators, who are presumed to have been invalids, as no other ancient building appears to have this provision. There was a passage upon every seat behind the back, for passing to and from each place without disturbing the occupants of the others. Access to the different tiers of seats was had by twenty flights of stairs, about two feet in width, which extended from the bottom to the top of this immense amphitheatre, at equal distances. A large part of the seats and steps still retain their original places, and very few of them have been removed from the ground; so that this may be regarded as one of the most considerable and massive of the antiquities of Greece. Like the other Grecian theatres, this had no roof, the performances being held in the open air.

At a small distance from the theatre is a stadium of large dimensions. It is not in so good preservation as the former. Its form, however, is perfect, and many of the huge stone seats remain in their places. It is oblong, and, like the theatre, was formed at least in part by excavating the earth.

The only remaining ruin worthy of special notice is a bath, partly at least below the surface. I did not measure its extent, but it can hardly be less than seventy-five or a hundred feet in length. The walls of massive hewn stone remain almost entire, to the height of eight or ten feet. A spout to introduce water into the bath is made of red granite, each block more than one foot square. Rows of massive stones, prepared with large grooves for conducting water, may be seen in the neighborhood of the bath and elsewhere, indicating the existence of others of which no relic now remains. There is also a large mass of brick-work, in the Roman style, presumed to be the remains of a public bath or of a temple. A rivulet running near was said to have medicinal virtues, and, as the highest recommendation, this was alleged to be the birth-place of Esculapius.

CHAPTER XIII.

NAPOLI.

From the site of these ruins to Napoli, though the road is hilly and rough, it can hardly be denominated mountainous. There is a small agricultural village at the distance of not more than a mile, with some fields, apparently fertile, though badly tilled. Then succeeds, for a distance of ten or twelve miles, an uncultivated waste, much of it formerly tilled, but now overrun with shrubs and bushes, none of them amounting to trees of the size of a man's arm. These the peasants were cutting and carrying in bundles, bound with ropes upon the backs of donkeys, to sell for fuel in Napoli and Argos. This wood was seldom more than one or two inches in diameter. The land, I was told, belongs to the king, and the peasants get the wood without any expense but the labor.

We met in this valley many flocks of sheep and a few of cattle, proceeding from the mountains of the Morea, where they spend the summer, to the islands which give sustenance in the winter. The shepherds were accompanied by their families, with their tents, their only dwellings, and their furniture—kettles, beds, and corn upon droves of donkeys. The women carried large packs also, and many of them had their children tied in a kind of long narrow box, not unlike a miniature cannon slung upon their backs. These groups, of which we met a large number, were wild and picturesque. Their peculiar costume, and their swarthy complexion, strongly reminded me of the North American Indian. The sheep, of which we met several large flocks, were small and lean, hardy in appearance, with long coarse wool, which is made into a shaggy coarse cloth, worn by the shepherds and other peasants without dyeing. The sheep are also milked, and the butter and cheese made from them is much used in the country. I have tasted the butter, which is pale, and of a vile quality.

December 6th. I took an early walk through the streets of Napoli, and along the quays. Many of the houses are well built of stone, three or four stories high. Two or three streets are of respectable width, but the rest are narrow, inconvenient, and excessively dirty. Even at sunrise in the winter, the stench was offensive enough, and in the summer it must be intolerable, and pernicious to the health of the city. Napoli has long been distinguished as a sickly city. The plague has several times committed great ravages, and autumnal fevers prevail from year to year. These have been ascribed to the vicinity of some marshes, which are, however, separated from the city by the bay. A more probable, and of itself a sufficient cause, is the filthiness of the streets, which, under a less powerful sun, might be expected to scourge the population with diseases. Here, where there is hardly ever a cold day, when to the present moment the foliage has not been discolored by winter, and flowers are in full bloom, the plague and all its family of maladies is but invited by such criminal and universal inattention to cleanliness.

There were a few, perhaps a dozen or more, small coasting vessels in the harbor, which is very well sheltered and spacious, though of no great depth. Many retail shops make some display of cheap wares suited to the consumption of a poor population, but there is very little appearance of activity or extensive business. The trade of the place has declined since the seat of government was transferred to Athens, and though Napoli is better built and has suffered less from the revolution than perhaps any other city in Greece, it exhibits the same neglected appearance and tendency to decline which I have observed elsewhere, Athens only excepted.

With every advantage of situation, its trade is said to have fallen off, and is threatened perhaps with still further decline. It is strongly fortified by its natural situation, and by the military works which have been thrown up by its successive owners. Its principal fortress is the Palymede, a mountain which rises almost perpendicularly, on all sides but the north-east, to the height of more than a thousand feet above the sea, which washes its base. The city is itself a regular fortress, surrounded by a wall and ditch, and having within a lofty citadel; but this citadel, as well as the town and harbor, are overlooked and perfectly commanded by the towering Palymede, which rises south of the town, and is separated only by the fosse and wall. The ascent from this side is by a long flight of stairs, covered with arches of masonry.

We ascend by another flight of almost endless steps, which is uncovered, and leads with many zigzags to the summit. The labor of ascending these steps, which, I think, must amount to a thousand, is occasioned by their bad construction. They are made in many places of small stones, many of which are loose or displaced—they are placed edgewise, or, if horizontally, so as to form unequal and variously inclined surfaces. In our ascent we were met by a company of convicts, preceded and followed by a strong escort of soldiers. This was the first intimation I had that this aërial stronghold is a prison as well as a fortress. One more perfectly secured I have not seen. When the approaches are properly guarded, as they are constantly by sentinels, escape is strictly impossible without wings.

We were shown into the workshops, where the prisoners are employed in manufacturing cotton cloth. In a second building, they make coats and shoes for the army. This seems to be a part of the system lately introduced, as the buildings are not yet complete. The commandant, who seemed much interested in the processes, and to whom we were introduced in the workshops, apologized for the slender scale of the manufactures, and said it was but a beginning. He accompanied us through the fortress, showing and explaining all in the most obliging manner. The fortifications were mostly constructed by the Venetians, and many fine pieces of ordnance bear the arms of that republic. Some of a very large size were cast nearly two centuries ago. They do not seem to be impaired by time, and are perfectly fit for use.

The Turks have added to the works of defence, but the style of their workmanship is very inferior to the Venetian, though of a later date. The different bastions bear the names of the heroes of ancient Greece, Themistocles, Aristides, Miltiades, &c. The garrison at present consists of one hundred and eighty men. I should think two or three hundred necessary to man the defences completely. The whole fortress, strong by nature and art, seems to be impregnable. Certainly it is capable of being made so, if any place in the world is. Its immense elevation removes it quite out of the reach of an enemy's fire. Its batteries command every point both of sea and land within gunshot. Large cisterns are constructed in different parts of the fortress, to catch and preserve the rain-water, which is the only supply.

The view from this place is extensive and beautiful, though bounded on all sides, except a very narrow vista into the Archipelago, by high mountains. Taygetus is seen in the distance in the south-west, covered with snow. Argos and a number of agricultural villages are seen to the north, scattered over the lovely and fertile Argive plains.

Having ordered a carriage to be ready at the hotel to carry us to Mycenæ, we hastened to complete our survey and take leave, but the polite and hospitable commandant would compel us to enter his apartments, which were tastefully furnished, and commanded a most enchanting prospect.

We were entertained *à la Turque.* First, a long pipe was presented to each of us in succession, to take a few whiffs, the commandant in his turn doing the same. I had not been polluted with the contact of cigar or pipe, I believe, for full twenty years, but ventured to orientalize for once. Then coffee was introduced, of which each of us was presented with a small cup, with sugar, but no milk. It was of the finest quality. We then rose and took leave. Our entertainer, however, led Mrs. C. down several flights of stairs to a little flower-garden, which was neatly laid out and well cultivated in a nook of the mountain, and after presenting her with a bouquet, bid us adieu, leaving us with the most favorable impressions of his politeness and good feeling.

We parted with our landlord a few minutes later, bearing with us less agreeable recollections. Our accommodations had been of the worst sort—dirty rooms, dirty beds, and, in spite of a change made at our express invitation, dirty sheets. For these accommodations (two beds) and for a supper of soup and rice, and a breakfast of mutton-chops and coffee, he charged us fifty drachmas. After a vain attempt to obtain some deduction from this extravagant bill, we paid it and left him with an assurance which we are likely to make good, of not favoring him again with our custom.

We were soon in our carriage, the only vehicle which we had seen in Greece out of Athens. It was drawn by two of the vilest horses we had anywhere seen, and by dint of good humor and kind words to our driver, who was delighted at my addressing to him some words of ancient Greek, which he repeated to me in the proper modern pronunciation, we rolled along the fine road towards Argos, with a degree of rapidity and comfort which, in this kingdom, no one may hope to realize who does not happen to journey upon this same highway over the Argive plain on the eight or ten miles of good road in Attica, which are said to constitute the whole amount of artificial highway between Macedonia and Cape Matapan. I suppose there is not a carriage in the realm of King Otho beyond the precincts of Athens and Napoli.

CHAPTER XIV.

TIRYNS AND MYCENÆ.

THE plain of Argos, celebrated for its fertility, both in ancient and modern times, is a beautiful tract of level land, extending about eight or ten miles from Napoli to Greece, and of unequal width, ranging from six or eight to not more than three or five miles. It may contain sixty square miles of excellent land—the best, I think it is reputed, in Greece,—fertile in corn, wheat, vines, tobacco, and vegetables. It reaches the bay of Napoli on the south, and is surrounded on all sides by high rocky mountains, bare of verdure, and of the most dreary aspect. They have nearly the color of ashes. A number of gray craggy rocks, and several conical mountains of no great extent, rise upon different parts of the plain, without, however, occupying any considerable portion of its surface. This is the season for ploughing, and we saw not less than a hundred yoke of oxen at work on this broad field.

At about two miles from Napoli are the ruins of the very ancient city of Tiryns. Long before the Christian era, this city was, as it now is, a heap of ruins without inhabitant. From the solidity of the structures, and the massive and imperishable materials of which it was composed, these ruins may remain other thousands of years, and excite the wonder of coming generations, These remains, which are of the class denominated Cyclopian, from the massiveness of the materials, and from our entire ignorance of the authors and the age of these stupendous productions of human art and industry, consist solely of an enclosure, two hundred and forty-four yards in length by fifty-four in breadth. The enclosed space is too inconsiderable for the area of a city, and must, therefore, have been the citadel only. This is made quite certain by its situation.

These walls are reared upon a mass of rock, or a small mountain, which rises from the plain of Argos, and is precisely one of those commanding and secure positions which the Greeks always chose as the nucleus of a city. In the early days of this people, when war and the dread of violence were the most common pursuit and the most urgent motive, a proper site for a citadel, where the people who built their houses around its base might flee for protection in times of danger, was an object of the greatest importance, and controlled, in the selection of a site for a new town, as completely as a good harbor does in these days of commerce. Such a site was the abrupt rock, commanding the neighboring country, and out of the reach of any higher eminence, upon which the ancient walls of this venerable citadel now stand.

The exterior walls of the city, and the habitations of

men, which were constructed of more frail materials, have thousands of years since disappeared. No vestiges of these, not even a mound to puzzle the antiquary and provoke conjecture, remain at the present time. Nothing is seen but the citadel, which was constructed for their security; and now that they have vanished from the world, and even history has failed to make any authentic record of them, this serves as a perpetual and impressive monument of their high civilization and stupendous energy.

The thickness of these walls is from twenty to twenty-five feet. The highest part now standing is about forty-five feet. It is evident, however, both from the appearance of the wall itself, as well as from the mass of stone that lay in disorder at its base, that it was originally much higher, not less these data would lead us to conclude, than sixty or seventy feet. They are not perfectly straight, but bend a little, to follow the direction of the rocky height upon which they are founded, not, however, following all its irregularities. There are two gateways still remaining—one small, and still entire, the other partially destroyed, and much larger,—both very peculiar in their shape and construction. The former is on the western side, looking towards Argos. It is pointed at the top, and there is a large accumulation of rubbish upon its threshold. It is now nine feet in height, and seven feet wide at the base. The other is fallen in at the top, but from what remains, is presumed to be of a similar form with the last. It looks northward to the mountains, and seems to have been a very large and the principal entrance to the citadel.

The most singular feature of them is the great size of the stones of which they are built. Some of them measure twelve or fifteen feet in length, by four or five feet in thickness, with an equal width. Most of them are from four to five feet square. They are rough or unhewn. They are laid without mortar in the most solid manner, the interstices being filled up with smaller stones. They were undoubtedly quarried at no great distance from their present situation, and are of the same sort as the neighboring hills and mountains. But the wonder is, how they were ever raised from their native bed, and transferred to their present position by a people reputed to have been ignorant barbarians, and centuries before the invention of those mechanical contrivances, upon which labors much less ponderous and difficult are now dependent for their achievement. It is this difficulty that has led men to ascribe these magnificent works to a race of giants, who peopled the earth long before the birth of authentic history,

The ruins of Mycenæ, about seven miles further south, and at the extremity of the Argive plain, are of the same class, but much more extensive, and constructed of still more gigantic materials. You pass over the lower hills that bound the plains to the southwest. You ascend a mountain of no great elevation. The next ridge before you, which is of great height, and of a waste, savage, bare and craggy aspect, opens, retreating to the right and left, giving space for a broad gap, nearly at right angles with the ridges. In the midst of this gap rises a lofty, nearly conical mount, abrupt and precipitous on all sides. On the summit of this mount is the citadel of ancient Mycenæ, the enemy and rival, and finally the prey of its more fortunate neighbor, Argos.

The history of Mycenæ and Tiryns is little known, as they were destroyed before the period of authentic annals began. They were prosperous and powerful in the days of the Trojan war, and took an honorable part in that enterprise. We do not hear of them in the more known periods of Grecian annals, except as deserted, though magnificent ruins. Such they were certainly at the commencement of the Christian era, and they seem in the second century, when we have a description of them by Pausanias, to have been in nearly their present state. They are believed by critics to have been built as early as about 1800 years before our era began.

In approaching these ruins from Napoli, the first object that engages the attention, is a magnificent structure, which is, with the exception of its entrance, entirely covered with earth. A large tumulus rises from the side of the last ridge which you descend in going to the citadel. The entrance is not visible until you pass the tumulus to the right, when a door or gateway, which, however, has no appearance of having been closed, except with earth, is perceived immediately opposite to the citadel, looking towards it, and distant perhaps eighty rods. The approach to this entrance is by a passage between two lofty walls, constructed of hewn stone, of vast size and in perfect preservation. The earth rises to the top of these walls on the outer sides, so that they are not visible until you have arrived at the entrance of the passage. It is not possible to determine the height of the gateway, as there is a large accumulation of earth and rubbish, probably several yards deep. It is about ten feet wide, measured upon the surface of the present entrance, and perhaps fifteen feet high. It is not a parallelogram, but grows narrower as it approaches the top.

Immediately above the door, is a triangular window of the same width at its base as the top of the door, but terminating in a point, thus forming with the door a pointed arch. The lintel of the door is formed by a single stone extending horizontally across the passage, and resting upon the massive walls. The sides of the door are of great depth, forming indeed a passage not so wide as that by which the approach is made, but five or six yards in length. This is covered by the lintel, and another immense slab of hewn stone, extending from the lintel to the interior of the edifice, nearly twenty feet in width, four or five feet thick, and hardly less than thirty in length. It reaches far to the right and left of the doorway, and forms a part of the interior wall.

It is certainly the largest mass of wrought stone I have seen. How it was ever raised from the quarry, and placed in its present position, is a question which must engage every observer, and probably it will never be solved. The interior of this edifice is circular, rising in the form of a cone and terminating in an apex. It is about fifty feet in diameter, and is built of huge blocks of hewn stone, without cement. The whole is in good preservation, and seems likely to outlast the most solid structures of the present age. It seems probable, from the nails which are found in the walls, and other holes in the stones from which the nails have fallen, that the whole interior was lined with metallic plates. A door nearly filled with rubbish leads from this large apartment into another of an oblong form, about eight yards in length. It is not walled, but merely excavated from the earth, which is so hard that there is no appearance of any change of form in the room since it was made.

There are thirty-four ranges of stone visible in the circular room. Many more seem to be hid by the accumulations at the bottom. In passing by the usual way from this structure, which is usually called the tomb of Agamemnon, another of similar construction, but more dilapidated, and nearly filled with earth and rubbish, lies close to the path. This, too, was undoubtedly the tomb of some distinguished Grecian. Others are mentioned by books of travel, but I did not observe them, and I examined the premises with some attention. I presume that the vestiges are much less considerable.

Upon approaching the citadel, the first object that arrests the attention is a magnificent gate (no doubt the principal entrance), called the Gate of Lions. It is approached like the door to the tomb of Agamemnon, by a passage about thirty feet wide. The walls on either hand are formed of hewn stone of huge dimensions, and in imperfect preservation. The gate is nearly filled up with fallen stones and rubbish. There is only enough room to creep under its lintel into the citadel. The gate is about ten feet wide, and no doubt widening towards the bottom, like that of the tomb. It must, to maintain the proportions, have been nearly twenty feet high. The lintel is fifteen feet long by seven broad and four thick. Above the gate is a triangular stone eleven feet long at the base and nine feet high. It fills a niche in the wall, and has sculptured upon it two lions, from which the gate takes its name. This is probably one of the oldest specimens of sculpture in the world. The hinder feet of the lions rest upon the base of the triangular stone, just above the lintel of the gate,—the fore feet rest upon the base of a column which rises between the lions and increases in size upwards. The lions stand nearly erect, facing each other. They are chiselled in high relief, their tails not bushy, but smaller than those we see in menageries. The heads of the lions are broken off, but the remaining parts are entire, and one is astonished to see how well they have resisted for so many centuries the influence of the seasons. The stone upon which they are sculptured is a green marble; that of which the walls of the citadel is composed, as also the tomb of Agamemnon and the ruins of Tiryns, is a very hard species of breccia or pudding-stone, of which all the mountains of this part of Greece are chiefly composed. There is another gate or entrance to the citadel much smaller than the gate of lions, and in good preservation.

The walls of the citadel follow the sinuosities of the rock upon which it is built, and it receives from this circumstance a very irregular form. It is more the shape of a triangle than any other figure. The walls are constructed partly of hewn stones and partly of rough polygons, all laid up without mortar or cement of any kind. The interstices between the polygons are filled up with smaller stones. The citadel is separated from a high and very large mountain, which stands very near it, upon the north, by a deep ravine, at the bottom of which is the dry bed of a rivulet. Over this a bridge is said to have existed, of which a portion is still pointed out. I saw nothing, however, which had the appearance of having ever formed a part of a bridge, and I descended nearly to the bottom of the ravine, to examine any remains that might have belonged to such a structure. Only one portion of the ruins can, with any semblance of probability, be regarded as having been connected with such a structure. This is too remote from the bottom, and has much more the appearance of a bastion. It is built upon a projecting part of the rock, is a continuation of the wall, and I could see nothing to lead to the supposition that a bridge had existed at this point, except the fact that this is the nearest point to the opposite mountain. That mountain is precipitous,—almost perpendicular. It would be impossible to build upon it, or to find a square yard that might be cultivated for a garden. No enemy could occupy it for the purpose of annoyance, at least any part of it from which the missiles of ancient warfare could reach the citadel. It is difficult, therefore, to conceive any motive for erecting a bridge.

Several parts of the wall now standing are perhaps forty feet in height, but these masses of stone lying in disorder at the base, have fallen from the top, and diminished the height, which was probably not less than sixty or seventy feet. When it is considered that the walls everywhere rest upon a rock of great elevation, some idea may be formed of the strength of this ancient fortress. I think the wall is nowhere less than twenty feet thick. It is in several parts much more. It is all constructed of huge stones, of which an old writer has said, "two mules could not draw one."

In front of the gate of lions is an open space of considerable extent, paved and possessing, it is probable, other ornaments beside the sculptured lions, where, according to the custom of primitive times, courts and markets were held, and public business generally transacted. The walls of the citadel project so far as to form, outside of the gate, a large oblong space, well fitted, and no doubt used for such occasions. Such were probably the "void places" at the entrance of the cities of the Israelites, where the prophets, on great and solemn occasions, delivered their messages before kings—where Boaz gave public notice to the kinsman of Ruth of his intention to redeem the inheritance of her family. If so, this ancient citadel affords a striking illustration of the customs frequently referred to in the Bible, and proves that other primitive nations had the same usages.

The ruins of this once powerful city, recalled to my

mind the prophetic denunciations contained in the Holy Scriptures against Nineveh, Babylon, Tyre and other great cities, devoted by divine justice to perpetual desolation. Several small patches upon the top of this lofty citadel, once covered with human habitations and with splendid temples and palaces, are now ploughed and sown. The peasant and his hardy beast clamber up the precipitous rock and over the piles of ruins, by paths hardly practicable for pedestrians not accustomed to mountain steeps. I was also strongly reminded of another figure by which the prophetic writers mark the utter ruin and devastation of the most populous and proud of human dwelling-places. I was clambering along the fragments of the Cyclopean wall and the crags of the original mount which overhang the deep and savage gorge, in search of the remains of the bridge, said to exist there. My eye was resting upon what has been taken for the abutment of the bridge, but which I regard only as a bastion, when a fox, roused by the sound of footsteps approaching so near his desolate habitation, started from his hole under the mass of ruins, and after fixing his gaze upon us for a moment, bounded down the precipice, and disappeared in the depth of the ravine.

I looked upon these magnificent remains of former days, with a deep and peculiar interest. Here was a city that had seen a career of prosperity before the annals of authentic history began. I looked upon specimens of fortification, architecture, and sculpture, which have existed nearly a thousand years. Here was the tomb of the hero who led Greece to the conquest of

Troy. Ancient authors saw Mycenæ two thousand years ago as I saw it yesterday, in ruins and uninhabited. They, like visitors of the present day, were filled with astonishment at its stupendous and imperishable structures, and felt a kind of religious awe for a race of men, who were capable of undertakings surpassing in massiveness and durability all that has been accomplished by their successors. Were they civilized and scientific? Or were they of a race possessing physical powers so vastly superior to ours? Who can answer these inquiries? In the meantime, Tiryns and Mycenæ are likely to exist with little change for thousands of years more to provoke the same inquiries, and to check the scepticism and humble the pride of new races of men, who, like us, may be disposed to cherish too little respect for those who have occupied the stage of life before them, and to claim for themselves a decided superiority in all that pertains to the arts and improvements of life.

CHAPTER XV

ARGOS AND CORINTH.

Dec. 7th. We returned from Mycenæ to Argos after dark, crossing the dry bed of the Inachus several times as we approached the latter place. We found lodgings, as usual, upon the second floor of a coffee-house, dirty, open and cheerless, but such as we expected, and we were therefore satisfied. This is market-day, and the little town was thronged with peasants and loaded donkeys at an early hour. It gave us a very favorable opportunity of seeing the people of the Argive plain. We had evidence of the fertility of this region, reputed the best land in Greece, in the abundance of grain, fine turnips, parsnips, cabbages and onions, with which the streets were filled. The market is held in the open air here, as everywhere else in Greece. The costumes of the peasants made a very picturesque appearance. All wore the high red cap. The tunic, trowsers, and leggings, were of a coarse woollen stuff, made in the country, of undyed wool.

The morning was rainy and cold, so that most of them wore the capote of dingy brown, coarse and shaggy stuff, said to be proof against rain. They have almost always some glaring ornament upon the head or other part—some gorgeous needle-work in bright red, which, seen at a little distance, appears ornamental. Argos is built upon level ground, near the western edge of the plain which bears its name. Immediately west of it rises the mountain, upon which stands the citadel. It is of great elevation, and might be made a fortress of great strength, though the proximity and more important situation of Napoli render it unnecessary, as far as the general defence is concerned. Upon the south-east side of this hill are the ruins of a large theatre.

The stone seats, rising one above another around the stage in a semi-circular form, are many of them still in their original position. Like the other theatres in Greece, the performances were in the open air. The site is elevated, and commands a noble view. There are no other ruins in Argos of any importance. Some fragments of an ancient wall remain upon the Acropolis—at least so we were told. Nothing has been discovered of the splendid ancient temples which are known to have existed at the commencement of the Christian era.

The present town has a population variously estimated at from five to six thousand inhabitants. They are mostly employed in agriculture. The climate is insalubrious. Fevers prevail in summer and autumn, and the people are many of them pale and sickly in appearance. A few of the houses are well built of stone, but nearly the whole town is built of sun-baked bricks, or of cobble-stones laid up in mud. The roofs upon the chief streets project, and are supported by rough posts, forming a kind of arcade or shed for the exhibition of merchandise. Everything has the most rude and clumsy appearance. Haste and cheapness seem to have been the only considerations that prevailed in their erection.

Argos is about four miles from Napoli, three from Tiryus, and six from Mycenæ. It is known to have been the conqueror of the two latter places, and to have incorporated their inhabitants with its own population. It gives one a striking idea of the state of ancient Greece to see three rival and independent cities within an hour's ride of each other. These are states which made wars, and acted important parts in human affairs. Certainly such states could only have been powerful and important relatively to each other. Greece herself owed her power and political influence to the uncivilized state of other nations. She would have cut a sorry figure in the modern system of European politics. These are conclusions forced upon the mind by a consideration of the small extent of the country, weakened still more by its division into petty sovereignties. It is this very circumstance that gives the highest idea of the genius and intellect of a people who achieved so much upon the theatre of human events, and have the high honor of being the teachers and civilizers of the world.

We set off before 10 A. M. for Corinth. It was rainy, and a heavy wind, which increased as we advanced, blew directly in our faces. I never made a more disagreeable journey. After leaving the Argive plain, we entered the mountain region, consisting of high, savage and bare ridges of breccia. After a ride of two hours and a half, we arrived at the pass of Dervenaki,—the Thermopylæ of the late Greek revolution, where a small body of Greeks, stationed upon a mountain which commanded the only road from Corinth to Napoli, destroyed a large body of Turkish troops—an event of great and decisive importance in the history of that struggle.

From this point we made a detour to the vale of Nemea, to view the ruins of the temple of the Nemean Jupiter, and the theatre of some of the fabulous or real exploits of Hercules. The vale is perhaps three miles in length, by one or one and a half wide. It is mostly uncultivated, and bare of trees, though once a forest which furnished Hercules with his club—the potent weapon with which he slew the Nemean lion and other monsters. The ruins of the temple are beautiful and interesting. Only three columns of this once magnificent temple are now standing. Two of them support an architrave of the Doric order, four and a half feet in diameter, and said to be thirty-two feet high.

It is easy to trace the outlines and extent of the temple in its perfect state, when it had fourteen columns on each side. They seem not to have been demolished, like many other noble monuments of the arts, by the hands of Vandal men, but to have fallen by an earthquake, or some other great convulsion. This is apparent from the position of the ruins, no part of which seems to have been removed. The materials are a soft stone, composed of sand-shells and pebbles.

Not far from this temple are the ruins of another smaller building; fragments of fluted columns are seen on all sides, and it is probable that these are the remains of another ancient temple. Still farther on the road by which we returned to the main route to Corinth, is the fountain of Nemea, which still gives an abundant supply of pure water. The fountain is a modern structure.

After leaving the fountain, the road leads over a mountain of no great height, but forming one of the most difficult passes for a horse that I had yet attempted. The path is in some parts worn deep into the rock, and scarcely six inches wide. In other places the descent is steep, and the animal was obliged to reach down a great distance to obtain foothold. These difficulties were increased by the sinuosities of the road, which made it necessary to shift the direction suddenly to the right or left, often upon steep declivities. These sagacious animals had then an opportunity to show their good qualities, and so perfectly did they understand the roads of this region, that they carried us over in safety. Upon an even surface they frequently stumbled, but upon the more difficult and precipitous parts of the route, they seemed to be sensible of the necessity of using greater caution, and seldom made a misstep.

On approaching within two hours of Corinth, the country assumes a new appearance. Instead of mountains of bare bleak rocks, are immense sand-hills, which have the appearance of having been blown up from the Gulf of Lepanto, which begins to be seen through the ravines or from the tops of the hills. The valleys are washed by the rains into deep gullies, often with the sides perfectly perpendicular to the height of twenty or thirty feet, and conformed to each other with the regularity of two parallel walls through several sinuosities. A meagre vegetation of shrubs covers the tops of these hills of sand, but the sides are often bare, and exhibit the appearance of having fallen off in large masses, through the agency of rain or other causes.

These sandy elevations, with occasional ledges of rock, continue till we enter the plain of Corinth, which is a tract of level country from one to two or three miles wide, extending for ten or twelve miles along the shore of the gulf, which is here narrow. On the opposite shore, a rugged high mountain rises from the water's edge. There are olive plantations of considerable extent upon this plain. Large portions are uncultivated, and it is not fertile. The olive trees are smaller than those of Attica.

Corinth has a beautiful situation between the gulf, from which it is a mile and a half distant, and the Acropolis, to whose base it approaches very near. The descent is gradual, affording the best possible facilities for a town, easily drained, and yet not inconveniently hilly. A few of the houses are substantially built of stone, the most are mud cottages. The population is twelve hundred. It must have been much larger before the revolution, judging from the ruined houses, which here as everywhere else in Greece, attest the barbarous spirit in which that fierce contest was waged. The Acropolis is naturally one of the strongest places in Greece, and, commanding as it does the isthmus, which unites the Morea to the continent, it must ever possess great importance as a place of defence. A single temple of all the splendid structures which adorned ancient Corinth, the most opulent and luxurious town of Greece, now remains, or rather seven columns remain to show where a magnificent temple of Neptune once stood. It is known that all the magnificent structures of Corinth were destroyed by Mummius, who disgraced the Roman name by his barbarous destruction of this noble city. The city was subsequently rebuilt, and again destroyed by the barbarians. It has since suffered greatly by war, as from its position it must ever be an important point in any system of offensive or defensive operations in Greece.

We found the only two khans, or inns, which this little town possesses, already occupied, and we were refused a place to lay down our beds. Having a letter from the Rev. Mr. Hill to the governor of this province, who resides in Corinth, we sent our dragoman to his excellency, to inquire if there was a prospect of finding lodgings in his capital. He returned with our messenger, took us to his house, and entertained us with a hospitality and urbanity not soon to be forgotten. He is a gentleman of education and intelligence, speaks English well, and is full of information, as well as patriotic in all that concerns his reviving country. He served in the navy during the war, and has since held important posts under the government.

CHAPTER XVI.

THE ISTHMUS.—AFFAIRS OF GREECE.

DECEMBER 9th. This morning (Monday) we set off a little after nine to embark at the port of Lechœum for Salona. We passed through the plain which continues for a considerable distance in this direction, until it is gradually lost in a barren waste of sand and covered with low shrubs. We passed by the remains of two canals, begun by the ancients across the isthmus. The Venetian wall, also, comes to the gulf of Lepanto, between Corinth and our place of embarkation. The isthmus is here only six miles wide. The ridge which runs along between the two seas, is of no great elevation, and might probably be canalled without enormous expense.

There are two traditions with regard to the causes that led to the abandonment of the attempt made by the ancients. In one instance, it is said, their progress was stopped by a hard rock which they were unable to excavate. Before modern skill and enterprise, the mountain referred to above would soon yield, even if it consisted of flint. The first attempt was abandoned, because it was ascertained that the water in the Archipelago is higher than in the gulf of Corinth—a difficulty which, if it really did exist, would easily be remedied by locks.

The Greeks and Romans had little skill for civil engineering. We were told by the governor that an examination has been made by a competent engineer, who reports that the communication is practicable, and may be effected at no greater expense than twelve millions of francs. This amount puts the enterprise, at present, beyond the resources of Greece, and perhaps the commerce of a country so poor and reduced would not be sufficient to maintain a canal and pay the interest of the investment. Certainly it would give great facility of intercourse between the nations of Western Europe and the Levant, and should Greece rise again to wealth and commercial prosperity, this will be one of the earliest enterprises to which the attention of her government and capitalists will be directed.

The navigation around the Morea is tedious and dangerous. It is really the greatest obstacle to visiting Greece. The way from Patras to Athens, laid open by such an improvement, would be performed in one-third of the time now occupied in going around Cape Matapan, and with an exemption from a multitude of risks and discomforts.

The hospitable governor accompanied us to the point of embarkation, a ride of two hours and a half, and by his interference shortened the delays by which the smaller functionaries of Greece, as well as those of the older absolute governments, contrive to embarrass a stranger, and, I believe, their fellow-subjects also, whenever they have an opportunity to exercise the faint emanation of royal power which rests upon them. We had much reason to be grateful to this hospitable and worthy man. He gave us much information with regard to the affairs of Greece, past and present. Though the agent of an unlimited and despotic power, he is a decided liberal, and such, I have reason to believe, are all the Greek authorities, though too many of them are restrained by their poverty and dependence upon royal favor from exercising a valuable influence in favor of free institutions. To them, however, they all look forward as a blessing which cannot long be withholden from a gallant people.

They wait, though not very patiently, till the people, so long inured to anarchy and misrule, become a little accustomed to the operation of laws,—till landed proprietors, now poor, for the want of capital to cultivate their estates, shall have acquired a little independence; and till King Otho shall have the benefit of more age and experience to enable him to see that his honor and interest will best be promoted by identifying himself fully with his people, and by ruling them in sympathy with the hopes with which they called him to his throne, and with the pledges given in his behalf when the Bavarian regency entered upon the government during his minority. That regency flagrantly violated all its pledges, and all Greeks feel a lively hatred towards the whole race, the king only excepted. They treated the brave nation as a conquered people. They possessed themselves of the most valuable offices, civil and military. They had ten thousand troops of their countrymen, whilst the veterans who had waged war with the Turks so heroically, were disbanded without any substantial reward, or even provision for their immediate wants. The indignation of the people was roused. Acts of violence were committed upon the intruders in different parts of Greece, and certainly scenes of blood would have ensued had not the government dismissed the mercenaries.

Only a few Bavarian soldiers are now to be found in the army, which is recruited with natives. A large proportion of officers remain, but they are gradually leaving the country. The minister of war and one judge only occupy high stations. Several of the professors of the university too are Germans. Not more, perhaps, remain than the public service demands. Their superior science would qualify them to do important service in a country which is so destitute of educated men, had not their presumption and avarice made them odious. It is said that the King of Bavaria, whose influence made the selection of the higher functionaries, did not select able men. True or false, that is the opinion of the Greeks, who feel themselves insulted by this instance of bad faith, no less than injured by the whole system of administration, and that sovereign is the object of much dislike.

The municipal system of France has been substantially introduced into this country. The system of the Turks was so bad, that it is said nothing of it has been retained; though, from a multitude of difficulties which are met with in bringing a nation under an entire new code, and in abrogating altogether the laws under which they have lived for centuries, the work of transition is but very partially accomplished. In the large towns, much better success has attended the attempt, than in the remote villages and among the mountain population. It must be the work of years to complete the transformation.

We embarked at the port, Lechœum, a place of only three or four cottages, with the ruins of some forty more built by refugees from Turkish cruelty. There were four decked-boats in the harbor, which is the extreme eastern point of the gulf of Lepanto. We hired one for thirty drachmas to carry us to Scala, a distance, as we were told, of thirty miles. The other boatmen, who demanded sixty and fifty drachmas, used loud and angry words towards our padrone, for having underbid them, and so deprived them of a good opportunity of imposing upon strangers. Here we took leave of our kind entertainer, who gave us letters to the Governor of Salona and other authorities on our route.

Our crew consisted of four men, who were barely sufficient for the management of the boat. We made half the distance with high spirits. The wind was favorable and the sea calm. We sailed about noon. At two o'clock the wind changed. Subsequently we had calms, relieved now and then by light breezes. From two o'clock till dark we made no perceptible progress. We were finally compelled to spread our quilts upon the grated floor of our low cabin, and lie down for the night. We arrived at Scala some time between twelve and six o'clock in the morning. The coast of the gulf of Lepanto, which we passed by daylight, and indeed the whole shore from Lechœum to far beyond the bay of Salona, which was visible enough during the early part of the voyage, is abrupt and bare; it is indeed a high mountain without any arable fields or verdure. On the left, the bay is bordered by a more variegated and hospitable region. The level ground continues for at least eight or ten miles. The country then becomes hilly and mountainous, but it is cultivated, and the neighborhood of the ancient Sicyon is fertile in currants.

Dec. 10th. The harbor of Scala, in which we found ourselves at anchor this morning, is a small but well sheltered bay, having apparently no great depth of water. We landed in a small boat, which, however, could not reach the shore. We stopped to procure breakfast and engage horses in a khan, as it was called, but which was entirely open in front and without floor, and was occupied as a coffee-house, market, and baker's shop. Several men were employed in moulding black bread, and several bushels of the bread, perfectly dry, lay on an elevated platform at one side of the room. It was designed, I understood, for sailors, many of whom frequent this port, though not more than a dozen small vessels, or rather boats, were in the harbor, and the village has not more than eight or ten houses. We saw a caravan of a dozen camels here employed in the transportation of merchandise and produce, between this port and the interior. After rather more than the usual amount of higgling and wrangling, which Demetrius fortunately transacts for us, we obtained decidedly the worst horses which have yet fallen to our lot in Greece, and got under way for Delphos a little after 9 A. M.

CHAPTER XVII.

DELPHOS.

THE road led us through a beautiful and fertile plain of no great breadth, but said to be ten miles in length from Salona, which was six miles to our left on our way to Scala and to Delphos. We passed through a beautiful and extensive olive-yard, two miles from Scala. Another still more extensive lay at our left, extending far towards Salona. As we looked back from the lofty hill which we mounted, in approaching Krisso, a most lovely view was spread out before us. On the right was the valley before referred to, reaching to Salona, and nearly to that town, verdant with luxuriant olive-trees,—then the town, built upon the declivity of the mountain, in a most conspicuous and delightful situation.

Beyond the town was a scanty verdure, which, however, gave a varied and cheerful air to the back-ground in keeping with the lovely plain below. Higher up the mountain was a bleak bare rock, like the most we have seen in this country. Finally, the top was covered with snow, which glistened in the sun with very peculiar lustre. The whole valley was surrounded with mountains of majestic height. Upon our left, or rather before us, lay the beautiful vale through which we had just passed, Scala and the gulf of Salona, Galaxidi, which occupies the opposite side of the bay, and ranges of mountains which bound the horizon.

The village of Krisso has apparently about a hundred and fifty houses, built of huge bricks dried in the sun—mere mud walls, which, in America, would not resist the climate for a year. The streets are narrow, foul, and precipitous. From this village, our journey of nearly two hours to Delphos, was one high rocky mountain, as rough and savage a road as could be desired. Our horses, bad as they were, kept their feet admirably. To the right of this wild and hazardous route, and not much less than a thousand feet below it, is a deep ravine—the bed, nearly dry, of the river Pleistus, which receives at Delphos the water of the Castalian fountain. Beyond this stream the Kirphis rises suddenly—a lofty and almost precipitous mountain of perfectly bare rock. Along the Pleistus, the valley which joins that of Salona, near Krisso, continues without intermission to Delphos, though often narrowed to eight or ten rods by the encroachment of the mountain. It is certainly fertile, and smiles with olives and little patches of wheat.

The whole declivity between our road and this lovely vale, steep and impracticable as it seemed, is under cultivation, except where the rocks are absolutely bare. It is terraced with a skill and industry of which I have seen no other example in Greece. Every spot where a little soil has retained its original bed upon the rock, or been deposited by rain, is carefully tilled; when practicable, oxen are driven up the narrow steep pathways to draw the plough. When this is not possible, they are tilled with the spade or hoe. Some little fields, containing hardly four or five square rods, are yet secured by terraces and sown in wheat. This description is applicable to the whole route from Krisso to Delphos.

Nearly midway, I think, between these places, we saw several tombs cut out of the face of the mountain. The entrance is semicircular in form, three or four feet deep horizontally, with an excavation of sufficient depth to receive a human body. This was covered with a large slab of stone. These sarcophagi, however, have been broken up, and their contents removed. One of them was much larger than the dimensions given above. The semicircle is, perhaps, ten feet in diameter. The depth is at least eight feet, and there are three sarcophagi, one in front of the entrance, and one on either hand.

We descended from a lofty mountain, by a rough and irregular path, practicable only for the horses of the country, into the modern village of Kastri, which certainly stands upon the site of the ancient Delphi. The entrance is near the pass where Perseus, king of Macedon, caused an ambuscade to be laid for the destruction of Eumenes king of Pergamos. Apart from the associations which belong to this celebrated spot, I have never seen a spot better calculated to inspire wonder and awe. The whole vale of Delphi, including under that name the whole region bounded by the surrounding mountains, is made up of rugged hills and steep declivities. The immediate site of the ancient city has an inclination so great that a pedestrian ascends from its lower edge with extreme difficulty. The temples and houses were built upon terraces rising one above another like the seats of an amphitheatre. It would have been impossible to support the foundation of an edifice of any size without such walls. The surface forms an angle with the horizon scarcely less than forty-five degrees.

These terraces were built in the most substantial manner, with large blocks of hewn stone. Many vestiges of them remain in a very perfect state. Indeed, they constitute the most considerable of the remains of Delphi, and attest the scale of magnificence and massive solidity upon which this renowned city was constructed. Two of the most considerable and perfect of these noble walls now support the superincumbent weight of Christian churches. Both are shabby, mean structures, and form a melancholy contrast with the works of those who formerly reared temples and dwelling-places on this sacred spot. Some of these fragments of the ancient terraces extend twenty or thirty yards in length—one is, I suppose, twenty-five feet high.

One of the first objects that attract the attention of the traveller who visits Delphi, is the classic fountain of Castalia. Its situation can hardly disappoint the most extravagant anticipations. The valley is bounded on the north side by Mount Parnassus, which is here nearly perpendicular, and of great height. Its appearance is savage in the extreme. The gray and broken rocks are perfectly bare. Many enormous masses, loosened perhaps by some great convulsion, have tumbled down from the heights above, and now lie in wild irregularity at its base. Others have a threatening aspect. This is the appearance of the mountain along the whole eastern side of the valley, which lies so immediately under its precipitous side, that a person looking towards the mountain cannot see the top, which, from that position, seems to be lost in the clouds. At the immediate spot where the fountain rises, there is a deep fissure in the mountains, apparently made by some convulsion. On either side of the chasm two projecting rocks rise between one and two hundred feet perpendicularly.

From the base of the rock, upon the right, the Castalian source springs forth. There is a scarcely perceptible horizontal fissure, elevated not more than two or three feet from the earth below. In this is inserted a spout, or rude trough, through which the water pours forth in a copious stream. It is received in a square basin, cut out of the solid rock, of the depth of three or four feet. The descent to this is by several steps also cut in the rock. The mountain above this fountain, and on both sides of it, has been cut to the height of twenty or thirty feet into a perfectly smooth face. In this are several niches, which probably were designed for statues or offerings. Between these and the fountain a kind of chapel is excavated, consecrated, no doubt, to the presiding divinity, and now, it is said, dedicated to St. John.

The water is pure and sweet, and not, as has been

represented, unusually cold. From the fountain the water flows rapidly across the steep inclined plane of Delphi, through a very deep and crooked ravine. Its high banks are adorned with a few venerable olive trees. Many high rocks overhang this classic stream. Others lie across the deep bed, producing a succession of wild cascades. The length of this little stream—it might more appropriately be called impetuous torrent—may be half a mile. It enters the Pleistos between two perpendicular rocks, not less, I conjecture, than fifty feet high, nor more than twenty feet asunder. The old town of Delphi was divided into two parts by this interesting stream.

The two high projecting rocks above the fountain, which were held to be sacred, gave to the poetic mountain the name of Biceps Parnassus. The one on the right hand was called Hyampeia, the other Nauplia. From the former Esop, the fabulist, was thrown; and Nauplia was the Tarpeian rock of Delphi, from which those who were obnoxious to the gods or their priests were precipitated. High above the sacred fountain are seen clinging to the rock ivy, and a variety of shrubs, some of them flowering. The fig-tree, which is said "to send its roots into the fissures of the rock, while its wide-spreading branches shed a cool and refreshing gloom over this interesting spot," has disappeared. "The majestic plane-tree in front of the spring, defending it from the rays of the sun, which shines on it only a few hours in the day,"* is still in its place, but it no longer cheers and shelters the Castalian spring, as it is

* Condor's Greece. Vol. ii., p. 278.

not nearer to it than six or seven rods. Even travellers take poetic license on this inspiring spot.

The chasm which separates the two sacred rocks is not more than five or six yards wide. The tops of these tall cliffs are nearer to each other than their bases. Hyampeia leans over towards Nauplia. This chasm runs back into the mountain, I conjecture, several hundred feet, diminishing in depth, not gradually, but so as to form three terraces or platforms rising at intervals one above another. These are ascended by ancient steps cut in the marble rock. Wheler and Clarke were unable to ascend these steps. They present, however, no considerable difficulty. The steps are polished by ancient use, so as to have become slippery, and they have rather an inconvenient inclination over the chasm. I ascended them, however, as did my companion, without harm. The third terrace is inaccessible. Seen from the second, it has the appearance of the mouth of a cavern. I threw into it several stones, which disturbed some wild fowl who found shelter there. They soared aloft, with much noise, amongst the higher peaks of Parnassus.

CHAPTER XVIII.

DELPHI.

SOUTH-EAST of the fount, and at the distance of three or four hundred yards, are the remains of the ancient gymnasium. A part of its site is occupied by a church dedicated to the Virgin. The location is known from the description of ancient writers, and is clearly identified by some massive walls, probably the terrace which supported the structure, which are in excellent preservation. The church has been rebuilt once or oftener, has still some ancient pillars (four) in its vestibule, and other fragments of marble in its walls. Indeed, there seems to be a prevalent ambition to distinguish not only churches but private houses, and these mere cottages or mean hovels, with some noble vestige of antiquity. You see fragments of precious and finely-wrought marble in the walls of a stable. The houses, built of huge bricks baked in the sun, have their corner-stones from the huge blocks which formed the terraces of Delphi. The combination is grotesque, but not uninstructive. It is a mighty and quite unparalleled display of modern skill and enterprise, to remove one of these masses from its place, and raise it a few feet in a modern wall. Indeed, they are seldom seen more than two or three feet high. It is hardly conceivable by what art this fallen and uncivilized race have been able to demolish the works of their ancestors. They can construct only such as are the most frail and clumsy.

The research of travellers and antiquaries has not been able to fix upon the site of but one more of all the magnificent structures which are known to have adorned this sacred metropolis. The splendid temple of Apollo has been so completely destroyed, that the most patient inquiry has not been able to bring to the light a single well authenticated vestige. The stadium, however, had a position so peculiar, and was constructed of such indestructible materials, that it has obtained a more honorable destiny. It is in the western, highest part of Delphi, above the present village. The ascent to it is all but impossible, and is another instance of the higher value of the ancient Greeks for a lofty and imposing site than for a convenient one. The stadium, which is of an oblong form, like that of Athens, was more than six hundred feet long. It was bounded on the north by the side of the mountain, east and west by high rocks, and on the south by a rapid descent towards the town. Here a magnificent terrace was built to support it, a considerable part of which remains. The stones are hewn and massive. One is four yards long. A number of stone seats remain. On the eastern side six courses are cut in the solid rock.

The valley of Delphi is secluded from the world by

lofty mountains. Parnassus on the north, and Kirphis on the south, rise up and overshadow it like cyclopean battlements. Towards the west the elevation is less, though very considerable, whilst the circuit of mountains towards the east is completed by many swells and broken ridges, among which the valley is imperceptibly blended and lost in an Alpine background.

The village of Kastri is one of the most crowded, filthy, and mean in a country where all are miserable enough. The streets zig-zag without reason. They are so narrow that you can hardly ride through them on your mule, and so precipitous as to test the skill of that sagacious animal. To add to the difficulty and disgust, piles of manure and offensive offal are abundant. It was by such approaches that we arrived near the sacred Castalian Spring. And here, as if to teach us how closely allied are the sublime and the ridiculous—how near a neighbor, sentiment is to vulgarity—our approach to the source of poetic inspiration was literally blocked up, not by the sacred nine guarding the portals of Apollo from the profane, but by just twelve washer-women, the most coarse and unclassical of the genus, half clad in hairy-stuff petticoats of undyed wool, ragged and dirty, and extending just below the knee! They were washing foul clothes in the stream just below the basin, with water that issued from the sacred fountain!

Upon leaving Delphi by the Thebes and Athens road, we passed some ruins which were without the walls of the city. A confused mass of large hewn stones, with some fragments of columns, indicated perhaps the site of some temple or other considerable structure. This was an ancient cemetery, and many massive sarcophagi, excavated in blocks of hewn stone, about seven or eight feet long, by three or four in width and height, lay upon the ground in all directions. They had all been opened; the ponderous lids, some broken, were near each one. Of course, nothing remains of their former tenants. One of white marble is only partially disinterred. It seems to have been recently discovered. The lid is entire, though it has been removed. It has some beautiful emblematical figures sculptured upon both its exterior sides. I was struck with two eagles in bas-relief of exquisite workmanship.

The valley of Delphi, throughout its whole extent, exhibits a more improved and industrious tillage than I had yet seen in Greece. Olive-trees occupy much of the lowest ground. The terraces upon which the old town was built are sown in wheat, and for many miles along the road the sides of the mountains were cultivated to the highest possible point. The higher parts of these declivities are terraced with great labor, though unskilfully, and planted with the vine, which seems to thrive well, almost up to the region of snow. Many barracks rise up amongst these vineyards, upon which the small stones gathered from the arable land are piled to such a height as to have the appearance of low pyramids. Our way was along the side of the mountain, elevated, I should think, much more than a thousand feet above the level of the vale upon our right. After nearly three hours, we mounted still higher upon what seemed to be a spire of Mount Parnassus.

The weather, which during the forenoon, and till two o'clock, was so warm, that I had to shelter myself from the rays of the sun with an umbrella, was now intensely cold. Our road continued to ascend, and to become more precipitous and difficult, till we arrived, a little after sunset, at the village of Arakoba. This place has nearly two hundred houses, rudely built, after the fashion of the country, upon the top of the ridge. A more wild and ill-adapted situation could hardly be found. The narrow dirty streets are precipitous. The people are peasants, cultivating the vineyards and olives upon which we had gazed with so much pleasure for the last two hours, as well as the region still farther north.

The produce of these fields, as well as the fuel, which at this aërial spot is an important article, is transported from the deep glens and steep declivities where they grow, to the top of the high and nearly inaccessible mountain. It probably never occurred to these primitive men that a better arrangement could be made than the onerous one which they have no doubt inherited from their forefathers. The spot had the advantage of good water, and is reputed to be signally favorable to longevity. Its remote and difficult position ought, it should seem, to confer upon the people the boon of security from the violence of war. This quiet village, however, was the scene of a fierce battle between the Greeks and Turks, and, like other towns of this country, was destroyed.

We stayed in this village not at the ordinary khan, but with an acquaintance of our interpreter, who has a brother a merchant in Athens. He was a proprietor and agriculturist, superior in wealth and respectability to the ordinary peasant. It gave me an opportunity of forming some notion of the style and domestic habits of this class—a thing I had much desired. The house is built in the usual village fashion, partly of small stones, of all shapes, laid in a mortar made of clay, partly of sun-dried bricks of a large size. A wall constructed of these at first shows the different strata of which it is composed, but after a longer exposure to the weather, exhibits only a uniform surface of earth or dried mud. Such a structure would be decomposed by the vicissitudes of our American spring. Here it stands for years.

I thought when I first saw the slight and ill-looking houses, of which not only the agricultural villages, but the cities too, are to a great extent composed, that they were cheap and hasty constructions, run up after the desolations of the Revolution, to be replaced by better as soon as circumstances may permit. Upon a careful examination of the old walls, which cover no small part of the surface of all the towns in Greece, I have found them uniformly built in the same barbarous way. It is the architecture of the country, as substantial and sumptuous now, I presume, as it has been at least for two centuries, or the period of the Turkish rule. The house of our entertainer was floored with rough planks, no common luxury here, where you see the bare earth through almost every open door in the villages. There was no glass, though there were windows in one of the rooms closed with plank shutters.

There were no windows in the room where we spent the evening. Two small holes through the tile roof served in their place.

The family were seated upon some old blankets, thrown down around the fire. There was a kind of chimney, but most of the smoke passed off by the windows in the roof. In most of the houses I have seen this is the only provision, the fire being made upon a sort of hearth just under these apertures. The smoke, of course, pervades the room, and passes off leisurely. Some very coarse chairs were brought for us, as we declined sitting upon the floor, and asked for chairs, or some substitute for them. We saw also a coarse table. A few indispensable implements for cooking and for eating made up the sum of household stuff. No beds or bedsteads were in use. A mat, an old capote, thrown upon the floor or upon a low bench, are the substitute. I believe the people sleep in their wearing-apparel—at least I have seen many do it. The table and chairs of this family may be taken, I suppose, for luxuries, since at most of our lodging-houses we do not find them,—at least we seldom enjoy both in the same place. A few dollars would furnish the house of a peasant in the usual style.

A mode of living so comfortless I have nowhere seen, except perhaps in Ireland, where deep poverty prevails to an extent that leaves nothing to the masses beyond the bare means of a wretched existence. In Greece, the *idea* of comfort seems to be wanting amongst the peasantry. Those who have means have no wants. The poorest hut in the United States contains several articles which to them would not only be unheard of luxuries, but of which they could not conjecture the use. Cleanliness is quite unthought of. Everything, —the entrance, the floors, the tables, the utensils, the clothes, the person,—is disgustingly filthy. As to food, judging from what I have seen, and more from what I have heard from Greeks, as well as foreigners well acquainted with their habits, I am sure that the subsistence of five Greeks costs less than that of an American laborer. A black, coarse, but not unpalatable bread, which costs in common times less than two cents per pound, and a few olives, which cost hardly a tenth part of that sum, constitute almost their only food.

The use of animal food, including cheese, butter and milk, as well as meat, is prohibited by the church for several months in the year. But the whole year is Lent with the masses, who do not think of eating flesh. It is perhaps difficult to assign the causes which have led to a mode of living so very frugal and abstemious. Perhaps it has descended from the ancient Greeks. I fear that there is no good reason to believe that civilization ever proceeded beyond the large towns. Perhaps the barbarous government under which this people have so long been degraded, has had its influence upon their modes of living. Under a system of legal plunder and rapacity, the possession of property becomes a crime, and every symptom of luxury and comfort is studiously avoided, through forethought and fear. Whatever the cause may be, it is undeniable that one meets here with few proofs of that pervading civilization which never exists without being manifested in the decencies and conveniences of common life.

CHAPTER XIX.

LIVADIA.

DECEMBER 11th. Our journey to Livadia, a distance of seven hours and a half, according to the measurement of this country, which allows about three miles to the hour, led us through one of the most desolate parts we have yet seen in Greece, though far from being the most rough or sterile. I remember seeing only two human habitations in a distance of fifteen miles. Much of this region is too mountainous for tillage, but we passed through a good deal of land which has been cultivated and is now evidently capable of a very profitable agriculture. It is overrun with brambles and useless shrubs. It bears little grass, which, however, is grazed by flocks of sheep and goats. There are in Greece vast quantities of arable land lying waste, more useless than abandoned fields in the United States, as nature does not here clothe such lands with a new growth of forest trees. With the exception of a few stunted pines, I have not yet seen a forest tree in Greece. It is not easy to conjecture why, in a country like this, which, with 800,000 inhabitants, and certainly not 8,000 square miles of good land, cannot be thought thinly peopled, so large a part of the arable land remains untilled.

The vast extent of the public domains, with a most preposterous system of managing them—the iniquitous system of collecting the revenue by tythes, which tends directly to throw out of cultivation all but lands of the first quality—the want of roads and consequent want of good accessible markets—together with a prevalent want of capital, are possibly the chief cause. I suspect, too, that there is a disinclination to agricultural pursuits. It seems to me that the people show a decided preference for town life, however mean, with some petty trade or mercantile speculation. It strikes me that the number of shops, in all the cities and large villages I have seen, is out of all proportion to the population and business. Everything is subdivided, and the articles of trade and merchandise seen in a dozen shops ought to be in one.

The land is very good in the immediate neighborhood of Lavidia, where we passed the night. The city has a considerable population; I could not learn the precise amount. Under the Turkish rule, when it was the seat of government for a large part of Greece, it was an important place, and contained, it is said, twenty thousand inhabitants. It may have six thousand now. It is built upon the edge of the extensive and rich plain which bears its name, and extends back upon the side of the high mountain that overlooks it from the south. The view is very imposing and beautiful on approaching the town as we did. No illusion, however, was ever more completely removed than was this upon closer inspection. A town so badly laid out, so meanly built, and so shamefully dirty, I have certainly not often seen. Yet the people are said to be rich, and they certainly possess, in the fertile plain they cultivate, an inexhaustible source of opulence. The situation is decidedly unhealthy, and the pale and sickly faces one meets with, aggravate the unfavorable impression made upon a stranger by a contemplation of the interior deformities of the city.

Livadia, the old Lebadea, has no antiquities, though it existed, as is well known, and was a large and populous city in the early days of the Grecian republics. I saw a few fragments of wrought marble and some broken pillars in the walls of a church near the citadel. Antiquarians have discovered nothing which they have thought worth recording. It is, however, a connection with the mythology of Greece which gives to this locality a peculiar interest. It is well ascertained that the allegorical fountains of Memory and Oblivion are within the limits of this city. They are south-east of the present Livadia, just beyond the limit occupied by human habitations.

On this side of the city is a citadel, a high and commanding rock, fortified at the top, and once thought impregnable. It is now neglected. This immense rock appears to be one end of the high bare mountain which lies behind the city, and it is severed from it by a profound gulf of nearly perpendicular sides, and not more than twenty-five yards in width, which intervenes between these threatening cliffs. A winter torrent of no great magnitude meanders and leaps along this dark chasm for nearly a mile—its bed piled up and obstructed by vast fragments of rock that have fallen from the overhanging mountains. Altogether, it is a scene of peculiar and savage grandeur. Just as the termination of this ravine, next to the city, and under the eastern side of the rock of the citadel, rises the fountain of Memory. It runs sluggishly from the rock, rather below than above the surface of the earth. Its water has the appearance of being stagnant rather than a living stream. Almost immediately opposite, across the bed of the winter torrent above described, is the fountain of Oblivion. It springs from under a high bank—at once a copious stream, which, with the humble aid of the fountain of Memory, which immediately joins it, turns several mills in the first quarter of a mile, and flows away to the plain.

The ancients called this stream the river Hercyna. It is said, in a very respectable book of travel, that the larger of these fountains still retains its ancient name, Lephe—a manifest corruption of Lethe. Another traveller (Dr. Clarke) has said that its waters are "troubled and muddy." To my eye they are beautifully transparent and clear. I walked from my khan half a mile, just after daybreak, provided with soap, towel, and tooth-brush, and there performed my morning ablutions. The water is rather warm for a living spring. It is soft to an uncommon degree, and pleasant to the taste.

Not only are these fountains of great poetical interest; the place was manifestly consecrated by religious observances. Only a few feet from the fountain of

Memory, in the eastern face of the lofty mount of the citadel, a chamber is cut out of the solid rock, not less than a dozen feet in length, eight or ten high, and nearly as many in width. Near this apartment are several niches cut deep into the rock, manifestly for containing statues and votive offerings. These remains leave no doubt, that this spot was once consecrated to the religious sentiments, with which the mythology and poetry of the ancient Greeks were so intimately blended. This chamber contained, at no remote era, the remains of some elegant painting, no doubt antique. All is, however, now blackened and obliterated by smoke. The chamber has apparently given shelter to some houseless family during the devastating war of the revolution, and no vestige remains of whatever it might have previously preserved to gratify the taste of the amateur in the fine arts.

CHAPTER XX.

LEUCTRA AND PLATEA

DECEMBER 12th. We rode more than four hours along the great fertile plain that spreads out east and north, from Livadia towards Bœotia. It can hardly be less than fifteen miles in length, by ten or twelve wide. It is a perfect level, bounded on all sides by mountains, and it was probably once a vast lake, which has been partially drained by some convulsion of nature. No inconsiderable portion of it, on the side most remote from the city, is still too low and humid for cultivation. A part of it is still a lake, and was anciently called the lake of Copais. In rainy seasons a large tract is overflowed with water, and generates disease in the villages as well as in Livadia.

This plain, as well as the more elevated land that borders upon it, is extremely fertile, and produces wheat, Indian corn, rice, and cotton, abundantly. The cotton-plant is below the height of even inferior lands in the United States, owing probably to bad culture. It is not planted in rows, so as to be tilled with the plough and hoe, as with us, but sown broad cast. This large tract contains a considerable number of populous villages. The village of Kaprena is upon its border, not more than three miles from Livadia. It was in plain view as we left the latter town, and during almost the whole of our journey along the plain. It occupies the site of the ancient Cheronea, where the liberties of Greece fell a prey to the victorious ambition of Philip of Macedon. After a very fatiguing ride of about eight and a half hours, we stopped upon another renowned battle-field, where the invincible Spartans were first defeated in a pitched battle by the Theban Pelopidas.

The city of Leuctra, though not large, must have been very well fortified, and probably contained several large temples and other public edifices. This is apparent from the very considerable remains which lie scattered over rich corn-fields that occupy this fertile region. Large blocks of hewn stone are to be seen half buried by the plough. Many stand upright at regular distances, apparently designed to mark the line of division between different proprietors. There are three or four piles of these massive stones, which were formerly Greek chapels, and were probably demolished by the Turks during the late war. Fragments of columns and well-wrought marble architraves are confusedly intermixed, in these rude edifices, with the large oblong masses that once formed the citadel or the walls of Leuctra. Two or three fountains are constructed of the same kind of materials.

I saw two or three beautiful bas-reliefs, in white marble, half concealed in the mud. I especially recollect one block of precious marble, with a vine exquisitely chiselled and in perfect preservation. This probably formed a part of the frieze of some very sumptuous edifice. Upon another was sculptured a man on horseback, which, though greatly mutilated, seemed to have been wrought by a skilful hand. The circuit of the walls is distinctly marked, not only by vestiges of the stone-work, but by a mound of earth and loose stones, which rises in many places as high as eight or ten feet, and forms a large quadrangle. I did not measure the length of the wall, but think it not less than half or three-quarters of a mile. I have no book in my possession which notices these ruins, though they are too considerable to have been passed unobserved.

The khan of Leuctra is decidedly the worst we have yet encountered. It has neither floor nor chimney, neither table nor chairs. In this most filthy of nations, this spot is entitled to the bad eminence of being remarkably foul. To complete the catalogue of disagreeables, besides Mr. and Mrs. C., myself and our dragoman, the room was also occupied by our muleteers and several other persons. The Greeks tumbled down upon the ground, and fell asleep like so many hogs. We made the best use we could of some old mats and what bedding we had with us, and then spent a nearly sleepless night in a vain and unequal controversy with swarms of fleas. I have reason to remember the khan of Leuctra. I ought not to omit the only alleviation of our unpleasant situation. We made an excellent supper on some wild ducks which Demetrius bought upon the plain of Livadia at twelve and a half cents apiece. These delicious fowls abound amongst the pools and marshes that cover so large a part of that extensive valley.

Dec. 13th. A ride of three hours on a very wretched road, rendered all but impassable by deep mud, brought us from Leuctra to another spot memorable in the annals of Greece. The ancient Platea was built about a mile north of a high ridge of mountains, and just upon the border of that extensive tract of rich land that stretches with little interruption from Livadia to Thebes, and has ever been regarded the best agricultural region in Greece. Its fertility seems in no degree exhausted by centuries of unskilful cultivation. I could not discover that any attention was bestowed upon manures. The ploughing is of the worst possible description. It is shallow and unskilful—a sort of ridge is formed by throwing two furrows towards each other, covering at least as much of unbroken surface as is stirred by the plough. The wheat springs up from the dark rich soil thus imperfectly prepared a broad, rank shoot, and the stubble of the former harvest, sufficiently attests that the matured grain is answerable to its early promise.

The great battlefield under the walls of Platea, is of the most luxuriant fertility. One might be led to think that the blood of the warriors slain upon some of the most celebrated fields of ancient and modern times, has imparted an inexhaustible richness to the soil. Waterloo, Leipzig, and Dresden, are the most productive corn lands in western Europe, and the renowned plains of Mantinea, Leuctra, and Platea, have a striking resemblance to these in the color and quality of their soil. They are the best lands in Greece. The remains of this ancient city are considerable—sufficient to mark its position for many centuries to come, though they possess none of the sumptuous magnificence which belongs to those of Athens, and to some other single monuments of Grecian taste and skill.

Two or three large heaps of massive hewn stones, intermingled with blocks of wrought marble and fragments of columns, sufficiently mark the position of some of the most considerable public edifices of this city. The modern Greeks, with that preposterous ingenuity by which they are perpetually putting their puny works in humiliating contrast with the splendid creations of their noble ancestors, have constructed churches of these beautiful materials, arranging them without taste or skill—a bit of curiously wrought architrave in the foundation—a huge block of gray breccia upon the fragments of a marble column—those masses which were too ponderous for the unaided human strength or clumsy machinery, wrought into the wall edgewise or perpendicular, as they were able—the interstices and inequalities filled with bricks and broken stones in the most bungling manner. Fortunately, the no less barbarous Turks have nearly demolished all these grotesque constructions. Besides these temples and public buildings, there are considerable remains of the walls of the city, which are constructed of large blocks of hewn stone. At least they were faced interiorly and without, with these stones laid without cement, whilst the space between was filled up with smaller stones laid in mortar or with earth.

The foundations of the northern wall remain to a considerable extent entire: one course, and a part of the way, two or three courses of stones, remain in their original position, and above the present surface of the ground. The accumulation of rubbish is eight or ten feet in height, and no doubt the wall remains entire at least to that height. It narrows gradually from the base, and the part now visible is about ten feet thick at the top. There are two or three projections in the northern wall, which were probably towers. There are similar indications at the two terminations, or at the angles made by this with the walls on the east and west sides of the town. A mound of earth, together with scattered blocks of stone, distinctly marks the whole extent of the wall that enclosed the city.

The interior of the city, which is under tillage, is raised from five to ten feet above the surrounding field, by the accumulation of rubbish. I looked with peculiar interest upon these memorials of the little city of Platea, which was distinguished amongst the cotemporary Grecian states, by its gallantry and good faith. When more powerful states were terrified at the approach of the hosts of Persia, Platea alone sent a thousand men to fight for liberty by the side of the Athenians at Marathon. Her citizens distinguished themselves throughout the war, and much in the memorable action which has given immortality to her name. Platea, too, was true to her alliances, and remained ever the fast friend of inconstant but glorious Athens.

CHAPTER XXI.

THEBES.

FROM Platea to Thebes is a ride of about three hours through a lovely and fertile region. For the last four or five miles, our road lay through lands belonging to the government, which, though equal to any in the world in quality, are here as elsewhere wholly uncultivated. Several large flocks of sheep were scattered over this untilled region; the shepherds and their huge dogs sauntering listlessly along the sides of the road, to gaze and bark at passers-by, for want of some more pressing employment. The public lands seem to be used as a common, where cattle and sheep graze without restraint, and where the people from the towns and villages cut wood for fuel, whenever they can find a stunted thorn or holly fit for that purpose.

This is one principal use of the public domains. They seem not to be preferred by cultivators; though let at a lower rate than private lands. The government is not liked as a landlord. Other proprietors aid the tenant in various ways; by advancing seed-corn, by furnishing half or all the oxen and donkeys, and the implements of husbandry. All these accommodations are paid for in the division of the crop, but they enable the tenant, who has little or no capital, to begin. Even those who do not need such advances are said to be fond of obtaining them, from the inveterate habit contracted under a rapacious government of hoarding all acquisitions, and exposing nothing that can be secured or concealed, to the risk of business investments. It is from the same cause that many in easy or even in affluent circumstances appear like beggars in their dress and habitations. Under the Turkish domination, the knowledge that a man possessed property led almost certainly to some judicial fraud or barefaced act of violence to rob him of it. There is now probably no fear of such atrocities; but habits change slowly, and Greece will long wear the ugly scars of wounds really healed. They must for a time remain barbarous, because injustice and oppression, no longer dominant, have made barbarians of them.

Thebes is not built upon a mountain, nor does it contain any lofty cliff, which could afford a retreat to its inhabitants in times of peril. Of the principal towns of ancient Greece whose site I have visited, this is the first which appears to have been chosen in reference to any other advantages than those of defence. Athens and Corinth, though addicted to commerce, chose their positions by the side of mountains, rather than upon the borders of those safe and capacious harbors that were in their neighborhood, and offered such facilities for commercial enterprises. Security from external violence was the first want to be provided for. Thebes is in the midst of rich corn-fields. It is four or five miles from any high mountain, and between it and the nearest range spreads one of the most lovely and fertile plains in Greece. The ancient walls contained several hills of considerable elevation, and no large tract of level ground, so the city may be said to have been built upon hills. It has no splendid remains. The old wall is traceable in many places. It was built, like the ramparts of other Grecian towns, of large square stones. Many of these remain in their original position. Others have been converted into fountains, churches, and foundations. The remains of an ancient fosse outside of the wall are also observable. No fine temples have been discovered, and yet a multitude of antique columns of various orders and of marbles are seen partially buried, or inserted in the walls and in terior of modern churches.

These certainly belonged to ancient edifices; and from the many manifestations in different parts of the town, where the rubbish has been partially removed to found new houses, or for other purposes, I am persuaded that precious monuments of art lie profusely scattered under the accumulations of rubbish which are here of very unusual height, and seem to have been little molested by the curiosity of the antiquary. Extensive excavations, judiciously conducted, may add much to our present knowledge of Grecian sculpture and architecture. At least it may demonstrate that Thebes has been too hastily declared to possess nothing of the curious and instructive memorials of the past, which seem to be the only valuable heritage of these fallen cities.

Here are several towns evidently of the Venetian age, built of the ruins of more beautiful and substantial structures than these merchant princes were able to construct. There is something painful in marking the progress from bad to worse in the memorials left by the successive masters of Greece, since the days of her glory; from the Romans, the Byzantines, the Venetians, the Turks, and so far, I fear, we must say the modern Greeks, the deterioration has been uninterrupted, and has followed every change.

Thebes is now meanly and stragglingly built, a cluster of mud cottages here and there, with little attention to streets or any other principle of regularity. Few of the houses are of solid construction. It is in the midst of modern as well as of ancient ruins. The rubbish from fallen structures is an immense pile and of great depth, extending over much of the town. I am not aware that any considerable attempt has been made at excavation in Thebes to disinter ancient remains. Such must exist here as well as in the other large towns, and probably would richly repay the expense of the search. Under a settled and enlightened government, something of the kind may soon be attempted. Thebes acted no very distinguished part in Grecian politics, nor was she ever honored by many literary men. Still, she had wealth, and a large population, and, it is to be presumed, public edifices in some measure commensurate with them. The columns and other fragments already disinterred are certainly inferior to what might have been expected in such a city, so long the metropolis of the most fertile state in Greece.

December 14th. I have had another opportunity of examining the situation of Thebes, and it certainly had more strength as a military position than I at first supposed. Immediately west of the city is a deep valley, the descent of which, though not precipitous, is very steep, and susceptible of easy and efficient defence against all the modes of warfare known to the ancients. The hill which overlooks this valley is the highest in the city, and upon it probably the ancient citadel was situated.

We were disappointed in not finding more tolerable accommodation in a place of so much importance, its population being hardly less than five or six thousand, and the surrounding region certainly the most fertile in the kingdom. The only inn or khan is one of the worst in a country where all are intolerably bad. We had our choice of several rooms upon the second story, and selected the one which, though probably the best in the house, proved to be immediately above the stable. In the stable, which was very large, not only horses and asses had quarters, but also the muleteers and guides, to the number, if a judgment might be formed from their incessant vociferations, of at least a dozen. I do not think they were all silent during an entire quarter of an hour throughout the night. The asses, too, were vocal, and huge dogs ever and anon joined in the chorus. The horses, though ordinarily silent and quiet animals, were adorned with bells similar to those put upon cows in America, which they wear at all times, and were thus enabled to act no inferior part in this dismal concert.

In a room next to us were stretched a half dozen or more Greeks, who either talked or snored incessantly. Hard by was a man ill with a fever. He groaned or raved at almost every breath. Another annoyance still more intimate we had in the fumes of the manure from the stable. The night was warm, and the odor was nearly suffocating. To finish the catalogue of misfortunes, swarms of fleas devoured us from the moment we attempted to sleep. Such a night of restlessness, and almost of agony, I have seldom experienced. I rose without refreshment, feverish and excited. A walk at daybreak in the balmy atmosphere revived me a good deal, and I set out upon the journey of the day, assured at least that I could hardly fare worse during the two additional nights which I must pass before returning to my comfortable hotel in Athens.

CHAPTER XXII.

BŒOTIA.

The level country which we had passed in travelling for the last two days, continues with little interruption to the long arm of the sea, that separates the island of Negropont from the mainland of Greece. Through this beautiful and fertile region, the more agreeable to us on account of its striking contrast to all that we had hitherto seen in Greece, lay our route for the day. The road was very good for horseback travelling, and even a carriage might pass with little difficulty over the greater part of the route. Such a luxury, however, has not probably been seen in Bœotia since the fall of the Byzantine empire. At first, we rode by ploughed fields of that dark, rich mould which we had so much admired around Leuctra and Platea, and from thence to Thebes. Then succeeded a large tract, which I took to be of the government domain from its being allowed to lie waste, though of exuberant fertility. After the first two hours, the soil is lighter but still very productive.

This is the season for sowing wheat, and a multitude of ploughs, drawn always by oxen, were in motion here and everywhere upon this magnificent plain. I have not seen any other animal attached to the plough in Greece, nor have I seen the ox employed in any other way. He is a small lean animal, more active far than the ox of New England, but certainly not half so heavy. The yoke is, I think, nearly six feet in length. I have seen a multitude of oxen in all parts of agricultural Greece,—certainly many hundred pair,—but scarcely a dozen cows in my whole excursion. All other cattle seem to be equally scarce. They are probably consumed in the large towns, whilst the oxen are reserved for agriculture. The cattle and sheep of Greece were nearly exterminated by the war. Horned cattle are yet very scarce, whilst sheep, which are more prolific, are now as abundant as ever. I much doubt whether the country is favorable to milch cows. It is dry, and the grazing land neither good nor abundant, at least in the parts I have visited. The grass and other vegetation that grows upon the mountains and other uncultivated lands, is sufficient to maintain the flocks of sheep, though the mutton is lean and insipid and the wool coarse. It is at least as much for the dairy as for these products that sheep are reared.

I have not tasted their milk, but I have their butter, which is strong and unsavory. Milk is very scarce. We have inquired for it at every stopping-place, but have obtained it only once during our whole journey. It is said to be out of season for this luxury. Swine, I think, are very scarce, as well as cattle. I have hardly seen so many as a dozen since I left Athens, where a great number are at large, and are no slight nuisance. The feathered race are much more abundant than quadrupeds. Chickens are to be had everywhere at low prices. Turkeys and geese, though less abundant, are often seen. I have seldom seen such flights of wild fowl. Wild ducks, wild geese, and pigeons we have seen almost every day in immense numbers. Flocks of crows follow the ploughman in every field, and devour the wheat which his imperfect ploughing has left uncovered. These mischievous birds are amazingly bold, and the confidence with which they approach the laborers in the field, is a proof that not much pains is taken to destroy them. They must be very destructive in parts of the country so much cultivated in grain as this is. I was told that the peasants do not shoot them, though no game-laws exist to prevent it, with the exception of a tax of three drachmas per acre for the privilege of hunting.

We stopped to rest and prepare dinner at about one-half the distance from Thebes to Oropo. To save time, Demetrius rode on before with orders to make ready against our arrival. We found him, however, just beginning to make a fire of fagots, and learned from him that he had found much difficulty in obtaining a place for these indispensable rites. He had applied to several persons without success, and at last was reluctantly received into a house with but one room and one door, occupied at the same time as a stable and a human dwelling-place. The first object that met my eye as I entered the door, was the oxen standing in the stall immediately before me. A small part of the room, from ten to twelve feet square, was appropriated to the family, and could be reached only by walking in the rear of the cattle. Here Demetrius was making a fire of fagots for the furtherance of his culinary designs, in the middle of the room, upon the bare ground, which was at once the only floor and the only fireplace. Mrs. —— had spread her bed upon a pile of fagots in the yard, for the purpose of taking some repose. I had found an old bee-hive, of which I made a seat also in the open air, as being the more comfortable quarters. We were waiting for the fruit of Demetrius' efforts, when we received a visit from the chief magistrate of the village, who approached us with the usual salutation, *ora hal'usin*, and invited us to go and occupy a fine room in his house.

We directed Demetrius to interpret to him our lively gratitude for his proffered hospitality, and our pressing haste as the reason why we declined the honor of being entertained by so respectable a personage. Demetrius performed the duty assigned to him in a most surly manner, evidently to the displeasure of the functionary, and then turned away in evident anger. Upon inquiry we learned that according to the custom in villages where there is no public house, he had at first applied to the hospitable Demarch, informing him that two gentlemen and a lady, Franks, wished for shelter for an hour. He was rudely answered by the Demarch, who refused to receive us into his house. He had waited, it seems, until he knew it would be impossible for us to comply with his invitation, and then came with proffers of kindness, fearing, probably, that we should make complaint against him for refusing what, according to usage, was our right. He urged his suit vehemently and ulmost angrily. He begged us to stay two or three days without charge, but having discovered his insincerity and villany, we paid little further respect to this servant of the crown, but were rather willing to allow him to discover our contempt.

He was evidently annoyed at the coolness with which we treated his overtures, though he continued to hover about till we were ready to leave. A military dignitary honored us with his company, having his pistols in his girdle. Indeed, no inconsiderable part of the population of this humble village were assembled before we had finished our humble repast, and gazed upon us and all our operations with a staring curiosity, which showed that such visitors were not often seen amongst them.

Our road to Oropo soon brought us near to the long sound of Negropont, and we had a beautiful view of an extensive range of the coast of that island. The city of that name, and another small town which our servant called Newtown—a translation, no doubt, of the Greek words having this meaning, made for the double purpose of making the matter comprehensible to us, and making known his own knowledge of English, were visible upon the opposite shore, and had a very pretty appearance. Some half a dozen of the small craft of the country were sailing toward these small ports, indicating, no doubt, pretty correctly, their commercial importance. After a narrow strip of flat land along the beach, lofty mountains arise as far as the eye can reach either way from one point of view. Far beyond these appeared others still more lofty and covered with snow.

One of these, of a conical figure, and apparently the highest in the island, had been visible for the greater part of our journey from Delphos. It had attracted our attention and remark by its peculiar and resplendent whiteness. I know not if imagination had not much to do with the impression, but it seems to me that the snow-capped mountains of this country have a lustre, a dazzling brightness which I have nowhere else observed. I made this remark when, from a distant part of the Morea, I saw the white tops of Parnassus and Helicon. The impression was strengthened at all the various points of view which, in a tortuous route by land and water, in valleys and over high mountains, I successively occupied. I am sure that the atmosphere of Greece has a transparency that does not belong to the northern climates of Europe. I think that, in this respect, it surpasses Italy. Distant objects are brought nearer, and I have several times been seduced into a fatiguing walk or ride to see objects which proved to be greatly more remote than to my eye, trained to estimate distances in a less transparent atmosphere, they had seemed to be. The same remark I had frequent occasion to make in Italy, which, however, I think is inferior to Greece in this respect.

Our path was along the beach for two hours or more, and, for a great part of the distance, in the water, with a bold high shore rising far above our heads. It was refreshing to breathe the pure sea air, and look upon its clear blue waters, and I could not but be struck with the contrast between nature and the improvements of civilization, such as we had recently seen them. My meditations, it is true, did not tend to a very profound philosophy. I was chiefly struck with the reflection that God's works are all *clean*—the sea—the blue sky—the green fields and the bare mountains upon which my eyes had so often wandered of late—all are *clean*, and I could not but regard the prevailing and disgusting filthiness that fills the habitations and dishonors the persons of the people with whom I had of late become familiar, as proofs of depravity as well as barbarism. Surely cleanliness has strong claims to a place amongst the virtues. Is it not always found where eminent moral purity exists? Does not the opposite vice tend to corrupt by degrading the mind? Let them smile upon these speculations as trivial, who have never travelled through Greece and spent twelve nights in a khan.

We slept this night at Oropo, an estate belonging to the Russian consul in Athens. It is an extensive and rich tract of land, which he purchased at a very reduced price of the Turks, when, at the close of the war, these fallen tyrants expected to be expelled from Greece, and were fain to obtain for their possessions even a part of their value. The house where we took lodgings is occupied by his agent, and is of a very superior order to the inns to which we had lately been accustomed. We had a tolerably clean plank to sleep upon. At first we were told that the rooms designed for travellers were all occupied, and that we could not have a place. We were indebted to my honorary title for the comfortable shelter to which we were finally admitted. The occupant of the house was ill, and after refusing us a place, asked Demetrius if either of the gentlemen was a doctor. Yes, was the reply. Demetrius, it seems, had all along taken me to be a physician. They then agreed that we should occupy a private apartment, reserved, I presume, from its superior style, for the use of the owner when he visits his estate.

I had hardly entered and congratulated my friends upon the unwonted comfort we were allowed to enjoy, when I received an invitation to visit the sick man and make a prescription. I assured Demetrius, and through him the sufferer, that I was no physician, and explained, as well as I could, how it sometimes may happen that a doctor is not a physician. The sick man was sadly disappointed, and even angry. He accused Demetrius of telling a lie to obtain lodgings. Against this charge, Demetrius indignantly protested, solemnly declaring, I doubt not, with perfect sincerity, that he had, up to that moment, believed me to be a doctor of physic. I am far from undervaluing the literary title which I wish I was more worthy to possess, but I do not remember that I have before derived from it any advantage so undoubted and satisfactory.

We met with Prof. Moore, of New York, at this place. We had made the voyage from Trieste to Athens in his company. He had just set out to visit the interesting places embraced in our tour, but had adopted a reverse order, beginning where we hope soon to end the excursion. He was three days from Athens, having been misled by his guide.

CHAPTER XXIII.

MARATHON.

December 15th. From Oropo to Marathon is a distance, according to our guide, of eight or nine hours. We made it in a little more than six, moving only in a quick walk. We stopped at a village about half way to prepare some refreshment, and, with the exception that the Demarch did not disturb us with his civility, had a fair repetition of the scene of yesterday. Our inn was again but a single room, used both for a parlor and a stable. Our horses entered by the same door with us, into the same apartment. This is the usual arrangement in Greece. The news of arrival again assembled the villagers, who only ceased from gazing at us intensely when we had mounted the horses and left the place.

These people remind me more and more every day of the North American Indian. In complexion they are lighter, but not unlike him. They have the same vaulting walk, the same erect and daring attitude. Perhaps the strongest part of the likeness is in dress. The moccasin of raw hide, made by perforating the edge with holes, and lacing it over the top of the foot with strings, is decidedly Indian. So is the coarse-stuff legging, fitting the ankle and calf of the leg closely, and tied below the knee. The tunic, too, is only a white shaggy blanket, hanging down not quite to the knee, with holes for the arms, and sometimes with sleeves. The Greek as well as the Indian wears a large knife stuck into his girdle, with the handle ostentatiously exposed. Their habitations are as similar as the difference of climate and building materials will permit. I speak here of the peasants of the interior. The dress of the females is a little different. They are barefooted. Their under-garment reaches to the ankles, and is usually ornamented with a gay border. Over this is worn a tunic like that of the man, reaching about to the knee, then a sleeved-jacket, reaching only to the waist. This and the tunic are often ornamented with needle-work, mostly red, in front, at the bottom, and down the middle of the back. A kind of sack is often thrown across the neck before, hanging to the waist behind, laden with a bunch of often very large beads, and little metal plates of the size of the smallest coin, worn, I suppose, for ornament, and as an aid to devotion. The men usually wear the Greek cap, which is always scarlet, high and cylindrical, surmounted with a tassel of blue, hanging from the centre of the crown. As a substitute for this, I have often noticed a common cotton shawl or large handkerchief wound about the head, not unlike the turban. The female peasantry often cover the head in much the same way. In the larger towns there is some variety in their head-dress, and many of them wear a red or yellow shoe, sharp at the toe, and of bungling workmanship.

The country between Oropo and Marathon is variegated, but chiefly mountainous and barren. The road must be called good here, but still it is only a path, and so precipitous, narrow, and obstructed by loose stones, or sharp shelving rocks, that in America I should without hesitation have pronounced it quite impassable, and should have thought the rash man who attempted to ride over it was doomed. Here, such is the effect of a fortnight's training, and such confidence in the ill-looking little horse of Greece, that I threw the rope carelessly upon his neck, to ride down or up the mountain, or hang upon its precipitous sides without any concern.

Before entering our hotel in Marathon, we rode over the celebrated field of battle between the Athenians and the Persians. It answers well to the description given of it by historians; only the plain is much more extensive than I had been led to expect to see it. I was a full hour in riding across it. It is almost a perfect level, though it seems to be sufficiently dry. The river Marathon, upon which the left flank of the Athenians rested for protection against the Persian cavalry, is now perfectly dry. Nor is there any marsh to answer to those mentioned by the historians. Many such changes have occurred in Greece, and one every day crosses the dry channels stated by the ancient writers to have been rivers in their age. The plain is bounded by the sea on one side, and by a semi-circle of mountains on all the others.

The immense army of the Persians was, according to the historians, drawn up across the plain in a line parallel to the sea and facing the mountains; the Athenians at the base of the mountain, were protected on either flank against the overwhelming numbers of their enemy by water or marsh. If the river was then flowing, as no doubt it was, it justifies the account, as far as the left wing was concerned. Perhaps, too, there was a marsh upon the right, though now it is a dry corn-field. The surface, however, is depressed in that part of the plain, and the changes in climate or other causes which have certainly dried up the river, would most likely exhale the moisture of the marsh. I have seen it objected to the received accounts of this battle, that there is not room for the evolutions of such armies.

I felt at first sight of this noble area that this objection is groundless. The host of Xerxes might have encamped upon it. An opinion which has gained some currency, transfers the contest from the semicircle of mountains to the pass between the sea and Mount Pentelicus, which is a mile and a half nearer Athens. This position would have suited the small band of Grecians admirably, by giving perfect security to their flanks and by contracting their enemy's front to the length of their own little host. It would have guarded also the most important pass to Attica. This theory, however, seems to me to contradict the accounts given by ancient historians.

There is near the centre of the plain an immense earthen mound, said, but rather improbably, to have been raised over the slaughtered Persians. It was more probably reared by the victors in honor of their own countrymen. There are also at no great distance the ruins of two ancient edifices, pronounced by history and tradition to be monuments of those who had a part in that great day.

Many doubts have been raised upon this point, and a popular traveller, whose work I had in my hand whilst surveying these ruins, declares that none exist except some brick foundations in quite another part of the plain. Yet I saw, as everybody may see, massive blocks of Pentelic marble, evidently ancient, and the remains of some great demolished structure. There are two such ruinous heaps not more than fifty yards apart. Doubtless they were rude monuments, reared in honor of the brave, by their grateful country.

I have been curious in my travels to visit the theatres of great battles, not, I trust, from admiration of deeds of blood. The battle field, however, decides the fate of nations—modifies for better or worse the various forms of human government, and retards or sometimes promotes the progress of human happiness. They are often the landmarks of history. They usher in new eras in the affairs of men. It is instructive and inspiring to stand upon such ground and contemplate the vast results which have sprung from the achievements or disasters of a single day. To my mind, history never speaks so distinctly as when I stand upon the spot where its heroes acted their parts. I make a détour very often to visit the grave or the birth-place of a great man, or the *locale* of a great event. In the same spirit I made a journey of two days to visit the plain of Marathon. I had from my boyhood looked upon the conflict of which this field was, two thousand three hundred years since, the bloody theatre, as one of the most interesting recorded in history. I had formed in my imagination a picture of Marathon—of its semi-circle of mountains, from which the brave Greeks rushed upon their foes—and of the sea upon which the discomfited Persians found a refuge after they had crimsoned its shores with their blood.

The sight of this plain verifies the historical narrative in a most satisfactory manner. So just had been my impressions, that I found myself looking upon the whole scene as one with which I had formerly been familiar. My impressions were erroneous in one respect only. I found everything on a much larger scale than I had imagined. This was precisely the reverse of what I have felt with regard to other places which I have seen in Greece. My imagination had expanded the cities and states of this classic and heroic land into dimensions, suited in some degree to the illustrious achievements of which they have been the theatres as well as the actors; and it has often cost me an effort to maintain undiminished my admiration for gallant republics and kingdoms, through whose entire territories my horse could walk in two hours.

I had no such difficulty at Marathon. The height and grandeur of the mountains, and the great extent of the plain, far surpassed my conception of them, and tended greatly to enhance my ideas of the splendid heroism and immense results of this most important of battles. When we look at this action as a brilliant display of courage and skill—when we admire the handful of intrepid men who braved and overwhelmed the mighty host of enemies who came to take away their liberty, we have taken only a narrow and unphilosophical view of the subject. We must consider that Greece at that time contained the learning, the liberty, and the civilization of the whole world. The Persian invasion was an assault of barbarism upon civilization. The battle of Marathon was a conflict between light and darkness. Had the Persian host prevailed, who can estimate the influence upon the future destinies of the race? Greece would have become a province of this immense despotism. Her shining galaxy of free and independent republics,—inconsiderable certainly in wealth and extent, but on that very account more favorable to liberty, to the growth of manly principles and high sentiments—to the elaborations of just political sentiments—to the improvement of the individual and of the social condition of man—would have been extinguished.

Even in Greece, civilization was not yet fully developed. She was not yet prepared to be the teacher of nations. Her literature and her arts were in comparative infancy. Phidias and Praxitiles were unborn. Thucydides and Xenophon had not written. Aristotle and Plato had not taught mankind. Greece was as yet but a nursery full of the germinating seeds of knowledge and improvement. But she had not yet commenced her mission as the teacher of the nations. Had Persia prevailed at Marathon, this mission would never have been accomplished. Providence might have accomplished the work by other means, but for aught that appears, ages upon ages of ignorance and barbarism would have been the consequence. Rome, who was proud to acknowledge her obligations to Greece for the arts and sciences, would only have spread barbarism with her conquests, and Britain, Gaul, and Germany, who received civilization in exchange for their wild independence, might have teemed with naked savages, such as fought against Julius Cæsar. Miltiades and the Athenians fought at Marathon for the civilization of mankind in all future time. Then victory, all but miraculous, rolled back the desolating tide, and secured not the country only, but the world.

Marathon was the forerunner of Thermopylæ, Salamis, and Platea. It was easy for Greece to conquer barbarians after Athens had demonstrated its practicability. The impulse which achieved all these victories was given at Marathon. The devotion of Leonidas and his Spartans was nothing to the feat of Miltiades and his Athenians. They first established the principle that civilization contains an element of strength, independent of numerical force. All the glorious events of the first and second invasions by Persia flowed from this great achievement naturally, and almost of course. It inspired the Greeks with confidence in themselves, in discipline, in intelligence, in freedom. From that day liberty and learning and civilization were consecrated in the general estimation, as not only the glory, but also the safe-guard of Greece.

The progress of society was amazingly accelerated.

All the arts and sciences, for which we are indebted to the ancients, speedily attained to perfection. In the brief period that elapsed from the Persian to the Peloponnesian war, architecture, sculpture, history and eloquence, attained an excellence which has never since been equalled.

Perhaps there is no event in the history of Greece, upon which most men are accustomed to look with more lively regret, than its subjugation to Philip of Macedon. The battle of Chæronea is spoken of as the final destruction of the glory of Greece. In what did that glory consist? In her free institutions? These were immensely valuable no doubt, as they hastened the development of a high civilization. It is in this light we are to look upon Greece as the civilizer of the world. Her republics, her freedom, were nothing only as they tended to this great end. More faction and disorder—less of security—did not perhaps exist amongst any people on earth. Yet was it a state of things precisely the most favorable for qualifying Greece to enter upon the mission to which she was destined. Her civilization, however, was fully developed before the battle of Chæronea. The successful diffusion of this civilization called for a different political organization.

The multitude of petty sovereignties, jealous and belligerent ever, was incompatible with this duty. Division and rivalry had nurtured and developed civilization. For its dissemination union and subordination were requisite. These the battle of Chæronea produced. It subordinated the jarring and heterogeneous elements to one controlling influence. It prepared the way for combined and efficient action. It enabled Alexander, at the head of the Grecian race, to subvert the great barbarian power in Asia, and establish in its stead Grecian rule, and with it science and civilization. In this view, which is the only broad philosophical one, the battles of Marathon and Chæronea were but separate triumphs of the same principle. They tended alike to fulfil the mission to which Greece was destined by Divine Providence—the civilization of the world.

The establishment of the power and diffusion of the letters of Greece over so large a part of the earth, became a most important means for the spread of the gospel of Christ. All who have taken large views of the subject have seen the hand of Providence visibly displayed in preparing the way of the Messiah, in the general diffusion of the arts, the philosophy, and, above all, of the language of the most civilized people in the world. The Greek had become the universal language. All men who read, or reasoned, or wrote, employed it as the vehicle of thought. When the apostles, therefore, spoke or wrote the precepts of the new religion, they, of course, adopted it; and by this means had the world for their audience. Doubtless, God could and might have found other means for the diffusion of His word. Still, He chose to employ this widely-diffused language in giving to all nations a knowledge of His saving truth, and, we are compelled to believe, prepared the way for it by directing the events which had made the language of Greece universal. The fate of the language was suspended on the field of Marathon. Had a different result followed the conflict upon that renowned plain, the language, the civilization and the power of Greece would have been obscured together.

In such meditations I indulged on the field of Marathon. And thus it was that Miltiades and his gallant host stood up before me as the champions of civilization and moral light—as fighting not for Athens, but for mankind. And thus their memory, their cause, and the field where they triumphed, were hallowed. I admired the Divine wisdom that prepared afar off, and in days of old, for the diffusion of light and life. It was the eve of the Sabbath, and I trust I was led by the scene before me into a train of reflections not unsuited to the holy season.

The Golden Horn.

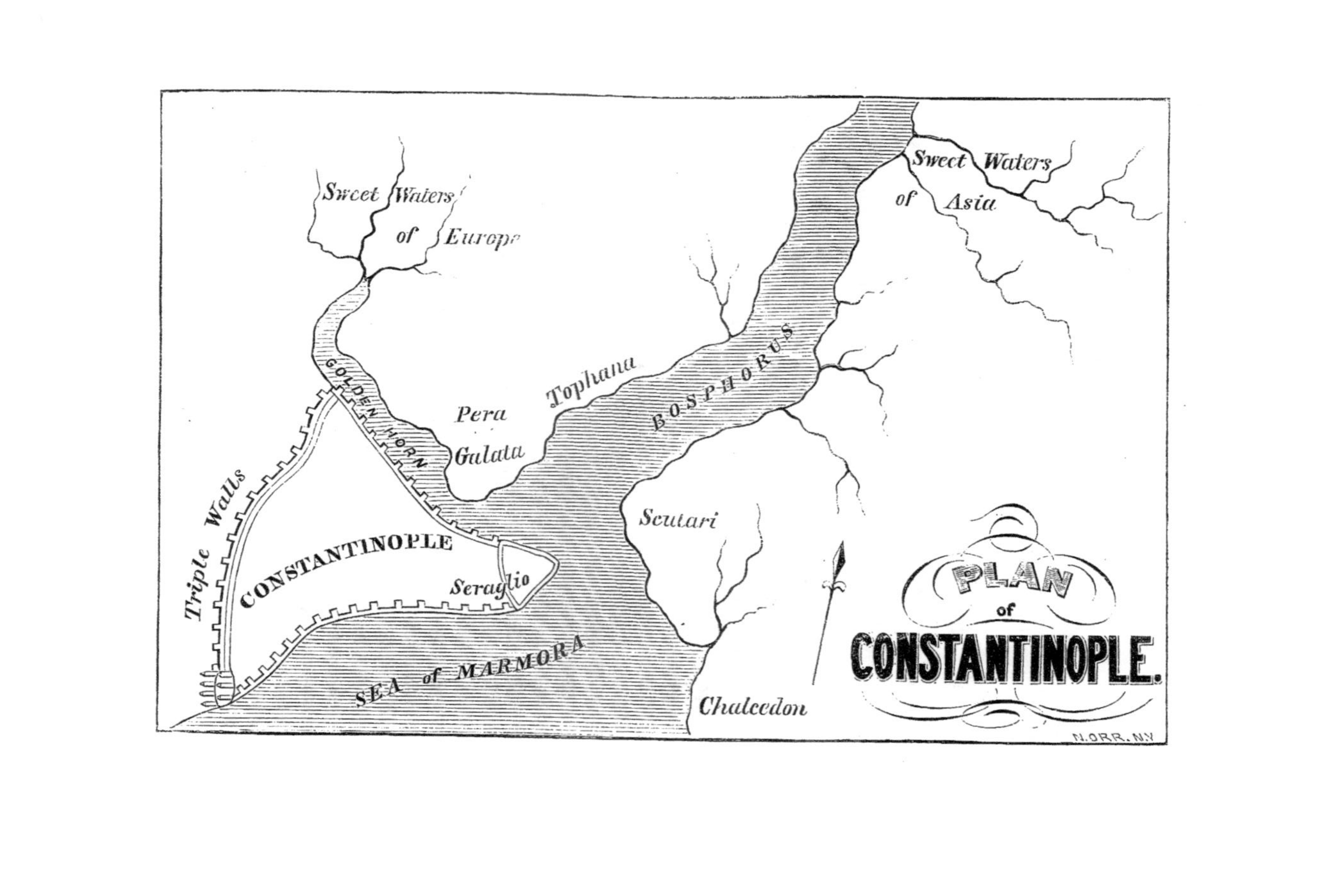
Sweet Waters of Europe
Sweet Waters of Asia
Pera
Galata
Tophana
BOSPHORUS
GOLDEN HORN
Triple Walls
CONSTANTINOPLE
Seraglio
Scutari
SEA of MARMORA
Chalcedon
PLAN of CONSTANTINOPLE.
N. ORR. N.Y.

CHAPTER XXIV.

CONSTANTINOPLE.

My first general view of Constantinople was from Mount Bourgaloue, to whose summit, shaded by low spreading pines, Turks as well as strangers frequently resort, for the extensive view it commands of the city and its environs. The undulating surface of this beautiful city appears to the spectator from this point like a level, so that its principal charm is lost by the too great elevation. Everything, however, is distinctly seen. The seraglio has the appearance of a forest ornamented with summer-houses. The noble line of mosques, that occupy the ridge of the promontory between the Marmora and the Golden Horn, is better seen than from any other point of view. I counted ten of these immense structures, which tower above the city, as well as the hundreds of other mosques inferior to them in their dimensions or position. Not less than eight barracks for the army are seen, chiefly in the outskirts of the town,—all extensive, magnificent establishments, occupying commanding sites.

Small clumps of cypresses in different parts of the town, and large forests in the suburbs, mark the sites of the cities of the dead, which occupy more ground than the habitations of the living. A multitude of ships in the harbor, between Constantinople and Pera, as well as in the Bosphorus, seemed to form a connection amongst the disjointed members of the great city. The view of the winding Bosphorus, and of the towns, palaces, and villages which line the European shore, as well as the gardens that cover the slopes of the hills, is truly magnificent. It extends above Buyuk-dere to the distance of seventeen or eighteen miles. The eye ranges over a vast region in the interior, composed of hills and valleys, little cultivated, which appear to be an immense plain, bounded by the horizon. In the direction of the Black Sea, the forest of Belgrade covers a large tract.

South of Constantinople are seen the edifices and villages that cover the shore of Marmora with little intermission to St. Stephano. The Marmora stretches south beyond the reach of vision, which extends to a large island in its bosom. Thence the view is bounded by a range of mountains that rise beyond the gulf. Near the head of the gulf, and at the distance of a hundred miles, the snowy tops of Olympus glitter in the sunbeams and dazzle the eye by their brightness.

Withdrawing our attention from this distant and glorious object, Prince's islands, six in number, rise from the Marmora five or six miles distant. Scutari is scarcely visible, as its aspect is west, but on the shore, a mile below, is the ancient site of Chalcedon, now a mean village, but beautified with many trees. An immense forest of cypresses, shading Mussulman tombs, extends from near this village east for several miles. Between this and the Marmora a part of the Sultan's army lay encamped, their green tents and floating banners presenting a fine appearance.

Looking east, with the back towards the city, the eye commands a noble view of the region stretching from the sea of Marmora—the bay of Nicomedia, as the arm of it is called—to the Bosphorus and Euxine. It is the ancient Bithynia—a region of hills and valleys, bounded by very distant mountains, which seem to encompass it in the form of a semi-circle. Farms and clumps of trees are seen at intervals, but the lovely region is mostly waste.

As we descended, we met several Turks going up with their pipes. Servants carried carpets, mats, and other appliances, to make their stay agreeable. Their horses, finely caparisoned, waited at a distance. Still nearer the village, which occupies the base of the mountain, we passed a company of Turkish women veiled, eating sweatmeats. They made the ascent in vehicles drawn by oxen, and furnished with cushions ornamented with tassels, instead of seats, to enjoy the shade in the hottest part of the day. We were an hour and a half descending the mountain. We saw on our way an Armenian cemetery, cultivated like a garden, with tombs similar to those of Europeans, and the kiosk where Mahmoud, the late Sultan, died. In recrossing the Bosphorus, we passed near a small circular structure, built on a rock that rises in the sea. Many traditions are afloat about its origin and design. It is the point to which chains were fastened, one of which extended to the Asiatic and the other to the European shore, to guard the entrance of the Bosphorus. Formerly some guns were mounted here. It is now, it is said, used as a lighthouse, though it had none of the usual appearances of one.

I passed from Galata to Stamboul with Mr. Hamlin, at 4 P.M. The city wall is at some distance from the water, the space between being built up. The custom-house, where we landed, is a handsome, solid building, with large ware-houses annexed. Soon after passing the gate, we came to the tomb of Sultan Ahmed. It is a beautiful structure of white marble, with rounded corners and a dome. It has a fountain and court full of trees, and is itself a place for prayer, being carpeted and matted. The Sultan's tomb is in the centre, under the dome. It is so concealed by the coverings of rich shawls, that its model cannot be seen. It is of beautiful marble, eight or ten feet long, eight high, and six wide, with a turbaned head upon its higher end. It is enclosed by a light railing, adorned with mother of pearl mosaic. Above it is suspended a splendid chandelier.

A number of smaller tombs of similar form, erected probably in remembrance of other members of his family, fill the edifice. All are covered with rich shawls, and the whole has a splendid appearance. Some men were engaged in prayer, which they left to drive us from the door. We proceeded to the wall which separates the Seraglio from the town, and followed its course to St. Sophia, a distance of perhaps half a mile. It is ancient, of stone intermingled with bricks, surmounted with turrets, and strengthened with square towers. Opposite to a gate on the west side of the Seraglio is the gate which leads to the Grand Vizier's palace, separated from the Seraglio by a street. The palace was burnt some time since. The site is very large. There were no signs of re-building, but I observed two large granite columns on the spot. Between the entrance of the Seraglio and St. Sophia is a large fountain of marble, gorgeously decorated with gold. By means of a small bucksheesh we passed into three courts of the Seraglio. We walked into St. Sophia also; and, despite the wonder and the hostile demonstrations of a group of Mohammedan boys, seated near the entrance with their school-master, I advanced into the interior, and was enabled, in the brief time allowed me by their indecision, to obtain a good view of this venerable and imposing edifice. The boys, however, followed me, and joined as they were by some men, they soon disregarded the air of stern authority I assumed; and throwing stones at me, and manifesting by unequivocal signs their anger at the intrusion of a Frank into their holy place, they obliged me to make good my retreat, which I happily did without receiving any injury.

A little south of this mosque is that of Sultan Achmet. We looked at the noble courts and gallery, but declined the invitation to enter for a bucksheesh. Immediately west is the Atmeidan, or horse course—the ancient Hippodrome—a quadrangle of three hundred yards long, by a hundred and fifty wide. It was formerly much more extensive. There are some interesting antiquities: an obelisk from Thebes, the pedestal of white marble, under which are blocks of red granite. It contains bas reliefs, a good deal damaged. One represents machinery by which the obelisk was raised—men pulling at ropes, &c., in the presence of the emperor and suite. Another side has a continuation of the same subject, and below a Latin inscription, signifying that Theodosius reared in a short time this pillar, which had proved too difficult a work for his predecessors. The third side represents chariot races, which probably took place on the occasion. The fourth has the inscription in Greek. The obelisk, which may be fifty feet in height, rests on four brass pillars standing upon the pedestal, from which it is elevated about one foot. It is in good preservation. The hieroglyphics have not suffered perceptibly from time, their angles being still sharp and perfect. On the north it is discolored, and covered partially with short moss,—a fact that points to the quarter whence the cold rains approach.

A few yards south of the obelisk is the celebrated spiral pillar which once supported a pillar at Delphos. It is of brass, formed of three huge serpents twisted together, growing smaller towards the top, from which the heads of the serpents are broken. It may be fifteen feet high, and it is much battered, and filled with stones. One hole is said to have been made by a cannon shot in the war with the Janissaries, under the late Sultan. The diameter is from twelve to fifteen inches.

A little farther south, and in a line with the two objects just described, is the lofty square column of Constantine Porphyrogenitus, built of blocks of marble, and covered originally with plates of metal, as is manifest from the holes of the nails which appear in the stones. The marbles are loose, and threaten to fall. The Atmeidan is still used for equestrian fêtes.

At the distance of less than half a mile, on the Adrianople street, is the burnt column, an immense pillar, nearly a hundred feet high, which has its name from having been discolored and fractured by the frequent fires that raged around it. It is so built around as to be unapproachable, but, as seen from the street, it has the appearance of porphyry. The joints of the column are or were concealed by metal hoops, much out of place. Wreaths wrought in the stone also encompass it at certain distances. A statue of Apollo once surmounted it. A Greek inscription is seen near the top, which I was enabled to decipher.*

A few rods south of the Adrianople street is a curious ancient cistern, now partially dilapidated and a good deal filled up. It was once used in supplying the city with water, which it probably received from the aqueduct of Valens. It is an immense reservoir, formed of thick solid walls, and covered with a roof of many arches, supported by a vast number of columns. It was too dark to count them, but the number is stated at 424. It is from this colonnade that it derives the name of Bin-bir-derek, or thousand and one columns. It is entered by a door on the south side, which

* "By the inscription we learned 'that that admirable piece of workmanship was restored by the most pious emperor, Manuel Commenes.' Tournefort's Voyage in the Levant." 1741.

leads to a flight of wooden steps. It has the appearance of a mound of earth rising eight or ten feet above the common level. There is a considerable accumulation of rubbish on the arched roof. Several holes, broken through the roof by accident or design, admit a feeble light. At noon it is sufficient for the purposes of the tenants of this subterranean abode—a dozen or more wretched, sickly-looking silk spinners, who were engaged in their occupation in the dim twilight, which had already settled upon these vaults at 4 o'clock in the afternoon, though the regions above were enjoying a brilliant sunshine. The ground was damp. We were conducted to a spring, the only water now in this cistern, of which we were urged to drink, and assured that the quality is excellent.

CHAPTER XXV.

WALLS AND TOWERS.

June 23, 1840. I set out at about eight this morning from Pera, the Frank quarter of Constantinople, to make an excursion to the Seven Towers. We crossed the Golden Horn upon the long bridge, not less certainly than half a mile long, built of wood, and resting upon floating rafts of timber. It is but little raised above the water, except at two points, where there are arches of considerable elevation to allow boats to pass under them. At the same points are draws, which are raised when a ship of war goes to sea from the navy-yard immediately above, or returns for repairs. Merchant vessels cannot pass above the bridge. Their most crowded resorts are immediately below it, on both sides of the Golden Horn. This bridge is in a sheltered situation, where heavy winds and seas have little power upon it. It is secured in its position by a multitude of anchors and strong cables attached to its timbers, at intervals of only a few feet. No tolls are paid by passengers, and the bridge is much used, though above the business parts of Pera, Galata, and Constantinople.

We obtained horses at the south end of the bridge, and entering the city by the nearest gate, proceeded at no great distance from the wall in a western direction. Our route, which we chose at hazard, willing to see as much of the city as possible, lay through the quarters occupied by the Jews and Greeks. Ballat, or the Jews' town, is perhaps the worst part of Constantinople, the streets more uncleanly and confined, and the houses in a more ruinous, neglected condition. Few of them are painted,—all, or nearly so, are built of wood, and the boards hang loose and ready to fall. The windows are broken and not glazed, and the open doors of the lower rooms disclosed scenes of filth and poverty. The shops, of which we passed a great many, are very meanly supplied with only the most common provisions and articles of merchandise. The large dealers and wealthy Jews, of whom there are many here, transact business in other parts of the city. I have been assured that even in these mean, ruinous houses, comfort and even elegance and refinement may often be found. The rapacity and injustice to which these unfortunate people, even more than others, have long been subjected in this country, have produced habits of caution. Apparent wretchedness is adopted as the best safeguard for real affluence and independence.

The aspect of the Fanar or Greek quarter is decidedly superior to that of the Jews. The houses are more spacious and in better repair. They are favorably distinguished from those of the Turks by the absence of lattice-work from the windows. The habits of the Greeks in this respect are more European than

Oriental. The women appear in Frank costume, and wear no veils. Indeed, their national characteristics are rapidly disappearing, and the Greeks of Constantinople seem likely to become fully Europeanized, even sooner than their brethren in their native land. No Greek, however, any more than a Jew, is allowed to paint his house in gay colors. These belong to the Turk, who alone may employ bright yellow, green, and white.

We dismounted to enter a Greek church, which is inclosed by a high wall in a large court. It is a plain but respectable edifice, in good repair, and decorated in the Greek style with many small paintings and engravings. The Virgin Mary has the place of undisputed pre-eminence in the pictorial part of their religion, no less than among the Catholics. This church, as I learned on a second visit to this part of the city, belongs to the Bishop of the Church of the Holy Sepulchre.

After leaving the Church, we passed out of the city at the Egri Kapoussi, or oblique gate, which is in the western wall, near the north-western angle, and a short distance only from the Golden Horn. We found ourselves at once in a vast field of graves, filled with Turkish monuments and shaded with cypresses. A paved road runs parallel with the wall from this point south to the sea of Marmora. Turning to the left into this highway, the best I have yet seen in Turkey, we soon reached a fountain built against the wall, which seems to be a place of considerable resort. The water designed for the use of the neighborhood runs through a pipe into a marble reservoir, situated in the usual manner on the outside of the building. We passed through a door into a large room, which receives from the aqueduct of Valens a large quantity of water designed for the supply of this part of the city. It is poured into a large marble basin by a multitude of pipes, through which it is filtered, and flows off in a copious stream to its destination. The play of the water produces an agreeable coolness in the atmosphere, and a number of cane-chairs or stools are placed upon an elevated part of the marble floor, where the Turks, during the heat of the day, enjoy their favorite luxury of smoking.

The west wall of Constantinople has an appearance of great antiquity, and was probably built by the Greek emperors. Tiles are mingled without much order in the rough stone masonry of which it is composed. Many parts are in a ruinous condition, though nowhere quite prostrate. These bulwarks might be of some use in resisting an assault, but would be easily demolished by a battery of heavy ordnance. There are two parallel walls, the interior the highest, distant from each other perhaps twenty or thirty feet. This space is in many places full of rubbish and planted with trees. Both walls are surmounted by small turrets, and along the outer at short intervals are massive towers, square, round, and octagonal, which rise forty or sixty feet in height. Outside of the towers is a fosse, twenty or twenty-five feet wide, faced with stone. It is in some places twenty feet deep. In others it is quite filled with earth. The soil which has accumulated in the bottom is rich, and a considerable extent is covered with fine wheat. Another portion is planted with fig trees, which also thrive well. A company of gipsies were encamped in this ancient fosse, near the Adrianople Gate. Their filthy, black turbans and tattered dress proved their fraternity with the same race in more western regions. Their tents were of coarse black wool, or hair, and not unlike those of the Bedouins, except in form.

The western walls and towers are among the most interesting objects that invite the attention of a traveller visiting Constantinople. Several of the towers have undergone repairs, and some of them seem to have been mostly rebuilt. The larger number, however, as well as the entire wall, are evidently in the state in which they were formed, upon the transfer of imperial power from the Greeks to the Mohammedan dynasty. Vestiges of the violence of war, no less than of the ravages of time, are everywhere apparent—partial breaches in the wall—half-demolished towers remain as they were when Mahomet II. entered the conquered city. Large trees rise from the very summits of these stately ramparts. The highest towers are so completely covered with running ivy as to conceal the masonry very perfectly, and several of them are rent from top to bottom, gaping wide and threatening to tumble headlong. The venerable, hoary aspect of these ancient bulwarks, their vast extent, the rich variegated verdure, and overhanging waving foliage, which mingle with shade and half conceal semi-dilapidated monuments of bygone ages—form altogether one of the most picturesque, historical, and impressive scenes to be found in any part of the world.

The Gate of Adrianople, which opens into the greatest thoroughfare of the city, seems to have been adorned with colonnades and other ornamental constructions, the fragments of which cover the ground. Cannon Gate, memorable as that through which the Ottoman conqueror entered the town, is upon a high ridge, but is not otherwise remarkable.

Of the Seven Towers, once celebrated as the prisons where foreign ambassadors were sometimes confined by the Porte, only three are now in existence. These have lately been rebuilt—two are round, the other is octagonal. I was told that the largest is used as a powder magazine. The entrance is on the outside of the city, through a court enclosed in a high wall of recent construction, and adapted to the new purposes to which the edifices have been devoted.

This western wall of Constantinople, which extends quite across the peninsula, from the Golden Horn on the north, to the Sea of Marmora on the south, I should conjecture to be not less than five miles in length. The region west of the town swells into gentle hills, but seen from any elevated position, a little distant, has the appearance of a boundless plain. There are a few gardens and cultivated fields in sight, but it is mostly a waste, affording, however, in the spring and autumn, pasturage to flocks of sheep. Near the wall, and to distances extending in some places several miles, this is an immense burying ground, crowded with Turkish monuments and planted with cypresses. In this neighborhood is the Armenian cemetery, which lacks the appropriate ornament of the dark waving cypress, reserved by custom, and it is said by law, to protect and beautify the resting-places of the faithful.

There are five gates in this end of the city, from each of which a broad highway has been cut through this vast necropolis to different parts of the country. Indeed, so vast a space has been devoted to the dead around Constantinople, that it is no longer possible to respect the sanctity of their abode without interfering greatly with the convenience of the living, and even an entire sacrifice of public convenience. Immense as the city is, I am quite sure that much more ground is occupied by tombs and graves than by the habitations of the living. The whole country about Constantinople, Scutari, and Pera, is occupied in this way, and a vast number of tombs and burying-grounds are enclosed within the walls. In forming roads, streets, and in building, it is no longer possible to spare them, and one often treads upon causeways or pavements made of sculptured grave-stones and monuments.

CHAPTER XXVI.

CONSTANTINOPLE.

WE re-entered the city at the Seven Towers, and passed through an Armenian quarter in returning to the bridge, where we must leave our horses. The houses are of wood, mostly unpainted, and in an almost ruinous condition. Still the occupants are many of them rich, and the slovenly and wretched appearance of their habitations must be ascribed to the cause already mentioned—the fear of exciting the envy and provoking the rapacity of their oppressors. This danger has, I apprehend, nearly passed away, but the effect of former days of cruel oppression, remain in this as in a thousand other instances, in the habits and vices of the people. The Armenians impose upon their women a bondage less severe than the Turks. Still their females always appear veiled in public, and the lattice that marks the front windows of many of their houses, demonstrates that a more domestic and private supervision is also maintained. In many of their houses, however, as well as those of the Greeks and Franks, a part of the front projects over the street, forming a sort of recess in the saloon, with side windows, which command a view of all that takes place in the street, up and down, as far as it follows a straight direction. In this niche the females may be seen seated, gazing eagerly at the passers-by. They sometimes draw the curtains which hang before the side-lights, to screen themselves from the view of the too curious gazer, but usually show no less willingness to be seen than to see. This custom is the natural effect of the restraints imposed upon females, and shows at least that they are not led to adopt the prevailing custom from any lack of curiosity, which is so natural to the sex, and indeed to the species.

We passed under the arches of the aqueduct of Valens, which conducts the water for the supply of Constantinople, from Belgrade, a distance of twelve miles. It has a ruinous appearance, but still answers the purpose of its erection. It is constructed of unhewn stone and mortar. The arches are of brick. It forms a striking object when seen from a distance, running along one of the most elevated ridges in the city. Through a great part of the distance, the water is carried under ground in covered channels of masonry and leaden pipes. The Turks have added a curious appendage to this subterranean portion of the aqueduct. Towers of fifteen or twenty feet in height, are erected at short and regular intervals, with a basin on the summit, into which the water rises by a pipe leading up one side of the tower. It immediately descends from this aërial reservoir by a second pipe on the opposite side, and pursues its hidden way until it is again exalted to an interview with the sun and atmosphere by a similar contrivance. It is difficult to conjecture the object, or more probably the mistake in hydraulics which led to the adoption of this novel expedient.

We passed, on our return, through a part of the city inhabited by Turks, not much visited by Franks, and had some experience of the bigoted hostility towards Christians, which has nearly subsided in Pera and the more frequented parts of Constantinople, but which still exists in full force in some remote parts of the capital, as well as in many provincial towns and villages. I was saluted by a stone thrown by a boy, which, however, did not harm me. Several others struck our horses as we passed. They fly with alarm at the least symptom of resistance or retaliation, though the persons who happen to be spectators of their rudeness, show no disposition to restrain them.

After returning with our horses to the point of departure near the bridge, and lunching at a neighboring restaurant, not much distinguished for the attraction of cleanliness, nor far advanced in the European improvements, which are so rapidly transforming everything Turkish, we returned again towards the central parts of the city, to examine an ancient sarcophagus, commonly called that of Theodosia. We passed at no great distance from the wall, a large steam mill, recently erected in a very substantial manner, unlike almost all other private buildings in Constantinople.

We succeeded in finding the sarcophagus after a good deal of difficulty, and threading a multitude of narrow, crooked streets. It stands in a small open space near a fountain. It is formed of a solid mass of breccia, nine feet in length, four and a half feet wide, and, including the lid, which is very thick and solid, about six feet in height. The figure of the cross, partially defaced by the zeal of the crescent, is yet distinguishable upon the sides and top. A hole has been broken through one of the ends, and it seems to have been used as a reservoir, though at present it holds no water.

This sarcophagus has not the elaborate finish which might have been expected from its being devoted to the sepulchre of a royal person. Indeed, this circumstance casts some doubt upon its claims to be regarded as the sarcophagus of Theodosia. Its form and proportions, however, are graceful, and it certainly belongs to an age as early as that of the Greek emperors.

Two or three fragments of large Syenite columns are seen at no great distance—a probable indication that some elegant public edifice once existed on the spot. Several large masses of ancient brick-work also are seen in this neighborhood.

The Lunatic Asylum is distant about a mile and a half, near the mosque Solomynia. We were stopped by the guard at the door, but were allowed to pass upon the promise of giving a bucksheesh, a term as common in the Turkish as in the Arabic language. It seems to be naturalized in all the languages of the Levant. Our ears were at once saluted with the clanking of chains, and the horrors of the mad-house in Cairo were suddenly recalled to my mind. I approached the grated cells and found them occupied by brown bears, who seemed happy enough in the situation, but were chained to guard against mischief and escapes.

After a few minutes spent in examining this menagerie, we proceeded through another gate guarded like the first, by several soldiers, who also demanded a buckshеesh, into another quadrangular court, where the lunatics are confined. The building is of a single story, being raised two or three feet above the pavement, and fronting on the court. The windows are grated with iron bars, without glass. The doors were open, and there are windows in the rear of the cells corresponding with those in front. The cells are of course well aired and ventilated. They are also tolerably clean—remarkably so, considering the little attention usually paid to this subject in the streets and houses of the Turks. Each of the unfortunate inmates had a mat with a quilt and blanket for coverings. A water pitcher and a drinking cup or bowl, both of coarse red earthenware, were near them. Considerable attention has evidently been paid to their comfort and health, and nothing is decidedly revolting to the feelings of the visitor, but the enormous, heavy chains with which every one is bound. They are not less massive than the chains commonly used in America for ploughing and hauling logs. The base links are fastened around the neck with a padlock; the whole is twelve or fifteen feet in length, and the end runs through the grates, and is secured in the outside of the wall. One of the patients was almost entirely naked, and seemed wild enough to require strict confinement.

The rest were perfectly quiet, either silent or chaunting in low melancholy strains. They looked pensive and contemplative, and generally kept their eyes fixed upon the floor, or only raised them to take a single glance at the stranger. Several of them were smoking, some were dining, and the provision seemed to be plentiful and wholesome. They were respectably clad, and the soldiers, as well as the citizens, who may have been relatives, entered their cells freely, and contemplated their situation with evident tenderness and respect. They even appeared unusually cheerful—a circumstance which was probably owing to the high veneration in which idiots and madmen are held by the Turks, who regard them as the special favorites of Heaven.

10*

CHAPTER XXVII.

COFFEE-HOUSES.—THE SERASKIER'S TOWER.

WE next proceeded to the long range of coffee-houses just outside of the vast courts of the Mosque of Solomynia. These coffee-houses are one of the most thronged and favorite resorts of the respectable Turks, who spend many hours of the day in smoking, and sipping their favorite beverage. The buildings are of one story, and consist of a row of small shops or stalls, where the refreshments are kept or prepared, with a covered gallery running in front. These are shaded with trees, and fitted up with divans and elevated benches two or three feet high, covered with carpets or mats, and running close to the street near the outer side of the gallery, where the shade of the trees and the fresh air can be most fully enjoyed.

Here the Turks may always be seen in large numbers, sitting cross-legged, their slippers off, and apparently buried in listless, thoughtless animal enjoyment. They smoke their immensely long, and sometimes intricate and highly curious pipes, with the utmost deliberation. Long pauses follow every puff. The smoke rises slowly, and scarcely discolors the atmosphere. One Dutchman or German raises a thicker and larger cloud of smoke than a score of Turks. Scarcely a word is heard. A single monosyllable, uttered in a low voice, or even a sigh, informs the watchful publican when the pipe is to be replenished, or a cup of coffee, or a glass of water or sherbet is wanted. You may observe one of these companies of absorbed and scarcely conscious Musselmen for half an hour, without seeing a single face lighted up with a smile, or indeed betraying any emotion.

The half-closed and inexpressive eye turns slowly towards the approaching stranger, and is probably riveted upon him in his seat, if his foreign dress and air exhibit anything peculiar. On the present occasion, after taking a cup of coffee, and resting for a few minutes, I made some notes with my pencil. This is almost the only thing that is capable of exciting the curiosity of these phlegmatic people, and this seldom fails to rouse them from their repose. Several grave, turbaned, serious personages immediately put on their slippers, and came close to me, to witness the process by which I was attempting to record some of the peculiarities of their customs and character. They were, of course, not the wiser for the examination, and they soon returned to their luxurious repose. The Turks are not only very curious to examine the writings of strangers, but very vain of exhibiting their own ability to write or to read a manuscript. I have often seen men of great apparent respectability make an ostentatious and rather ludicrous display of their accomplishments on board steam-boats, and in other public places where the presence of strangers afforded a temptation to such an exhibition.

This range of coffee-houses was formerly the great resort of the opium eaters, of whom so many travellers have given graphic, and, as I suspect, rather poetical descriptions. I repeated my visit to this place, in hopes of seeing some remains of this race, but without success; and was repeatedly assured, in answer to inquiries addressed to many intelligent Franks, as well as natives of the city, that no such persons at present exist. It is said that the freer use of wine and spirits by the Turks has produced this change; but those who have enjoyed the most favorable opportunities for obtaining accurate information, concur in declaring that the representations referred to, if not wholly fabulous, are grossly exaggerated; and I did not converse with a single individual who had ever known an opium eater, though many professed to have been at much pains to obtain correct information on this point.

The coffee-houses are the great places of congregation in Constantinople. They are instead of hotels, theatres, news-rooms, and all other places of amusement. The number of these establishments is immense, and they seem always to be well patronized. Many of them are fitted up with much elegance, or rather with much gorgeousness—marble fountains, gilded canopies, splendid carpets, are common decorations. The coffee is served in a very small gilded porcelain cup, holding not more than a common wineglass. It is usually very strong, and thick with the grounds, which are always found in the bottom of the cup. The Turks used to drink it without sugar, as the common people do now; but the wealthier begin to prefer this Frank innovation. Milk and cream are not used. A cup of coffee with sugar costs hardly more than one cent. There is indeed no place where such abundance of agreeable refreshments may be had at so low a price. Various preparations,—curds, ice-creams, &c.,—are sold at every corner of the street, and hawked through the market places, not only at excessively low prices, but of very good quality.

One of the best views of Constantinople and its environs is obtained from the Seraskier's Tower, to which we proceeded from the cafês of the Solomynia. It rises in the centre of a vast enclosure, which embraces the different offices and appendages of the Turkish War Department. The site is one of the most commanding in the city. Its situation is central, and the tower, standing upon a lofty eminence, is itself nearly 160 feet in height. The ascent is by a spiral staircase, consisting of 180 steps, each about ten inches high. Near the summit, the diameter of the tower is enlarged, and forms a spacious circular room with windows on all sides, from which a view may be had in all directions. A guard of several soldiers is stationed here, and here coffee and other refreshments are served.

The chief advantage of this point of view over those afforded by the tower of Galata, and the mountain in the rear of Scutari, consists in its commanding every part of Constantinople. Standing upon the high ridge about equally distant from Marmora and the Golden Horn, the plains which incline from this ridge both north and south are immediately under the eye of the spectator. From Galata half the city is concealed, whilst from Bourgaloue the whole of Scutari is unseen, and the city, too remote as well as too low, is seen indistinctly. From the Seraskier's Tower, Pera, Scutari, the harbor and shipping, the Bosphorus as high as Buyuk-dere, with all the natural and artificial beauty that borders its incomparable shores, as well as the Sea of Marmora with its islands, and the vast chains of mountains, including the white tops of Olympus, which bounds the view beyond it, are all seen with wonderful distinctness and effect. As to the city itself, the eye readily traces the wall in all its vast compass. The position and form of the bazars, palaces, mosques, colleges, and principal khans, are spread out as upon a good map.

The admirable taste shown by the Turks in choosing the sites for their public edifices, is one of the first things that strike the stranger who visits Constantinople, but it can nowhere else be so fully appreciated as from the summit of the Seraskier's Tower. Every commanding summit either in the city or its precincts, and certainly no other spot on earth can have so many and so splendid, is occupied by a palace, mosque, or other public edifice. Look which way you will, some noble structure, magnificent both from its simple proportions and lofty position, arrests the eye, and effectually screens all meaner objects, of which there is the greatest abundance, from fixed and minute observation. Common habitations, too, are marked by the trees, which abound in all parts of the city, and impart to it a rural and lovely aspect. Only the red tile-roofs are visible amongst the overshadowing foliage.

The graceful white minarets of the inferior mosques, surmounted always with a glittering, golden crescent; and the magnificent domes and loftier towers of the principal mosques, which crown the hill tops, rise conspicuous above the vast field of humble edifices, and the verdure which half conceals them. Fifteen of these noble religious structures crown the graceful summits of the peninsula, stretching in a waving line from St. Sophia, close to the seraglio, to the western wall of the city, a distance of five or six miles. Either of these fifteen mosques is decidedly superior to St. Paul's church in London, in magnificence of proportions and position. The beautiful spires of two hundred smaller mosques mingle on all sides with the dark foliage of the tall cypresses, and it is said there are at least twice as many more inferior places consecrated to Musselman devotion.

Most of the buildings belonging to the War Department are of slight and mean construction. They are small, made of wood, and some of them nearly ruinous in appearance. It is surprising that such inflammable materials should be used when it is so necessary to guard against fires. On descending from this tower, I observed an immense globular basket, painted red, and suspended by a rope from the top. It is of the size of a small cottage, and is employed, I was told, in giving notice of fires.

Just outside of the high walls that encompass the War offices, are long ranges of shops wholly devoted to the sale of vessels and utensils manufactured of brass. They are almost exclusively of Turkish workmanship, and they exhibit a very creditable state of this branch of the arts. The vast extent of the district devoted to this single branch of trade is an impressive evidence of the great population of the capital. These articles are mostly manufactured in the city. Many of the workshops are seen near the Golden Horn, below the bridge.

CHAPTER XXVIII.

THE BAZARS.

A WALK of a few minutes brought us to the Bazars, a characteristic and very interesting feature of Constantinople. They occupy a very large and central region of the city, and form a labyrinth of streets and avenues, which a stranger learns to comprehend only after frequent visits and careful observation. I never attempted to visit them after any particular plan, but wandered from one to another as chance or fancy directed. They are formed of long ranges of small shops, and occupy both sides of a narrow street, which is commonly arched above, so as to form one continuous arcade. Sometimes a simple awning of mats, or a timber roof, is substituted in the less important bazars, for the stone arch. They are lighted by windows in the roof.

The several shops or stalls which are open in front, for the exhibition of merchandise on sale, are closed at night by light sliding or swinging doors, and the whole bazar is closed at an early hour by gates at each end, which are opened at a fixed and rather late hour in the morning. Each of these bazars is devoted to some one branch of trade, and is a separate and independent establishment. There is a great number of them, but they mostly occupy one region of the city. Sometimes several of them radiate from a common centre—others branch off as accident or convenience may dictate, forming a vast number of irregular and bewildering ramifications. The display of merchandise is very imposing and brilliant, far surpassing in variety, abundance, and splendor, anything I have previously seen in the Levant. Indeed, there is nothing equal to it to be seen in London or Paris, where a vast amount of business is transacted with much less display.

The bazars for the sale of shoes and slippers are among the most splendid. They are more than a quarter of a mile in length, and the slippers, which are of bright red and yellow leather, and many of them richly embroidered with silver and gold, are suspended on either side of the street, so as to form an immense gallery, radiant on all sides with the most dazzling brilliancy. Another splendid range is devoted to the exhibition and sale of embroidered muslins, silk shawls, and other similar wares. Here, too, is a gorgeous spectacle, such as is nowhere else to be seen. A vast amount of these glittering wares are consumed here, and the art of embroidery seems to have attained a high degree of perfection. The fabric upon which so much skill and precious metal are lavished, is commonly coarse and of a very inferior quality.

The saddle bazar also exhibits a great profusion of articles of the most rich and splendid colors, and resplendent with gold and silver. Turkish bridles are always highly ornamented. The reins, instead of simple leather, are often composed of some rich stuff, scarlet, yellow, or green, and every part susceptible of such ornament, is bespangled with gold and hung with gay silken tassels. The seat of the saddle is usually composed of red or blue broadcloth, richly embroidered. It is, however, upon the ample housing, or cloth which covers the whole horse, back of the saddle, and hangs low down the flanks, that the most attention is bestowed. It is usually of a gay color, crimson, olive, blue, &c. Long heavy silk tassels are suspended from the corners and along the lower border, and the whole glitters with silver and gold, embroidered in bold relief in beautiful and showy figures.

A Turkish saddle is uncomfortable enough to the rider, but nothing of the kind can be more picturesque and agreeable than the sight of one of their noble, spirited horses, splendidly caparisoned, walking or ambling along the street, bearing a pacha with his retinue of footmen before and on either side.*

* Omer Pasha, who had recently entered the service of the Sultan, was at that time engaged in active service on the frontiers. Born of a noble Croat family, he commenced his military career in the service of Austria. In consequence of a quarrel with a superior officer, he emigrated to Turkey, and entered the Ottoman army, where his remarkable ability and his services procured him a rapid advancement. For fifteen years he has distinguished himself in all the struggles which the Ottoman empire has had to sustain. The most memorable expeditions were those of Syria in 1844, and still later those of Georgia and Kurdistan. During the last, he established everywhere the authority of the Porte, and, as a pledge of the submission of the rebels, led as prisoner their chief, Berderkhan

A very rich and splendid bazar is devoted to the trade in furs, of which a vast quantity are used in Constantinople. This trade appears to be wholly monopolized by the Armenians, who are likewise principal consumers of the article. Every one who is able, and nearly all are so, has his winter garments lined throughout with fur. Even in the extremely hot days of June, when I experienced the most oppressive heat in perambulating the streets of this great capital, I constantly met with Armenians, and often with Turks, burthened with an ample outer garment of broadcloth—a kind of overcoat, reaching the heels, completely lined with thick fur.

They wear it, perhaps, to keep out cold, no less than for show, and, moving as they always do, in a slow, measured pace, they feel the inconvenience of such unreasonable clothing much less than men of a more mercurial and bustling temperament would do.

There is a bazar for calicoes, and another for silks—for broadcloths—for red caps—for leather—for arms—for hardware—for haberdashery—for old clothes—for carpets—for pipes—for jewellery—indeed for almost every article which enters largely into the trade and consumption of a great capital. The complete separation of the different branches of business, forms a very striking characteristic of all considerable oriental cities.

Bey, the last representative of the turbulent feudality which had been so rudely assaulted by Mahmoud. Sultan Abdul-Medjid, more merciful than his father, pardoned Berderkhan Bey, and recompensed his conqueror, by having a medal struck at the close of the campaign, with which he decorated his royal person.

It is a great convenience to the buyer, to find a collection of all the wares of which he may wish to purchase, in a single locality. It must be favorable, one would think, to useful rivalry amongst manufacturers, as well as to a wholesome competition amongst sellers, to have their wares brought into a mart so conspicuous and extensive, and subjected to a ready and accurate comparison with those of all other dealers in the same line.

The bazars share with the coffee-houses in being the principal, and almost the only places of common resort in Constantinople. In passing through the streets which conduct to them, you might imagine yourself in the midst of a deserted city. Only here and there a solitary individual is moving slowly towards or from these favorite haunts. Pass the open gate, and the eye ranges over a living mass of human beings, extending the whole length of the street. When the spectator happens to be stationed at one of the radiating points, from which half a dozen bazars diverge in right lines, the spectacle is grand and imposing. Every avenue is crowded with men and women, clad in the most various, but always the most showy and dazzling costumes. The red caps of the men, the snow-white veils of the women, who appear in the bazars alone in still greater numbers,—the flaming robes of cloth, silks, and stuffs, in which the gayest and brightest colors always predominate,—the long beards,—the formal ample tartan,—the red and yellow boot and slippers,—the whole mass not rushing to and fro like the crowd in Chatham street or Broadway, but moving slowly like a funeral pomp, amidst the profuse and brilliant display of merchandise which I have already described,—such is the scene offered to the eye of the visitor, during the greater part of every day, by the bazars of Constantinople.

It is instructive to contemplate the calmness and dignity with which the Turkish merchant smokes his long pipe, and surveys a scene so calculated to awaken his hopes and excite his cupidity. He sits cross-legged upon his carpet, in front of his little stock of goods, ready, if called upon, to rise and wait upon a customer. He does not, however, show the slightest wish to receive your patronage, and really seems to have less interest than anybody else in the busy scene.

Not so the Jews, who engross the bazars appropriated to the sale of sewing silk, twist, braid and old clothes. They take down their gayest, most attractive merchandise from the shelf, and wave it before you. They entice you to their stalls by the most earnest gestures. They cry out to you in half a dozen languages, — Turkish, Greek, Italian, French, English, Spanish, of which they are always provided with at least a few words. They smile, entreat, and even pull you gently by the arm. If you persevere in your course, as is always most advisable, some ragged Israelite is sure to follow you, and offer you his services as a guide to the bazars or antiquities. He understands your language, whatever it may be, and has a perfect acquaintance with all the objects which you can possibly desire to visit.

The bazars for the sale of rich silks, furs, and jewellery, are kept by Armenians, who are also much more earnest in quest of customers than Turks, though they are honorably distinguished from the Jews by their superior dignity and decorum. They are indeed the chief merchants of Constantinople, and nearly all the principal business passes through their hands. Most of the manufactures too, which require extensive capital, are conducted by them.

Several of the principal bazars seem to have been built with a view to guard against fires, which are so frequent and destructive here. None of them, however, seemed to me to deserve the name of fire-proof; and some of the most lamentable instances of the loss of life, as well as property, have occurred in these immense passages, which are always filled with the most combustible matter, and have no way of entrance or escape but through the gates at the two extremities. These, on some disastrous occasions, having become choked with goods and a crowd hastening to escape a miserable death, multitudes have been consumed by the flames.

CHAPTER XXIX.

FIRES IN CONSTANTINOPLE.

JUNE 25. I walked this morning to visit the new and splendid Armenian church in the suburbs of Pera. We called on our way to see a Greek church, which, though not entitled to be called splendid, is substantially built of stone, and is every way of very respectable appearance, and commodious for public worship. It has the usual supply of worthless engravings, and paintings, and tawdry ornaments, which are always to be found in churches of this communion. It has afforded me much gratification to find that the Christians in the Turkish dominions, fallen as they are in morals and spirituality, have yet zeal, as well as liberty enough, to build good religious edifices, and to maintain with decency the solemnities of public worship. The Greeks have a large number of churches in Constantinople and its suburbs. They are erected, as in the United States, by voluntary contributions,—a source from which a sufficient revenue is derived for the maintenance of the clergy, as well as for founding schools and charitable institutions for the infirm and indigent members of the communion.

The Armenian church stands upon the border of what is called the burnt district, a name which it will retain only for a brief period, till a conflagration shall give some other portion of this great metropolis a claim to this distinction. A large tract, variously stated to have contained from three thousand to six or seven thousand, was devastated during the last year by this appointed scourge of the Turkish capital.* The scenes of confusion and distress occasioned by this disastrous fire were described to me as unexampled. The great frequency of such accidents here has produced a sort of indifference and recklessness in the minds of the people, whilst the actual occurrence of conflagration fills the public mind with a degree of consternation and despair elsewhere unknown on such occasions.

This is the natural result of the inadequate means employed here for checking the fury of the flames, and from the extreme combustibility of the city, which is little else but an immense tinder-box, ready to give aliment to an ocean of flames at the bidding of a single

* These fires are resorted to for the same reason that public meetings and petitions are got up in England—as an expression of the public discontent. Towards the close of the year 1851, the national feeling against the system of reform broke out openly, and showed itself even in the capital by the barbarous expedient of incendiary fires. Three hundred of the largest houses in Constantinople were reduced to ashes, and fifteen hundred houses in Scutari fell, including all the markets, magazines, and mills, and probably the whole town would have followed, had it not been for a violent fall of rain, which quenched the fire.

On the 17th of June, 1848, a tremendous conflagration desolated Pera, from the Golden Horn nearly to the Bosphorus, and a subsequent one, a few months later, left Pera a heap of ruins.

spark of fire. When a fire is fairly begun, nobody expects to see it suppressed till it has produced extensive ruin, and the firemen often begin to demolish houses, and take other usual precautions, at a great distance from the actual theatre of the conflagration. The people having no hope of saving their houses, soon abandon all attempts at it, and limit their efforts to securing their furniture and families.

The whole mass of the population, bearing the feeble and the aged, and laden with their domestic goods, is rushing from the point of danger, completely blocking up the narrow streets. Here they are met by another multitude with engines and other appurtenances, hastening from distant places to render assistance. Companies of mounted policemen are galloping to the same impassable streets, to guard against thefts and other disorders. They force their way through the dense masses, with little regard to the safety or aims of the crowd. It unavoidably happens that many lives are lost, and many more persons are seriously injured.

These occasions are said to afford curious illustrations of the little sympathy which exists among the different religious sects, or, as they are more usually called, the different nations which compose the heterogeneous population of the Turkish capital. If it is in the Jewish quarter that the desolating element is, Turks and Christians, who have been roused by the alarm, retire quietly to their beds, or shops, leaving them to manage their own affairs. The Armenians show the same indifference to the misfortunes of the Greeks, and *vice versa;* and the Franks of Galata and

Pera are equally left to their own resources during these frightful visitations. Personal interest, resulting from the ownership of property, or other causes, will of course produce many exceptions to this exhibition of selfishness and bigotry, but such, I am well assured, is the common usage.

One is able, in riding or walking through Constantinople and its populous suburbs, to read the history of their calamities in the fresh or antiquated appearance of the buildings. To be burnt up is the natural and expected end of a Turkish house, and to this result their structure and arrangement are especially adapted. Rents are enormously high, being calculated upon the principle that the average existence of a house is seven or eight years. If by any good fortune it escapes the flames for a longer period, it is reckoned so much clear gain to the lucky owner. He must, however, be at the expense of making general repairs, as the structure, designed only for so brief an existence, is built in the slightest manner, and soon begins to fall in pieces if spared by the flames much beyond the usual term.

Hundreds, probably more than a thousand houses, are now in the course of building in the burnt district. Several of these are lofty and spacious, but the material employed in a half dozen of them would not be more than adequate to the construction of one substantial and durable edifice of the same dimensions. The most important and massive portions of the framework are formed of timber scarcely more than four or six inches square, whilst the braces and rafters are either of small poles or saplings, or mere narrow strips of inch plank. It is slightly covered with clap-boards, a quarter of an inch in thickness, and two or three feet long, often nailed on without planing. The roofs are of tiles. One is astonished to find that these frail constructions are not shattered to pieces and blown away by the first strong wind.

They are, however, crowded together, and shelter each other. The narrow streets give little play to violent winds, and after all one is inclined to modify and apply to these tottering houses the proverb which will secure them against all other misfortunes in virtue of their having been made to be burned. To this appointed destiny, the great mass of the houses of Constantinople have a most observable and growing adaptation. The thin weather-boards twist and crack in the sun, become ragged and hang loosely upon the walls, and everybody, instead of making repairs, seems patiently waiting for the *coup de grace* of the predestined conflagration.

CHAPTER XXX.

ARMENIAN CHURCH AND CEMETERIES.

THE new Armenian church, the immediate object of my morning's walk, is on the verge of the burnt district, and its ample courts and solid walls afforded a shelter to a multitude of persons on the occasion of this great disaster, as well as a place of security for their effects. This edifice is situated in the centre of a large enclosure, formed of high walls, which conceal the body of the edifice from the view of those who are without. The entrance into this court is secured by massive gates, and the whole has the appearance of a strong fortress. The church is of ample dimensions, beautiful proportions, and solid architecture, and, to my taste, better adapted in its style and arrangement to the purposes for which a place of Christian worship should be consecrated than any I have seen in the Levant.

The entire structure is composed of solid marble—the walls are very thick—and the roof consists of an immense arch, which springs from their summit. Massive joists, cased in wood, run across the body of the edifice, to aid the walls in resisting the pressure of the vast weight which rests upon them. The galleries in Armenian churches are particularly devoted to females, though I have often seen them in the body of the edifice. There are three galleries in this church, rising one above another across the end remotest from the altar. The first is roomy and convenient, but the third can hardly be less than fifty or sixty feet above the pavement; and as far as hearing is concerned, its occupants might as well be on the top of the house. There are no pews or seats. The Armenians kneel upon the pavement, which is always provided with mats or carpets, and sit in the same place, cross-legged in the Turkish manner. So, at least, I have always seen them accommodated in the churches. A few pictures, of no merit as works of art, are suspended above the altar and on other parts of the walls, and a good supply of lamps, for illuminating the edifice, hang a few feet above the floor.

The spacious court around the church, like the interior, is paved with large slabs of marble. These, and the entire mass of materials employed in the erection of this fine edifice, are tomb-stones taken from an Armenian cemetery. On many of the large slabs employed in the court the inscriptions still appear, though all the stones have been dressed anew in order to fit them for their present use. A good deal of opposition was made to this desecration, as it was called, of the monuments of the dead. The time, however, has come when the living and teeming population of this vast metropolis are compelled to encroach upon the countless and interminable cemeteries which environ them on every side, and assert their superior claim to the occupancy of the surface of the earth. Perhaps nothing better can be done with the antiquated monuments that literally cover and encumber the ground adjacent to Constantinople, than to employ them in the erection of churches. It is even possible that the more thoughtful worshippers will derive useful moral lessons from these "sermons in stones."

Armenian burying-grounds are to be found in all directions around the city. One large and important one, which I visited, is a little north of Pera, upon a hill which commands a noble view of the Bosphorus and Constantinople. It is thinly shaded with large, spreading trees, and contains many tombs and other monuments, of chaste design and good execution. They are not unlike the memorials seen in an American or English cemetery.

Their massive solidity particularly strikes the visitor who approaches the spot, as I did, through the vast Turkish burying-ground, which stretches from the Bosphorus along the north side of Topana and Pera almost to the one just described, belonging to the Armenians. Here the monuments are all slight and frail. Marbles six feet in height are only eight inches wide, and one or two thick, and they are chiselled with the most fragile tenuity, in order to give them the form of the human head and neck. These are unfit for building the walls, or even for paving the courts of churches; but they are temptingly convenient for bridging a wet-weather stream, or forming a hasty causeway over a mud-hole, for which less honorable purposes they are often used.

The Armenian monuments are covered with the usual inscriptions in their own language, commemorating, as we who cannot read them may safely conclude, the dignities and virtues of the departed, in the spirit of vanity or affection which dictate such things in all places and ages. In another respect, however, they are quite peculiar. Upon many of the monuments the instruments of the trade followed by the deceased in his life-time are conspicuously sculptured. On one stone is seen the hammer and knife of the shoemaker,—on another, the tailor's shears. On one I saw the anvil and hammer of the blacksmith.

A plough of primitive form, attached to a yoke, was the coat of arms which pointed to the resting-place of the peasant—whilst an inkstand and pen, which are sculptured upon many tombs, denote the truly Armenian vocation of accountant and scribe. There is something touching in these simple memorials, and it is impossible not to admire the true independence and good sense, which is not ashamed to proclaim in a way so public and enduring, that honored parents and beloved relatives lived by handicraft employments. It is said that some have carried this peculiarity so far as to sculpture upon the tomb the instruments of punishment by which their relatives have been executed for alleged crimes. I did not meet with any instances of this kind, though I took some pains to discover evidences of a usage so very curious.

Armenian funerals are attended with some peculiar

rites, the most interesting of which is the taking leave of the deceased, immediately before the interment. It is usual on such occasions to give the most unrestrained indulgence to expressions of grief, which are said often to be heart-rending. I had no opportunity of witnessing such a scene, but I often saw evidence of the strong propensity of the Armenians to linger about the graves of their deceased relatives and friends.

Dr. Walsh, who enjoyed many advantages for becoming acquainted with their views upon this and other subjects, says that they believe themselves to hold spiritual converse with the departed, which is the principal cause of these visits to their tombs. With whatever views they pay these visits, it is certain that the burying ground is their favorite resort, where they spend many of their spare hours. Whole families, parents and little children, may be seen gathered around a tomb in silence and seriousness, or in animated and joyous converse. The grave slab is often their mat, and often the table upon which they spread the cake, fruit, and wine for their fête champetre. I have seen it too employed as a card-table, where the idle or profligate play for piastres, hour after hour. All the burying grounds, Turkish, Jewish, and Christian, are chief places of public resort. If this custom were not so common in other parts of the East, I might conclude that it originated here, from the vast number and extent of the cemeteries, which hardly leave any other places for public promenades and sports.

CHAPTER XXXI.

NAVY YARD.

After my return from the churches, I paid a visit to the Sultan's navy yard. Nothing can be finer for the purpose of building and repairing ships, or of being made the maritime depôt of a great nation. It is upon the Golden Horn, which here forms a large bay on the Pera shore, a little above the floating bridge. The water is of sufficient depth to afford good anchorage for ships of the line, in water close to the shore. It is perfectly sheltered from all winds, and though almost in the heart of the capital, is completely removed from all interference with merchant vessels, which moor just below the bridge; whilst public vessels pass through the draws, of which there are two, into the harbor of the navy yard, immediately above it. We passed under one of the draws in a caïque, the only craft which passes beyond this limit.

In approaching the landing-place, near the gate of the arsenal, as the vast enclosure of the navy yard, with its contents, is usually called, we passed by some old ships of war, the remains of the fleet destroyed by the allies at Navarino. They are in a state of decay—

several of them have been broken for their timber and other materials; and the rest, including an immense vessel of, I believe, one hundred and twenty guns, must soon share the same fate. One would think that the perpetrators of that outrage on the dignity and independence of the Ottoman empire, would be anxious to see these interesting memorials of their blind and criminal policy, completely annihilated. This wish will be consummated long before the disastrous consequences of that breach of good faith will cease to operate disastrously upon Turkey and all Europe. Russia should be excepted, which is likely to reap the whole harvest of a crime, in the perpetration of which she acted only a secondary part.

From the moment of the destruction of the Turkish fleet, which dismembered the Sultan's empire, and by its moral influence doomed it to inevitable weakness and ultimate extinction, the question of the East, as it is compendiously called, has been the first and the most difficult in European politics. It is becoming every day more complicated and unmanageable, and will only find its solution in the annihilation of the Ottoman empire, and probably in a general continental war.* As a moral question, the Christian may con-

* The real object of dispute, says an English writer in 1853, is at present the empire of the East, and the first place in the East. England and Russia alone aspire to that. England does so reluctantly and unconsciously, perhaps. But still the power whose flag floats at Peshawur and in Pegu, in the islands of Borneo and Canton—this is the power which the Russians look on as their rival; and with whom principally they seem to desire at the present moment to try a fall. England, in fact, pretends to dispute with Russia the empire

template such changes with hope, but its political aspect is certainly fraught with fearful omens. What good has been done by the battle of Navarino? Greece, too weak to be independent, and too corrupt and ignorant for freedom and self-government, has become virtually a province of Russia, under a stupid king, whose rule is decidedly more oppressive than that of the Turk.

The Pacha of Egypt, the sternest and most terrible tyrant known to history in the last thousand years, acting upon the policy sanctioned by Europe at Navarino, has wrested Egypt, Syria, and Arabia from Turkey; and the allies, having robbed Turkey of the elements of her natural and moral power, are now laboring to counteract her irresistible tendency to ruin by the arts of diplomacy. They perceive that they have demolished the only natural and efficient barrier to the dangerous power of Russia, which can only realize her ambitious schemes by pushing the limits of her vast empire to the Bosphorus and the Dardanelles.*

of Asia, and the paramount influence in Europe. Thus the struggle that is now commencing, and of which the present century will not see the end, is for no less than the supremacy over two quarters of the globe."

* "Though the establishment of the Turks in Europe is now of such respectable antiquity, that its fourth and perhaps fated centenary draws nigh, and though their rights of dominion have acquired a title beyond that of mere prescription, yet the nation itself is still only "*encamped*" on its conquests. They have never comported themselves either politically or socially, as if they anticipated in Europe any continuing home. Ottoman legends relate how a belief arose, even in the very hour of conquest, that the banner of the cross would again be some day carried to the brink of the Straits; and it

We experienced some difficulty in getting admitted into the Navy Yard, an order having been issued by the chief of this department, that no stranger should for the present be allowed to see it. The reason of this order is supposed to be the derangement of the establishment, from some late changes in the administration. The sentinel at the gate denied us admission, and refused the proffered buckshеesh with a decision as unusual as it was discouraging. We inquired for an American known to Mr. H., who was lately employed in one of the shops, and were allowed to accompany the soldier who went into the enclosure to look for him.

This gave us opportunity to look at several interesting objects. The American, however, was no longer there, and our guide was leading us, in spite of our attempts to turn to the right and left, directly back to the gate by which we had entered. We fortunately, however, met a Greek physician, who had been admitted to see a sick man, and contriving to send back our soldier with his fee, we accompanied Dr. —— through the establishment. It has the usual appurten-

is said that this misgiving is traceable in the selection of the Asiatic shore for the final resting-place of true believers. It is certain, too, that from the first definite apparition of the Russian empire, they instinctively recognized the antagonists of Fate. Europe had hardly learned the titles of the Czar, when the gaze of the Porte was uneasily directed to the new metropolis on the Neva; throughout the whole country, notwithstanding its chequered incidents, the impression was never weakened; and to this day the inhabitants of Constantinople point out the particular gate by which the Muscovite troops are to enter the City of Promise."—*Edinburgh Review, Jan.* 1850.

ances. There is an extensive saw-mill, worked by steam, a rolling-mill to prepare copper for sheathing vessels, a foundry for cannon and machinery to bore them, and a shop for the construction of boilers for steamboats. We saw an enormous copper-boiler, nearly completed, the second which has been attempted here. The machinery, which is from England, is very fine, and works admirably. Several of the workmen are also English.

We also saw a beautiful inclined plane, constructed of marble, with the appliances necessary for building a first-class ship of war. This, with most of the improvements of this fine establishment, is the work of Mr. Rhodes, an American gentleman, who was until recently employed as principal naval architect of the Turkish government. Many of their finest vessels, which are said by good judges to be equal to any in the world, are constructed under his orders. He deserved and enjoyed in an eminent degree the confidence of the late Sultan, who was both his patron and friend, and many attempts to injure him by intrigue, made during the life of Mahmoud, were signally unsuccessful. They have been renewed, however, with more effect under his youthful successor, and Mr. Rhodes has recently thought it due to his self-respect to resign his post and return to his native country. The Sultan has some foreign officers in his naval service, whose personal and national feelings were too deeply wounded to permit an American to enjoy quietly a station so important and conspicuous in the Turkish marine.*

* "The last anniversary of the birth-day of Washington (1854) was

The carpenters and other operatives work under the thick shade of a fine grove of trees, impervious, or nearly so, to the rays of the sun, whilst they admit a free circulation of air,—an arrangement, in this climate at least, where the sky is commonly serene, very superior to the close and dusty shops where such labor is usually performed.

I heard a pleasing anecdote of a change which has been introduced into the administration of this establishment since the publication of the Hatti Sheriff. The Turkish government, instead of obtaining timber for building ships of war by purchasing it at the market, or by sending its agents to cut it down in the forests, has long been accustomed to make upon the villages of certain parts of the country a demand for a prescribed quantity of oak and pine, to be delivered at the public depôts. Like everything else in this unhappy, misgoverned country, this usage gave rise to abuses, by which the various functionaries contrived to enrich themselves. It commonly happened, when the poor peasants, torn from their rural occupations at the most unpropitious time, brought their quota of timber to the depôt appointed, that the officer having charge of the business refused to receive it, under the pretext

observed in Constantinople, for the first time, with imposing ceremonies. In the harbor were several Turkish, English, French, Dutch, and Austrian vessels of war; also the U. S. ship Levant. In the morning, each ship displayed the American ensign at the masthead. At noon the Levant fired a salute of twenty-one guns, which was immediately followed by a similar salute from all the other ships of war in port. In the afternoon, Captain Turner of the Levant had a party on board his ship."

that it was not of the description called for by the order of government. The peasants must return to the mountains for another supply, which was liable to a similar condemnation, besides the certain ruin that must come upon their domestic affairs from such protracted absence. In order to extricate themselves from this perplexity, it was usual for these poor people to give a bribe to the officer to induce him to receive the tribute, which, as being condemned, they must also deliver for a mere nominal price.

This abuse exists no longer. The government buys its ship-timber at the market price at a much dearer rate, to be sure, than formerly, but without oppressing its helpless subjects. Such practical effects of the new system of reform are gratifying proofs of the sincerity of the government, and excite a hope that the system may be efficiently carried out in all departments of the administration.

After leaving the navy-yard, we went to visit a ruinous edifice near the west wall of Constantinople, commonly known as the palace of Constantine. It has a first and second story, and consists of three or four arched rooms, now occupied as a wretched dwelling. There are some columns of very bad execution, and of no order of architecture. A fragment of Greek inscription inverted is shown upon a broken stone.

The building is not Turkish, but it seems to have little claim to the character commonly assigned to it. It has the appearance of a Genoese structure, being composed of a mixture of brick and stone. The city did not extend so far west in the days of Constantine, and if built by him at all, it was a country villa. The modern occupants are Spanish Jews, a half dozen at least of whom, all women, fell into a high quarrel, which, as well as we could understand it, concerned their respective rights to show the premises to strangers, and the proper ownership of the gratuity we were expected to make. We were ready to depart before they had settled these difficult questions, and they turned upon us with such earnestness, and even fury, that we were compelled to use some violence to rescue ourselves. I never heard more inharmonious voices, nor saw woman apparently more degraded and disgusting.

CHAPTER XXXII.

HOWLING DERVISES.

RETURNING to the Golden Horn, we took a boat to the northern termination of the bridge, and walked through the extensive burying-ground which stretches thence to the tower of Galata. It is an inclined plane, sloping towards the south, and in this part, unlike most Turkish cemeteries, nearly bare of trees. The hour was 1 P. M., and the rays of the sun, which shone with intense brilliancy, reflected by the naked sand and the tomb-stones, produced a burning, stifling heat altogether intolerable. I reached my apartment panting for breath, and quite overwhelmed; and it was not until after a repose of several hours that I was able to prosecute the engagements to which the afternoon had been allotted.

The temperature of Constantinople is subject to great extremes, at least so far as I was able to judge from experience. The nights were invariably cool. I even thought I could perceive a kind of mountain chilliness in them. During the day the fiery heat of the sun, which acts with immense power, is tempered by a northerly wind, which blows down the Bosphorus from the Black Sea. It begins to be felt by eight or nine o'clock, A. M., and before afternoon becomes a gale, agitating the water in the harbor to such a dedree, that a passage in a caïque to Scutari, or even to Constantinople, becomes an adventure. It is only in the streets, and in such sheltered places as the cemetery of Galata, that great inconvenience is experienced from the heat of the sun. In passing from one of these glowing localities to some considerable elevation, or an open space where the Euxine breezes are enjoyed, a change is experienced almost as violent as that which is felt on leaving a heated parlor to encounter the keen northern blasts of an American winter. These vicissitudes, however, seem to produce no bad effect upon the health of the people of Constantinople. I was told by a physician, whose professional pursuits have made him well acquainted with the subject, that a residence here during the warm season is not only free from all danger, but often decidedly salutary to the more delicate pulmonary patients. The rest of the year he considers pernicious to this class of persons, from the prevalence of damp chilling winds, accompanied often with profuse rains, and occasionally with extreme cold.

At 3. P. M., I went with a number of friends to Scutari, to witness the performance of a strange sect of Mohammedan fanatics, called the Howling Dervises. They occupy convents, are wholly consecrated to religious observances, and possess considerable estates, the gift of zealous Musselmen for the maintenance of these establishments. I had no means of learning what are the distinguishing dogmas and more private duties of this sect, but they have on Thursday of each week an open exhibition of what, I suppose, they would call their public worship. It is regarded as one of the sights of Constantinople, and few strangers omit to visit it at least once during even a short stay in the capital. Their chapel of exhibition is nearly a mile from the landing-place in Scutari. We passed through an outer court into a large square room, a convenient space upon two sides being separated from the rest by a low wooden railing for the use of spectators. Some rude musical instruments and some old dirks or short swords were suspended in the area devoted to the religious performances. The latter, it is said, are sometimes used by the more fanatical of the fraternity to inflict wounds upon themselves by way of penance, which they regard as highly meritorious. The dervises, thirty or forty in number, stood in rows on three sides of the area appropriated to their performance. They were about to recommence their exercises, which are occasionally suspended for a few minutes for the purpose of taking breath.

The fourth side was occupied by a number of persons who were not dervises, but seemed, from the great deference paid them, to be distinguished personages, who countenanced the fraternity by their presence. I observed one of them, after some time, lay aside a part of his dress, and take a part with the rest as a kind of amateur performer. These persons were seated on sheep-skins, covered with long wool dyed bright scarlet color. Near the centre of the room sat a dervise, also upon a scarlet fleece, who appeared to be a chieftain in the fraternity, and on this occasion he opened their exercises by setting up a low, dull chant. In this he was accompanied by the dervises standing around the room, who, at the same time, commenced a slow and measured motion of the body, backwards and forwards, the feet alone remaining immovable. By imperceptible degrees the chant became more loud and quick, and with it the movements of the devotees corresponded. The hand described a longer arc, with perpetually increasing velocity. Each of the performers might be likened to a revolving pendulum inverted. The resemblance ceased, however, when, at the end of a quarter of an hour, the more supple and active nearly struck their foreheads against the pavement, and it became impossible to bend so low in the opposite direction, without losing their balance and falling headlong. Nothing could exceed the violence of gesticulation and preternatural energy with which they now performed these exhausting evolutions.

The heat of the day was extreme, and all were literally drenched with perspiration. Every muscle and fibre was called into play, and labored with observable and fearful effort. The eyes half closed and turned upward, rolled swiftly and frantically. The chant, which grew every moment more quick and loud, seemed at least to proceed not from the lungs, but from the lower viscera, which visibly struggled and agonized in sustaining this vocal accompaniment. These profound, abdominal notes, painfully loud and piercing, though half-stifled in their emission, would more properly give the name of grunting than of howling dervises to these deluded people. Now and then, however, the strained voice broke away from its imprisonment, and fell upon the ear of the spectator in shrill, frantic tones, which might without impropriety be called screaming or howling.

The chief, who led the performance from his seat on the scarlet fleece, seemed less moved than any one else, but he labored with all the arts of which long experience had made him a most perfect master, to work up the feelings of the performers to the highest pitch, and increase their already dangerous excitement into absolute frenzy. He artfully varied his chant, and made it more rapid, low, and piercing. He looked with approving sanctimonious smiles upon the most extravagant and rapt of the throng. He occasionally clapped his hands, and several times broke out into stirring appeals and exhortations. An instrument of music, a rude tambourine, occasionally poured in its hoarse, thrilling notes.

With several of the dervises the performance ended in convulsions, a result which seemed to be expected as well as desired, for two or three persons who took no part, stood watching for such cases, and hastened to receive the falling victims in their arms. They carried them to the vacant area in the middle of the hall, and employed friction, and striking the palms of the hands and the soles of the feet to restore them. The first unfortunate returned in a few minutes to his place and devotions, which soon brought on a return of spasms.

There was one poor fanatic who attracted peculiar attention by his general appearance, and the superior frenzy to which he attained. He wore a dark filthy dress. His hair and beard coal black, were long, thick, and bushy. At every vibration it waved in the air, and lashed the faces and eyes of those next him, as with a whip of scorpions, then falling over his own face and breast, quite hid them from our sight. A withered arm frightfully scarred and distorted, which he kept bare, and swinging through the air like a club, added to the really frightful appearance of this fanatic. He outstripped all his fraternity in extravagance, and at length leaping from his place, pitched headlong upon the pavement in strong convulsions. Every nerve and muscle was strained and distorted to the utmost, and his head and feet were brought almost in contact by the violence of his distortions. The usual means were resorted to for his recovery. The chief men came forward and kissed him, or rubbed their beards over his filthy face.

One who came in after the ceremonies began, and was received with the most profound respect, came and breathed upon him again and again. This man, as I understood, is a great santon, who works miracles, and a number of children were brought at intervals of the performance to obtain his blessing. He took them in his arms, laid his hand upon their bosoms, and, inclining his head, breathed upon their faces. The convulsions of the fanatic, however, were too strong to yield to such remedies, though often repeated, and, after waiting a considerable time to see him restored, I left the place whilst he was yet struggling in the arms of three or four of the dervises.

It was a strange sight I had been looking upon, and strange sounds conspired with it to put my brain in a whirl. My nerves had suffered greatly from witnessing such a scene, and I retired thanking God for the light of the Gospel of His Son. The Mohammedans, of whom a large number were spectators of this scene, evidently regarded it with the deepest reverence. Several of them occasionally advanced to the arena and took part in the exercises, but without attaining or apparently aspiring to the perfect absorption and frenzy which the practised and highly excitable nerves of the initiated enabled them to command, or, more properly, rendered unavoidable. Some half a dozen small boys also participated in the exercises. They seemed to be in training as noviciates.

CHAPTER XXXIII.

THE SULTAN.

JUNE 26th. This day, Friday, is the Mussulman sabbath. The public institutions are all closed, and other objects and places usually visited by travellers, if they are kept wholly or chiefly by Turks, are inaccessible. Without adverting to this fact, with which I was well enough acquainted, I proceeded to the city, at an early hour, with a view of examining some objects of minor interest, which I had overlooked or omitted in former excursions. A shabby, dirty Jew soon forced himself upon us as a guide, professing, as usual, to know everything, and to be able to secure us admission to whatever we might desire.

We followed him for some time without succeeding in getting access to anything, and after losing two hours or more, crossed the Golden Horn to Topana, having arranged to visit a mosque where the Sultan with his suite was expected to be present. At this hour of the day, every Friday, the Sultan is accustomed to perform his devotions in one of the mosques of Constantinople or its vicinity. It affords a favorable opportunity to see him and his principal officers, civil and military, of which all strangers commonly avail themselves. When the mosque selected for the day is upon the shore, the royal visit is made in barges. On other occasions the Sultan and his court are mounted on horseback, and the display of fine horses and gay equipages is said by those who have witnessed the scene to be very imposing. Notice is given in the morning of the mosque selected for the day, and travellers obtain information from the boatmen of Topana, who are usually employed on these expeditions.

We found, on making inquiry of the watermen, that the royal visit to-day was to be paid to a mosque on the Asiatic side of the Bosphorus, distant about eight miles. It was already 9½ A. M., and we had to contend against the wind as well as the strength of the current. We took a caïque carrying two men and four oars. These boats are very long and narrow, of a very light and peculiar construction. Their form is often compared to that of a swallow. They more resemble an egg divided longitudinally, with the ends much elongated, and made very sharp.

The boatmen occupy the centre of the boat, and when no passengers are on board, the prow appears very low, and is often submerged when the water is rough, whilst the stern rises several feet above the water. The passengers, who sit back of the rowers, restore the equilibrium, and the caïque appears only to touch the water by a few feet of the middle of its sharp keel. There is a fore and quarter deck, which cover a half or two-thirds of the entire length of the boat, and the utmost care is requisite in taking one's place not to overturn it. If alone, one must occupy the middle, and avoid any inclination of the body to the right or left. When more than one person is on board, still greater care is necessary to preserve the equilibrium of this most unsteady and ticklish of aquatic vehicles. So many precautions are apt at first to produce a little apprehension for one's safety, which is increased rather than diminished by the timed and measured movements of the men. When, however, everything is properly adjusted, and the frail bark is carefully disentangled from the vast fleet of small craft that is always to be seen about the wharf, nothing can exceed the beauty of its movements or the strength and dexterity of the boatmen.

The long, sharp beak, cuts the waves with inconceivable facility, and the graceful caïque, gently rising and falling with the heaving sea, glides along like the playful flight of a swallow through the air. The oars are of a form as peculiar as the boat. The paddle is light and elastic, but the handle swells into a thick mass, just below the hands, in order to balance the longer end, which plays in the water. To effect this with the utmost exactness, holes are often bored in the handle and filled with lead. The gunwale and benches of the caïques are commonly ornamented with carving, which is certainly rude enough, and sometimes a sentence of the Koran is inscribed in Turkish characters. Our boatmen on the present occasion were Greeks, who are seldom seen on the Bosphorus, being mostly employed in plying between Constantinople and the island and coasts of the sea of Marmora, for which larger boats are used. They proved to be as fine fellows as ever pulled at an oar, and carried us at a rapid rate towards the place of our destination.

As we approached the new palace, on the European side of the Bosphorus, the present residence of the Sultan, we had the mortification to see the royal cortege leave the wharf with a speed which bade defiance to all competition. Passing near the palace, I had another opportunity of admiring the beautiful architecture and graceful proportions of its immense façade, adorned with two lofty gates of unparalleled elegance, and with nearly one hundred marble columns.

Just as we were opposite the fortress, west of the palace, we were startled by the loud report of artillery. A great number of guns were discharged in quick succession. It was the customary salutation to the Sultan, who was more than half a mile in advance. The same order was observed at the other forts, of which we passed half a dozen. The salutation was reserved till the Sultan was removed out of the reach of all harm, even had the guns been loaded with ball. This delay, I believe, is not usual elsewhere, but it is well devised to secure the honored personage from the painful shock of such repeated discharges of artillery.

The gay Ottoman flag was flying everywhere, and soldiers with military music were paraded along the shore, to add pomp and dignity to the scene. We were left so fast by the royal caïques, that we began to feel some apprehension of being too late for the spectacle. A multitude of boats, however, were going in the same direction, and we presumed to the same place.

One of them bore a pacha, who was not likely to commit so important an error as to time, and our Greeks perceiving that we should feel secure against disappointment whilst in such company, strained every nerve to prevent the pacha's boat, which was worked by three men and six oars, from passing us. It was a perfect race for several miles. The Turks were ashamed of being outstripped by a boat of such inferior pretensions, and the Greeks were evidently impelled by national pride, and their undying hatred for the Turk, not less than by a wish to gratify their customers.

I never saw men in any circumstances make greater exertions. They threw off all their clothes but the shirt, which was drenched with perspiration. I was gratified to find, on reaching the point opposite the mosque where we were to turn across the Bosphorus, that we were still in advance two or three boats' length. Here our noble fellows slackened their oars, and allowed their fairly beaten antagonists to pass them. A point of etiquette had occurred, and they feared to take precedence of a high public functionary in approaching the landing-place. Not a word was said, not even a smile was seen, but the satisfaction of our men was evident and excessive, and we did not fail to congratulate them upon their achievement in a manner more undisguised than they would have thought it prudent to employ.

The Sultan was in the mosque, which was about forty yards from the edge of the water. The intervening space was filled with soldiers and curious spectators, including many Franks, who, like ourselves, were waiting in well chosen positions to see the object of their expedition, as he should retire from the place of prayer.

We were kept waiting fifteen or twenty minutes, which afforded us opportunity to examine the splendid caïques which were moored at the wharf. There were six royal barges, besides a multitude belonging to military and other officers. The two largest bore the Sultan and his ministers, and four of smaller dimensions seemed to be designed as guard-boats, two sailing before, and two behind, the royal caïques. These were of the most graceful form and splendid decorations. They must have been nearly eighty feet in length, and each was rowed by two or four men, selected for their size and youth, no less than for dexterity and strength. They were uniformly dressed in loose trousers, and a long shirt, with very broad flowing sleeves, all perfectly white and clean, and confined at the waist with a girdle. The prow and stern were very lofty, rising many feet above the water, and, like every other part of the boat, were literally covered with gold.

The Sultan's seat was on a sort of quarter-deck, covered by a canopy, of which the frame-work was gilded, and the covering of scarlet broad-cloth, and hung with curtains of scarlet silk velvet, deeply bordered and fringed with gold. The cushions were richly embroidered with gold, and the deck was covered with a sumptuous carpet. The ropes by which the boats were moored to the shore were of purple. A long carpet of blue cloth extended from the boat to the door of the mosque, in order that the descendant and representative of the

Prophet might not set his foot upon the vulgar earth. A man continued to sweep it with a brush, to prevent the accumulation of dust.

At the end of nearly half an hour, the attendants began to come out of the mosque, and, from the preparations amongst the bargemen and soldiers, it was evident the cortège was soon to move. A great many high officers of the state and army successively made their appearance. Several of them were fine-looking, venerable men, with gray moustaches. Hallil Pacha, the lately dismissed minister, and brother-in-law to the Sultan, was one of them. They wore green coats, stars of diamond on their breasts, and their swords and vests glittered with gold and precious stones.

After the due arrangements had been made, and soldiers were drawn up in two lines on either side of the way, with other preparations a little tedious to an impatient spectator, anxious to see the principal object, the Sultan at length made his appearance, preceded by a functionary, religious, I suppose, bearing before him a censer smoking with incense, and accompanied by high officers, who carried the folds of his ample cloak.* He had on a common red cap or fez, with a

* A writer in an English journal of October, 1853, referring to the impending war with Russia, states: "An ancient custom requires the Sultan to march to battle against the infidel at the head of his sacred troops. This custom has degenerated into a fiction. In accordance with it, however, the Padishah is preparing to quit his palace, and during the war he will inhabit the kiosk at Therapia, which his father Mahmoud occupied during the late Russian war, and which is being prepared for his reception, and is, we may add, vastly more comfortable than the tent of his great ancestor, Suleiman the Magnificent."

brilliant on the front. The collar of his frock-coat was covered with splendid diamonds, and a diamond star hung on his breast. He is tall, nearly six feet, well made for a Turk, and looks very serious, thoughtful, and rather pale. His forehead would be pronounced intellectual, and the expression of his countenance denotes energy and character. He is remarkably well-grown for a youth of seventeen or eighteen years old, and has an uncommon though still thin beard, which is unshaven.

The Turks raised their hands to their bosoms, and made a solemn inclination of the head,—the Franks uncovered and bowed, according to the custom of their country. The Sultan regarded them one by one with his piercing black eye, but deigned no other recognition of their homage to him. This is the custom here, and is less troublesome than the European fashion, which exacts from kings, when they ride through the streets, the toil of taking off the hat to every person who salutes them. The Sultan was conducted to his seat in the barge by high officers, who knelt before him as they adjusted his cushions and the folds of his cloak.

The cortège of caïques, as they pushed off from the shore and glided down the Bosphorus, was a truly magnificent spectacle. It was just twelve o'clock, and as the sun poured its flood of light through a cloudless sky on the *tout ensemble*, glittering with purple and gold, the scene took the hue of a gorgeous enchantment, and became too bright for the eye to look steadily upon it. The water which trickled from the gilded paddles, as they rose and fell with the most exact regularity, seemed converted into shining pearls. I was reminded of the triumphant procession of Cleopatra on the bosom of the Cydnus, when

> "The barge she sat in, like a burnished throne,
> Burnt on the water, the poop was beaten gold;
> Purple the sails,—the oars were silver;
> Which to the tune of flutes kept stroke."

It was by far the most oriental spectacle I have ever seen.

CHAPTER XXXIV.

TURKISH SOLDIERS.

JUST below the mosque where these ceremonies took place, a small stream discharges its waters into the Bosphorus. It forms a fertile vale, shaded with thick spreading trees. In the warm season, this is one of the most favorite retreats of the Turks, where they spend a few hours in the heat of the day. Here they bring their harems to enjoy the country air, who, sitting in groups and covered with white veils, feast on confectionary, whilst their watchful, taciturn lords, reclining at a distance on carpets or mats spread on the ground in the shade, smoke their long chibouks and sip black coffee.

The place is called the Heavenly Waters, and sometimes the Sweet Waters of Asia. I saw, both in going and returning, a great many Turkish soldiers, who were drawn up along the shore to do honor to the young sultan, and I was struck, as I always am, with their very unmilitary appearance. But one never sees amongst them the rude, disorderly conduct, and boisterous merriment, so common amongst undisciplined and ill-governed troops in other countries. This would be unnational and inconsistent with the sluggish temperament and grave manners of a Turk. I refer to the want of everything in their appearance and bearing which belongs to a regular well-trained soldier. They are mostly boys, many of them cannot be above twelve or fourteen years of age, and are scarcely half grown. The veterans are said to be on the frontiers in active service, whilst the young recruits are retained in the fortresses and barracks in and near the capital, to perfect their discipline.*

* A writer in an English periodical, November 1853, presents a striking picture of the gathering together of the Turkish troops in the city of the Sultan, at the commencement of hostilities with Russia.

"Since the war manifesto was publicly read at Constantinople, the war fever has been continually increasing, and every one is so intent on procuring arms, that even the most useful articles of household furniture are sold, if the necessary funds for the purchase cannot be raised in any other way. In the midst of a population roused to war, no lawless act whatever is heard of. European travellers, with their wives and daughters, walk fearlessly about the bazars of the capital; nor have we to record a single instance of insult to a Christian, either native or foreigner. The behavior of the Asiatic hordes in the capital and its environs, is described as exemplary. A stranger cannot walk through the streets of Constantinople without seeing the most evident signs of war. Troops of the line are marching and counter-marching; steamers are daily embarking men, horses, and baggage. The narrow streets and ricketty wooden houses tremble to the roll of heavy ordnance dragged over rugged pavement. But these are the preparations of the government, the mustering of the organized forces of regular warfare.

"Besides all this, we see the numerous volunteer corps of citizens arming themselves to resist their northern foe. The firemen of Stamboul—as stout, active, and rough a set of men as any city could furnish—march past, armed with heavy axes and pistols,

This is probably true, and it would certainly be little less than a sacrifice to send the juvenile bands which I saw about Constantinople, into the field against the veteran Egyptian regiments of Ibrahim Pasha. As far as I had opportunity to witness the military exercises of these troops, they were on a par with their personal appearance. They were ludicrously awkward in their motions and attitudes, straggled from the line, and obeyed the word of command without any pretensions to the observance of time.

The Turkish army, it is well known, have, ever since the destruction of the Janissaries, been trained according to European tactics. The military system of France, always the best in Europe, has, I believe, been adopted. French officers have been employed to communicate

much like the ancient janissaries. Troops of lazy apprentices, joined with gray-beard and respectable shopkeepers, who have buckled on their fathers' or grandfathers' sword, and burnished up some ancient firelock, are repairing to the Seraskier to tender their services, while rude Turkoman shepherds, from the mountains of Anatolia, armed to the teeth, are gazing with stupid wonder on the strange city life into which they are introduced for the first time. Bodies of irregular horsemen—Kurdish, Turcoman, and Arab freebooters, whose costumes and arms are those of the middle ages—are from time to time observed following some bearded warrior, the barbaric grandeur of whose arms and dress mark him as the chief of a clan. Those who have travelled the length and breadth of the Turkish empire, and who fancied they could recognise its various tribes and peoples, are now at fault, since the alarm of war has called from unknown solitudes tribes of whose existence they were ignorant. The other day a troop of strange people from a far country appeared, whose arms were scimitars and bows and arrows: they were clothed in loose white garments and peaked caps—probably from some remote valley of Daghestan or Northern Kurdistan."

instruction and discipline to the newly modelled regiments, as well as to guide the schools established for the education of military cadets. Hitherto these attempts at reform seem not to have been followed by any very flattering success. In the field, the new troops have uniformly proved inferior to their enemies, whether Russians, Greeks, or Egyptians, and upon parade they are certainly the most ungainly, slouching, unmilitary body of men I have ever seen wearing a soldier's uniform.*

Their costume is Frank, with the exception of the fez, or red cap, which is universally worn by all who have laid aside the turban, both in and out of the army, and from the well-known aversion of the Orientals to the hat, it is likely perhaps to be retained long after every other part of their picturesque, graceful costume shall have been supplanted by European fashions. This cap is cylindrical in form, is eight or ten inches in height, and the crown is ornamented with a blue silk tassel, often so long and thick that it spreads out over the whole hinder part of the cap, in a manner very pretty and picturesque. All the high officers of state and of the army, and the Sultan himself, wear this cap,

* If we may judge from an account given by a writer in Bentley's Miscellany in 1853, the progress of military discipline in the Turkish army has not been very rapid. He says, "The Turks have an undisciplined and raw infantry, soldiers young and officers untaught; an army, in fact, that should go through the schooling and the life of a campaign in order to become an efficient one. The one hundred, or the one hundred and fifty thousand soldiers in the pay of the Sultan, do not form an army sufficiently numerous to go through such an ordeal.

as well as the common soldier. It has no rim nor projection to protect the eyes from light and heat. This is a great defect in a climate where the whole atmosphere glares and glows during the summer, but, as the head is never uncovered, and the Mohammedan, when he offers his prayers, is obliged to press his forehead many times against the ground or floor of the mosque, such an appendage to the fez, however convenient on other occasions, could not be adopted.

Objectionable as the red cap may appear in our eyes, it is the only item of the soldier's wardrobe which does not misfit and disfigure him. A Turk in small-clothes is a ludicrous object. In his stately turban, long beard, and flowing robes descending to the feet, he is a respectable and often a venerable figure—his slouching, indolent movements, his bare feet and contemptible cross-legged posture, are masked and partially remedied by this ample, and often magnificent costume. In a close coat and trowsers, however, he always makes a sorry and contemptible figure. They never fit well, the pantaloons hang in bags below the knee, whilst they are tight upon the thighs—the waistband binds like a cord, whilst the seat and front emulate the discarded petticoat trowsers of the old regime.

It is no better with the coat, which, upon officers civil and military, is always a frock. They button it close under the chin as tight as a halter, and leave the rest open to flutter in the wind. It is always loose, and in wrinkles on the shoulders and back. Vests and cravats are not so commonly worn, and stockings are pretty much confined to ultra reformers and exquisites.

Add to all these borrowed deformities, the clumsy, shuffling gait, which is universal. The Turk, man and woman, shoves his feet along the pavement instead of lifting them up lightly as he walks. This arises from wearing slippers or shoes down at the heel, which is common with the men, and with the other sex universal. If a Turk puts on a pair of boots, he always wears over them slippers, which may be put off on entering a house or mosque. This slipper consists of a sole, and merely a covering for the toes, by which, with care and difficulty, it is retained upon the foot. From this results the awkward, embarrassed movement, which is observable in all. A company of Turkish gentlemen or ladies walk as slowly as a funeral procession, and with a fumbling, measured pace, which reminds one of horses turned out to graze in fetters. It may result from the same cause, that they turn their toes *in* instead of *out* in walking. I am more inclined, however, to attribute this peculiarity to the universal habit of sitting cross-legged, or of positively sitting upon their feet and ancles, upon which a Turk contrives to instal himself in regular form, as a Frank does upon a cushion. Such unnatural postures, begun in early childhood, can hardly fail of producing a degree of distortion in the limbs as well as of preventing natural and graceful motion.

These observations may be just or otherwise, but it is evident to me that a Turk in the Nazarene costume, as it is here called, is a much less handsome and noble animal than the American or European. His shoulders are narrow and badly set. He is disproportionately large in the girth, seeming commonly inclined to corpulency; the calves of his legs are small and ill-formed, and his feet and ancles, probably from their ungainly action, appear more or less distorted.

CHAPTER XXXV.

DANCING DERVISES.

On my return from this expedition, I stopped in Pera, just opposite the great cemetery of Galata, to witness the religious services of a Mohammedan sect, known as the Dancing Dervises. They have a handsome mosque and extensive apartments devoted to their use; while a number of sumptuous monuments and tombs in a cemetery, forming a part of the same premises, give evidence of their wealth and respectability. Having passed through the gate, which opens upon a very public street, we walked through an ample paved court, adjoining which is a garden, planted with shrubs and trees. From this court, by a second door, we entered the area which was already occupied by the performers in the scene we had come to witness.

It is a large hall, in the form of an octagon, with a railing on two sides, separating the space next the doors assigned to spectators from the large area devoted to the religious exercises. There were about twenty-five dervises present. They wore a very high cap, in the form of a sugar-loaf, without any brim. It was of a light gray color, and, I thought, made of wool, like the body of a hat. Their dress consisted of a close jacket of white cotton, and a broad petticoat of the same color and material, which was so long as to trail by several inches on the ground. A pair of slippers became visible when they lifted up these ample folds to move the feet. Over all each wore a dark cloak.

They were standing in a circle round the railing, and upon a signal given by their chief, whose costume differed in nothing from the rest but in an immense green turban, which he wore over his sugar-loaf cap, they began to move and follow him in single file, and at a pace indescribably slow, around the area. On the eastern side of the octagon, the point nearest to Mecca, lay a scarlet fleece on the pavement. Upon approaching this, each bowed slowly and profoundly, bringing his head almost to the pavement. Having passed it in front, he turned and repeated the same ceremony, and then continued his round.

Some instruments of music, which I was unable to see, struck up a lifeless, drawling tune at the commencement of this almost stationary promenade. It grew quicker by imperceptible degrees, and the pageant moved with a corresponding increase of celerity, though never I think so rapidly as a quarter of a mile the hour. This solemn procession around the area was made, I think, three times, when the chief, taking his stand at the scarlet fleece, clapped his hands as a sign for beginning the dance—the music at the same time playing a more lively air. Upon this, the dervises, as they successively approached their leader, bowed reverently to him, kissed his hand, and whirled off into the dance.

They disencumbered themselves of their cloaks and slippers, and commenced turning from left to right, at first slowly, but gradually increased the velocity of their motion, until they whirled like the spinning of a top. Their long petticoats became inflated with air, forming a cone six feet in diameter at its base. The arms, at first crossed upon the breast, were soon stretched out horizontally and at full length, forming with the body a perfect cross. The eyes, half closed in reverie, and the face, were turned upward, and the giddy performer seemed lost, as no doubt he was, to all earthly things and thoughts.

They continued these gyrations without intermission for about fifteen minntes, and the grace and regularity of their whirl, together with its amazing velocity, are really wonderful. At length, a signal was given by clapping the hands, when the dance stopped, apparently to allow the performers a few minutes of repose. It soon recommenced as before, and I was informed that two hours are passed in repetitions of the same exercises. There is nothing painful or disgusting in witnessing this spectacle, as there is in looking on the performances of the Howling Dervises. The men are cleanly and well dressed. The Sultan often patronizes this set by his presence, a circumstance which has led to evident improvements in their personal appearance, as well as their premises.

CHAPTER XXXVI.

THE GOLDEN HORN.

BETWEEN three and four o'clock, I set out in company with my kind host and hostess, Mr. and Mrs. Hamlin, to visit the Valley of Sweet Waters, at the head of the Golden Horn. The point at which these excursions usually terminate, where we went on shore, is perhaps seven miles from Topana, where we embarked. Good boats of two and three pairs of oars are always to be had here, whereas at Galata they have not usually more than one pair, being used chiefly for transporting passengers across the harbor to Constantinople. The longer transit of the Bosphorus is sometimes, though seldom, made in these small caïques, whilst in excursions up the Bosphorus to the Seven Towers, the Valley of Sweet Waters, &c., boats of two or three pairs of oars are almost invariably employed. They move with greater rapidity, and are more agreeable as well as safer.

The established fare in a small caïque from Galata to Constantinople, is half a piastre. An excursion of seven or eight miles in a four-oared boat costs from twelve to fifteen piastres. The charge for the same boat to Scutari is three piastres. The stranger should make himself acquainted with the established prices, especially for the shorter ferriages, and without making any inquiries or stipulations with the boatmen, should lay the amount upon the deck, or give it to the man at the time of his debarkation, but not before. In this way he will commonly shun all difficulty and altercation. Should he ask the price of the watermen, or offer two or three times the customary fare, he is taken for a stranger, and the most exorbitant demands are made upon him. In one instance, a boatman to whom we had incautiously given five piastres instead of three, his legal fare, seized our effects, and clamorously refused to let them go without the payment of fifteen piastres. These boatmen are nearly all Turks, and though very expert in their profession, they are certainly as great rogues as any of the craft with whom I have happened to have intercourse.

In my way up the Golden Horn, I had another opportunity of admiring the fine naval architecture of Mr. Rhodes. We passed between two steamboats moored in front of the navy yard, built by this gentleman for the late Sultan. The smaller was constructed for his personal use, to make short excursions on the Bosphorus and elsewhere. It has the most perfect symmetry of form, and the finish is admirable. The whole exterior is polished like a mirror, and reflects the moving boats and other objects around it. It is richly adorned with gilding, but all in a chaste and sober style, without any of the tawdriness usually exhibited in oriental workmanship.

The other boat is larger, being designed for longer voyages, and though less elaborately finished, it possesses similar excellencies of model and construction.* It is remarkable that this beautiful new ship is undergoing repairs and alterations. The persons who have been so fortunate as to succeed Mr. Rhodes, are obliged, for the sake of consistency, to make some practical demonstration of their sincerity in charging that gentleman with incompetency as a naval architect.

The head of the Golden Horn is bounded by an expanse of flat, alluvial meadows, through which the small river Lycus discharges its waters by several mouths. About a mile high up the stream, the valley is contracted into an inconsiderable breadth, and the lofty hills approaching on each side to within a few yards of the Lycus, and conforming their direction to its numerous sinuosities, swelling at the same time into a great variety of graceful slopes and elevations, constitute altogether a very picturesque scene. New and ever varying views are constantly opening upon the eye as you advance, not unlike the succession of pictures sometimes seen in cosmoramic exhibitions.

These beautiful hills are not wooded, and the same may be said of the valley, with the exception of some small, unpromising trees, which seem to have been planted and then left to their fate. A little labor and expense would make this one of the most enchanting spots in the world, an unpleasant reflection, which is

* In 1852, steam navigation increased greatly at Constantinople. More than twenty steamers were then plying daily in the Bosphorus and the Sea of Marmora.

constantly rising in the mind of the stranger, as he contemplates the inexhaustible variety of beautiful sites and prospects which nature has lavished upon Constantinople and its environs.

At the distance of perhaps five miles from the city, we passed a handsome kiosk close to the right bank of the river. I was told it belonged to a pasha, as indeed one never sees a tasteful well-kept house in town or country, which does not belong either to the Sultan or to some of his officers. Others are too poor, too uncultivated, or too cautious to aspire to these elegancies. We landed opposite to a guard-house, where a few soldiers are stationed to preserve order amongst the visitors of all classes who throng these grounds upon every fair day.

The valley here expands into a broader plain, still bounded by lofty hills. A large number of noble spreading trees afford shade to the groups who come here to breathe country air, as well as to the smaller number, who may have a taste for the more active pleasure of promenading. There are some mean-looking coffee-houses, at a little distance from which, chairs and the usual refreshments are brought by servants, who approach you with a profusion of salams and other solemn formalities, which pertain to Turkish etiquette.

A few rods higher up the river is a kiosk, or summer palace, belonging to the Sultan. It is in the midst of an extensive lawn, which is surrounded with a ruinous fence and long rows of very fine trees. A little above the palace. a dam is thrown across the river, now nearly dry, which forms, when there is water, a pretty fantastic cascade. The dam, like everything upon the premises, is dilapidated. The marble blocks, of which it is constructed, are broken or displaced, and the gingerbread work, designed, I suppose, to produce a play of cross currents and jets for the amusement of the Sultan's women and children, is nearly demolished. The kiosk is badly built of lath and plaster and wood. It is of a faded yellow color, and in a very ruinous condition. The Sultans display great taste and magnificence in their palaces, but they are veritable Turks after all, repairing nothing and building always in the slightest manner.

If the sovereign takes a fancy to a particular residence, it is fitted up, or more properly rebuilt with lath and plaster or clapboards, and the whole gaudily decorated with paint and gilding. In the meantime all other royal edifices are neglected, and in a few years become utterly ruined, until a new caprice in the Sultan, or the accession of a successor, chances to visit them with the renovating process. This barbarous and childish policy has the double disadvantage of being the most expensive, and of always keeping the royal palaces in such a mean and shabby condition as to be a disgrace to the nation. In a well-governed country three-fourths of them would be sold or pulled down, and in a civilized one the rest would be kept in repair.

My attention was called, on our return to the city, to a great number of small marble columns scattered over the slopes and summits of the hills that rise on either side of the valley. These monuments mark the spots where the arrows of the Sultans have fallen when they were pleased to amuse themselves with archery. The late Sultan Mahmoud is said to have been passionately fond of this diversion, and to have prided himself much upon his skill in drawing the bow. None of his courtiers or generals were able to compete with him in this exercise. They were probably too prudent and courtly to attempt it.

An American gentleman, who happened to be near on one occasion, when Mahmoud was engaged in his favorite amusement, sent to ask him for one of the arrows which had been honored by having been sent from his matchless bow. The Sultan, evidently gratified at the request, as a courtly compliment from an unusual quarter, gave the necessary orders for complying with it. The enchanted arrow, however, in its way to the favored stranger, had to pass through so many hands, each of whom must of course be rewarded with a handsome gratuity, that it turned out to be rather an expensive favor.

The beautiful village of Haskra, which is near the head of the Golden Horn, on its north side, is properly a suburb of Galata, forming a part of the vast city, which, under the various names of Pera, Galata, Topana, &c., stretches for several miles along this side of the harbor, and is only inferior to Constantinople itself in its lovely and commanding situation. Many respectable and wealthy Armenian families have their residence here. Their principal church, which is a fine substantial edifice, occupying rather a favorable site, has an anecdote connected with its recent history, illustrative of the temper of Mohammedanism, as well as of the policy adopted by the late Sultan and pursued by his successor.

As the church advanced towards completion, the bigoted moulahs in the neighborhood were chagrined by its respectable style, and, above all, by its commanding position, which made it a conspicuous object from the harbor, and even from a considerable part of Constantinople. They accordingly applied to the Sultan for a firman to forbid the further prosecution of the work upon the original plan, and to restrict the height of the church edifice so that it should not rise above the neighboring house, to wound the eyes of the faithful. Indignant at the spirit of intolerance and oppression which led to this application, the Sultan directed the Armenians to enlarge their plan, and erect an additional story. It is in consequence of this order that the new church is one of the most respectable and conspicuous buildings in this part of the city.

This village was lately the site of a flourishing Armenian school, which had at one time as many as five or six hundred pupils. It was established by a rich banker for the benefit of his people, and taught by an intelligent and pious young man, both acting under the good impulses which they had received from the labors of the missionaries of the American Board of Commissioners for Foreign Missions. In the persecution which subsequently arose, the banker, after resisting many attempts to break up this excellent establishment, ultimately became discouraged or intimidated.

The pious teacher was sent into banishment, from which he has just obtained permission to return.

The mosque of Eyoub, which, with the grounds around it, is much resorted to by the Turks for devotion, relaxation, and pleasure, is situated upon the Golden Horn, only a short distance from the western wall of the city. We spent a few minutes in examining the interesting objects in this locality. The mosque has nothing worthy of special attention, being inferior in its dimensions, architecture, and decorations to many others in different parts of Constantinople and its vicinity. It possesses, however, in the eyes of Mussulmen a peculiar sanctity, partly from its having been consecrated by its founder, Mahomet II., to the memory of Eyoub, who has a sort of fabulous reputation both as a warrior and prophet, and partly from its being the mosque in which all the Sultans are girded by the Mufti with the sword of state, a ceremony which answers to the ceremonial of a coronation in other countries.

Christians are not allowed to enter the court of this mosque, a privilege allowed them in all others in the city. We looked above the heads of the disorderly crowd of boys who rushed to the gate to forbid our entrance, and saw some magnificent plane-trees, which spread their deep refreshing shade over the greatest part of the enclosure, adding not a little to our desire to tread upon the holy ground. The space between the landing-place and the mosque is occupied with tombs. One, where a Sultan and his family repose, is of peculiar richness and beauty. In form it resembles the other royal tombs. It is of white marble, and is hung with rare and beautiful shawls. It is supplied with costly lamps and other rich ornaments of gold, all kept fresh and clean, so as to appear like a new erection. The Turkish fashion of endowing tombs as perpetual places of prayer, and of committing them to the care of persons who derive their subsistence from this appointment, is admirably adapted to preserve them from the neglect and ruin which speedily, almost universally, befall the cemeteries of even the most opulent and powerful in other parts of the world. Whether the object is worth the expense incurred in attaining it, or is even desirable, is another question.

There are many single monuments, erected over the graves of distinguished persons, of great sumptuousness and beauty, and they seem to be preserved with the same care as the royal tomb, from which they are only a few steps removed. On the opposite side of the way, for here is a street of tombs, is that of a child of Hallil Pasha, son-in-law to the late Sultan, and brother-in-law to the present. It is a fine structure, and was probably built for a family tomb. The pasha has within a few weeks or months fallen into disgrace, and it is a striking evidence of the speed and relentlessness with which justice or vengeance, as the case may be, overwhelms the condemned in Turkey, that the grave of this young prince of the blood royal, has been already despoiled of all its costly ornaments. Close to the water is an extensive coffee-house, thus completing the *tout ensemble* of all that a Turk most desires in this world—a mosque, a well-shaded cemetery, and facilities for smoking his chibouk and drinking coffee.

I have inadvertently omitted one more object necessary to the perfection of the Mohammedan Eden—a sumptuous fountain, built of white marble, and glittering in the sun with a profusion of gilding, which stands at a little distance from the Sultan's tomb.

In prosecuting our homeward voyage, we passed a boiler and some other fragments of a steamboat, lying neglected upon the shore. An enterprising Armenian, possessed of some wealth, attempted to build a steamboat for the conveyance of passengers or merchandise. Through want of skill or some other defect, his first essay failed, but, not discouraged by one failure, he soon set about constructing a second, hoping to profit by his former mistakes. His enterprise was arrested at this stage by the government, and a heavy fine imposed upon the unfortunate undertaker in addition to his heavy losses. The pasha, by whose department this affair was cognizable, alleged as the ground of his interference, that the man was foolishly squandering money, which, through the medium of taxation, might be useful to the state. This is a truly Turkish method of encouraging native talent and enterprise. The poor Armenian seems to have been too much disheartened even to gather up the fragments of his disastrous undertaking, which still strew the shore.

CHAPTER XXXVII.

THE SLAVE MARKET.

JUNE 27th. I passed over to Constantinople this morning at an early hour to visit a few interesting places, which, in my previous excursions in the city, I had, from want of time, or some other cause, been unable to reach. The slave market, which was my principal object, I had once or twice found closed, and, as a good deal of difficulty is often experienced in obtaining admission here, I was accompanied by one of the janissaries, or cafasses (as they are called since the fall of that military band), attached to the service of the American embassy, who was kindly furnished by Mr. Brown, the secretary of legation. They are a species of executive officer, employed by all the consulates and embassies in the Levant. They wear arms and possess certain powers and privileges, with the nature and extent of which I am not well acquainted. Access is readily given them to several places closed against the more unattended strangers, and their lordly blustering is of signal efficacy in opening one's way through a crowd.

I passed through the Egyptian Bazar, as the great

wholesale mart for drugs and medicines is called. I do not know the reason which led to the adoption of the name. It was, perhaps, applied to this bazar when Alexandria, or Cairo, was the great emporium from which medicines, as well as every other species of merchandise were brought. This is a very extensive establishment, apparently well supplied with all the variety of articles belonging to this branch of trade. It is kept almost exclusively by Turks. I saw only two or three Armenians here, and not one Jew, another curious example of the appropriation of certain branches of business by particular races.

Like the other bazars, this long street of shops is covered above, and as it is not ventilated, the atmosphere is strongly impregnated with an infinite variety of perfumes and odors. My head soon became unpleasantly sensible to their influence, and I should imagine that persons constantly employed here would be liable to very serious injury. The Egyptian bazar is only a few rods from the northern wall of the city, and nearer the harbor than any other of these great mercantile establishments. The slave market, on the contrary, is, I believe, the most remote from the harbor, being situated south of the ridge, which divides the city into two nearly equal inclined planes. No objection was made to our entering this mart of human beings, nor did I perceive any sentinels stationed near the gates or the streets leading to them.

It is an irregular quadrangle, approached by several narrow streets, which are closed by gates. A deep gallery, one story high, runs around this enclosure with a row of stalls, or small, badly lighted rooms in the rear. A noble building, provided with a similar gallery, stands within the area, which is partially paved in the prevailing style of Constantinople.

The slaves, of whom, I should conjecture, four or five hundred were exhibited to-day in the market, were almost exclusively black girls from nine to ten or sixteen years of age. Their complexion, their wooly heads, and general physiognomy, mark them indubitably as negroes, though their lips are not so thick, nor their noses so short and blunt, as those of the African race we are so accustomed to see in America. They are a good deal darker than the slaves I saw in the Cairo market, and have evidently been brought from a different latitude. Upon the whole, I should say they are a handsomer and more intelligent looking race than the Africans brought to the United States, or the first generation of their descendants.

Their dress was very similar to that most commonly worn in the field by female slaves in America—a long gown or robe of coarse white cotton stuff, and a parti-colored or red handkerchief rather tastefully tied upon the head. Several had the hair elaborately plaited, and all, or nearly all, wore large and showy finger-rings, ear-rings, beads, and bracelets. These trinkets were of various metals, and of rude workmanship. Some were evidently of gold.

The larger number of these girls were seated upon mats spread upon the ground, just in front of the galleries—a situation which gave free access to the buyers and sellers. A considerable number were seated upon a sort of counter under the back part of the gallery, the front of which was furnished with a similar counter, on which were many Turks smoking and drinking coffee, at the same time that they occasionally surveyed the slaves thus arranged in rows on either side of their divan, in a situation most favorable for inspection. These Turks I took to be buyers, who were prosecuting the business leisurely, according to their custom, indulging in the meantime in their indispensable luxuries.

Several of the dark rooms in the rear of the gallery were occupied by girls dressed in a superior style, and veiled, with the exception of the nose and eyes, in the Turkish manner. They had been selected from the vulgar herd for their superior beauty and accomplishments, and, being candidates for a higher destiny, were more expensively attired, and more carefully guarded from the approach and gaze of the crowd. I saw nothing indelicate or offensive in the negotiations between buyer and seller. The most active agents were elderly Turkish women, who passed amongst the slaves, making inquiries, and examining their forms and features. In one instance, a gentlemanly looking Turk conducted the investigation in person, but he did no more than cause the girl, who was pretty, and might be fourteen years of age, to stand on her feet that he might have a view of her stature and form. He also felt her arms and shoulders. She appeared confused, but, upon the whole, pleased with the attention.

I observed amongst the owners a black man of a singularly noble aspect and bearing. He was very tall and perfectly formed. His venerable beard descended upon his bosom. His forehead was highly intellectual, and his eye black and piercing. He wore a large white turban, and a rich flowing robe of purple silk. His broad scarlet girdle was very splendid, and his sword and pistols, elaborately inlaid and mounted with gold, must have cost a very large sum. I never saw so fine a looking black man, and I felt regret that one should be engaged in so odious a traffic, whose lofty attributes seemed to mark him as fitted to be the prince and benefactor of his people.

I was much struck with the universal cheerfulness of the slaves. Amongst them all I did not observe a single care-stricken or sorrowful countenance. They seemed desirous of attracting attention, and put on their smiles whenever they saw a person approach who was likely to become a purchaser. Of an age which forgets all the past, and looks upon the future through the medium of delusive hope, they seem elated at their condition and prospects, and evidently consider their removal from the wild and savage scenes of their native land to a great and splendid metropolis as a piece of great good fortune, which places them in the way of the highest promotion. These girls are not usually kidnapped, but voluntarily sold by their parents, who train them for this destination, and probably think that by selling their daughters to become waiting-maids or concubines in the rich families of Turkey, they make the best provision for their happiness.

These views are of course inculcated upon their children, who are taught to look upon the day when they are sold as the beginning of a more brilliant era. Nor are these expectations always, or perhaps usually disappointed. Slavery in Turkey and the East, is a very different thing from that of the West Indies and the United States. The Africans become, almost without exception, in-door servants in rich families, where they perform little severe labor, and are rather kept for play than use. According to the universal testimony of persons acquainted with Turkish habits, which I have had many opportunities of verifying by what I have seen in steamboats and elsewhere, the slaves are treated with great kindness, and even indulgence—rather as equals than as bondmen. They are well clad, eat the same food with their owners, and always approach them with an air of freedom and familiarity quite inconsistent with habitual oppression and hardship.

Manumission is favored by the religion and laws of the country, as well as by custom, and it is so common in practice, that there are comparatively very few hereditary slaves. When in addition to this it is considered that the rich Turks often choose their wives and concubines in the slave market, that the birth of a child makes the mother free, whilst the child of a concubine is entitled to the same rights as that of a wife, it will be perceived that the servile state in these regions is attended with many alleviations, and that it is not without some good reason that the unreflecting aspirants to so much possible and not very improbable good fortune, appear cheerful and contented with their destiny. It is highly credible that in a majority of cases, slavery under these circumstances proves a boon.

It is only in more civilized countries, where the demand for expensive luxuries, the pursuits of industry, and the commercial spirit always seek to organize and strenuously employ the physical energies of society, for the attainment of their objects, that the condition of slavery is liable to become less favorable to happiness, than a state of rude barbarian freedom, such as is enjoyed amongst the African tribes.

There were no white slaves in the market, and I was informed that none are ever exhibited here. They are kept by the dealers—almost always Jews—at their private houses, where they are instructed in such accomplishments as are likely to be valued in the harem, and of course increase their price. This course of education commonly embraces singing and dancing, and scarcely ever the less useful arts of reading and writing. To these private depôts the rich sensual Turk, who has resolved to add to the attractions of his harem, or more commonly some discreet female friend, proceeds to examine the merchandise and effect the purchase. Very high prices are often paid for this class of slaves, who are mostly from Circassia and Georgia. From one to two thousand dollars is not an uncommon amount to be paid for a girl. The blacks seldom command above one hundred and fifty dollars, and are frequently sold for seventy or eighty dollars.

In returning from the slave mart, we passed through the bazar devoted to the sale of arms. The Turks are peculiarly fond of highly-mounted swords and fire-arms, and they indulge in the utmost extravagance in the purchase of them. A scimitar often costs several thousand piastres, and a double-barrelled gun much more. The display of these articles in the bazar was imposing and highly curious. Damascus blades, though they seem to have lost a measure of their former reputation, are still highly appreciated, and, to my unpractised eye, these, as well as the gun-barrels made in the same place, were the handsomest as well as the best in the market. Immense expense is lavished upon the hilts and scabbards of the various descriptions of side-arms here exhibited, and the belts were often covered with gold and precious stones.

In viewing several of the splendid bazars of Constantinople, which are certainly more dazzling and magnificent than anything I have seen elsewhere, one is apt to imagine himself in the capital of the most wealthy and luxurious people in the world. Yet it is only in a few articles that a Turk indulges or can afford to indulge in great expense. He must have a rich carpet of the size of a table-cloth—an amber mouthpiece for his chibouk—gorgeous saddle and trappings for his horse, and, if a military man, splendid arms. These, with a showy dress, and some embroidered slippers and muslins, for his harem, seem to comprehend all that is greatly expensive.

He feeds on bread and fruit, drinks no costly wines, and has no carriages, and the most expensive items in the expenditures of an American or European are scarcely known to him by name.

CHAPTER XXXVIII.

EXCURSION ON THE PROPONTIS

In the afternoon I made a boat excursion with Mr. Hamlin to the Seven Towers, crossing from Topana directly to Seraglio Point, and coasting along the Sea of Marmora, under the southern wall of the city to its west extent. The whole distance is about seven miles. I never look upon the seraglio from a new point of view without being more and more impressed with the unparalelled advantages of its situation. Washed on three sides by the sea, with the most perfect enjoyment of its pure, healthful breezes, and yet in the heart of an immense capital, commanding the most delightful views of the beautiful cities of Pera and Scutari, together with an interminable prospect of water, and noble mountain scenery, with ample space for gardens, lawn and grove, this spot unites in perfection all that could make a royal residence attractive. Yet this palace was quite neglected, and even detested by the late Sultan. Perhaps his aversion grew out of the tragic scenes enacted here during the earlier and less fortunate part of his reign.

Just over one of the entrances to the seraglio, near

the Golden Horn, is seen a grotesque and semi-barbarous display of some immense bones said to belong to a whale. The Turks believe them to be the skeleton of a giant some way connected in his fate with their early history, and it is perhaps in deference to this superstition that this uncouth exhibition is tolerated in a place so little suitable to it. The navigation round this point is rendered difficult by the strong current with which the Bosphorus pours its immense volume of water against this barrier. The agitation may have been greater than usual to-day, aided as it was by a strong north wind. The mass of waters labored, and swelled, and chafed the shore, and, over a surface of many acres, bubbled like a boiling pot. Boats are carried down by the current with great velocity, and care is requisite to avoid being dashed upon the Point. The rowers in ascending the stream are aided by men on the shore, who tow boats for the distance of about a quarter of a mile. The shore is faced here by a wall of substantial masonry, the massive stones of which are fastened together with iron clamps. A range of buildings, forming a part of the palace of the seraglio, occupies a site close to the water, and along the eastern extremity of this immense enclosure. They have, as seen from the water, a light and agreeable appearance, and are admirably situated to enjoy the full advantage of the breezes that every day blow over this point from the Euxine or the Sea of Marmora.

A little farther south, on this side of the seraglio, is the gate through which persons condemned, or suspected of crime against the State, are conveyed, to be thrown into the Bosphorus. Death by the bow-string, and a grave in the deep dark waters, may be said to have been the common fate of Turkish viziers and statesmen, who have been so unfortunate as to become distinguished by their talents and wealth. Many inmates of the harem, who have incurred by any means the suspicion or the displeasure of their capricious lord, have been put in sacks, and made to expiate their offences or misfortunes in the same dark abyss. A number of mutes, maintained as spies in every part of the palace, and present at every interview and conversation which takes place within its walls, are employed as executioners. Upon an intimation given by the Sultan, these messengers of death proceed to the presence of the doomed victim,—to whom their approach probably conveys the first apprehension of danger, or even of a loss of the royal favor,—strangle him with a bow-string, and then cast the body, laden with weights, into the sea. No announcement is made of the fact, and it is only the mysterious and sudden disappearance of the victim that communicates to the world the sad intelligence, to which the tongue of the boldest would tremble to give utterance.

Philanthropy would rejoice to believe that these atrocities, which so long disgraced the Turkish court, have passed away with many other relics of barbarism. It is known, on the contrary, that secret executions were never more frequent than in the late reign. During his struggle with the janissaries, Mahmoud silently prepared the way to the victory, which he finally achieved by the secret destruction of their most able and popular officers. One after another, these leaders of the turbulent band were clandestinely led to their fate through the bye-ways of the seraglio, or conducted to some of the fortresses in the neighborhood of Constantinople, from which they never returned.

It is understood, too, that the accession of the present Sultan during the last year, was signalized by the mysterious disappearance of individuals suspected of evil sentiments or designs. For some time a fearful suspense hung over public affairs, and it was doubtful whether the partisans of reform or of the old régime would triumph. When victory was finally declared for the former, there is no reason to believe that they used their success with any peculiar moderation. The city was filled with dark rumors of secret executions, and it was generally believed that the mute emissaries of death in the seraglio were very actively engaged. The excitement died away, as any excitement must, depending on rumors which it is dangerous to repeat.

Near this gate of death, we passed a fishing-house, a peculiar structure, seen, as far as I am aware, only in the Bosphorus. Several long posts are set up in the water at some distance from the shore, secured against being carried away by the current, by cables stretched in different directions. On these posts a hut is erected, covered with mats or a light roof. Here a man is constantly stationed to watch the approach of the shoals of fish, and to give notice to his associates upon the shore to draw their net, which is spread in a situation to intercept their progress. A great many of these houses are seen in passing up the Bosphorus to Buyuk-dere and the Black Sea. The fishermen often take a vast number of fish, which supply the markets of Constantinople.

Another singular method of taking fish, much used here, I have also seen at Smyrna and other parts of Asia Minor. A brilliant light is kindled in a brazier upon the prow of a boat, which is rowed to the proper fishing grounds in the evening. The fish collect in numbers around the boat, attracted by the blaze, and are easily pierced with a spear. These boats have a very picturesque appearance as they move in different directions in a dark night, their blazing fires flashing upon the water as they shift their course, or are tossed by the gently swelling waves.

The walls of the city, on the side of the Sea of Marmora, have a general resemblance to those on the north, and west of the town. They, however, lack towers, and give some other proofs of being the work of a different and later age. The most striking of these is the great number of marble columns of various sizes, but mostly small, which are seen built into the foundations, all the way from Seraglio point to this western extremity, near the Seven Towers. I counted more than two hundred of these columns, and think there cannot be less than a thousand so employed. We should be led to conclude that this part of the wall had been destroyed by the violence of war, together with a large portion of the public edifices of the city, and that in the pressing urgency of the occasion, the precious and costly materials of the latter had been used in the reconstruction of the indispensable public defences.

I am not aware, however, that such a conclusion finds any countenance in the history of Constantinople. But for the employment of so many columns and precious fragments which have belonged to other edifices, the want of uniformity with other parts of the wall might be accounted for satisfactorily, by the constant and powerful action of the Sea of Marmora in undermining this shore. Many parts of the wall have evidently been destroyed by this cause. In several places, it has lately been repaired or rebuilt, and in many more it threatens a speedy fall. With some general conformity in the materials and workmanship, the whole wall for the distance of three or four miles, has the appearance of a patch-work made and mended at different eras, and with various degrees of skill and care. The difficulty of accounting for the profusion of wrought and costly marbles in the foundation remains to be accounted for, and seems to refer to a reconstruction after some great and general destruction by war or the elements. These fragments afford perhaps the most striking evidence now in existence, of the number and splendor of the beautiful edifices with which Constantine adorned his new capital.

At the distance of perhaps two miles from Seraglio point, we passed a large establishment for printing calicoes, which stands close to the water. It is owned and conducted by Armenians. Many samples of these goods were hanging in the open air for drying or some other purpose. The figures and coloring are in a better and simpler taste than we should expect in an oriental fabric. The calicoes seen in the bazars are far more gaudy. In this neighborhood is a small harbor, formed by an indentation in the shore and a sort of pier made by throwing large stones into the sea, which is here of no great depth. It seems to be occupied only by boats and very small craft—all of a description very inferior to those which frequent the Golden Horn. This little harbor is probably not used in winter, and it can afford no adequate shelter during the prevalence of any but northerly winds.

Still farther in the same direction, we passed an extensive region of the city, desolated by fire during the last year. A considerable number of houses have been rebuilt—some are large and respectable in their appearance, but all constructed of wood in the prevailing fashion, providing fuel for another conflagration. This is an Armenian quarter, and was the most wealthy and respectable of the several cantons occupied by that people in the city. The bankers and wealthy merchants had their residence here. The region is recommended by its facility of access, being approachable by boats, without the necessity of passing the heart of the town. The city wall, which elsewhere keeps close to the shore, makes a *détour* here, returning to the edge of the water after leaving a considerable district *extra muros*. This was involved in the conflagration like the greater part of the Armenian quarter.

An occurrence which happened during the fire in this extra mural region affords rather an amusing illustration of Turkish character. The people in their attempts to secure their household goods from the flames, brought them to a large open space in front of the gate, through which their secluded residence communicated with the city. As this was considered the place which afforded the greatest security, the accumulation increased to such an extent as to prevent all access to the gate. In the meantime the fire continued to rage, and at length approached so near the immense combustible mass, where the people had taken refuge, that the heat as well as the danger became insupportable.

In attempting to escape for their lives, they perceived with dismay their mistake in blocking up the only thoroughfare by which a retreat was possible. The only resource was a small door in the wall, which was usually kept bolted on the inside, as it was found to be on the present occasion. The key was fortunately known to be in the hands of a Turk who occupied a house close by in the city. The calls soon brought him to the gate, which they requested him to open for their escape.

To their utter consternation he refused, alleging the strict orders he had received never to unlock this door, but upon an express order from the pasha, who had charge of this department of the public service. They represented to him their desperate situation, their habitations in a blaze, all other means of retreat cut off, themselves hemmed in a corner, with the flames rapidly approaching—and the atmosphere already heated to a temperature frightfully high. The Turk heard all without emotion. He said he was sorry for their situation, which, however, had not been produced by any fault of his. His orders were positive, and he could not and would not turn the key without the permission of the pasha, advising them to send to his residence near the Seraglio, a distance of nearly two miles, in order to obtain his consent to opening the door.

In these desperate circumstances, the sufferers having found on the spot a large beam of timber, converted it into a sort of battering-ram, with which they now demolished the door, but only just in time to save the most exposed part of the crowd from perishing. They were too deeply impressed with the demerits of the obstinate porter to allow him to go unpunished. Some who had escaped with the largest measure of strength and spirit, seized the heartless villain and administered the bastinado upon the spot. They immediately reported what they had done to the pasha, who of course approved of their conduct.

The Grand Vizier, and some other high officers of government, with an appearance of concern for the sufferers, not very often manifested towards Christians, soon afterwards made their appearance, and attempted to arrest the progress of the flames, and protect the property and persons of the sufferers. As usual on such occasions, a crowd of thieves and pickpockets were gathered and eager for prey. Two men who were caught in the act of stealing the exposed property, were, by order of the Grand Vizier, thrown into a burning house and consumed. This is the terrible and summary punishment usually inflicted by the Turks on this class of malefactors.

We continued our agreeable excursion to the west termination of the city, and returned a little before sunset to Pera. I observed in returning some immense accumulations of rubbish and filth, the sweepings of the city, which had been thrown into the sea, and rose quite to the top of the wall. Instead of carrying these putrefying masses into the country to enrich the gardens and cornfields, everything is thrown into the sea without any regard to the injury of the harbor. No inconvenience seems to have been experienced as yet from this practice. It is thought by many that the current of the Bosphorus acts even upon the higher parts of the harbor, to sweep away all accumulations from its bottom and shores. The decaying masses referred to are objectionable in another point of view, as they emit an effluvium which taints the air for a considerable distance around them.

CHAPTER XXXIX.

ST. SOPHIA.

JUNE 29th. By the politeness and persevering efforts of Mr. Brown, Secretary to the American Embassy, we obtained permission this morning to visit St. Sophia and the other principal mosques. This privilege is granted to foreigners only upon application made by some ambassador to the Turkish Secretary of State for foreign affairs. The government, it is said, manifests no unwillingness to gratify the curiosity of strangers with a site of their religious edifices, but they contrive to make the favor too expensive as well as too difficult of attainment, to be frequently sought. Our firman cost about forty dollars, paid in fees to the different parties and guardians of the edifices which are visited, and to three or four attendants from one of the public offices, by whom we were accompanied. Mr. Brown, who speaks Turkish, and several other Americans, gentlemen and ladies, resident in Constantinople, were so obliging as to be of our party, which was swelled into a crowd by strangers of different nations, who usually take advantage of the issuing of a firman, to obtain a view of objects to which access is obtained with so much difficulty.

We went at once to the mosque of St. Sophia, the pride of the Mohammedans, as it was of the Christians of former days. As seen from without, this celebrated edifice exhibits nothing remarkable but the lofty central dome by which it is surmounted. This is always an imposing object, but the rest of the building fails to produce corresponding effect. The massive towers or buttresses, which have been added to the original edifice to give additional support to the grand dome,—the less elevated and smaller domes that surround the principal one,—the great number of appendages, built for the accommodation of the priests and other purposes, which surround and form a part of the mosque,—the multitude of small domes in the Turkish style, giving an immense extent to the roof, which descends in irregular and ungraceful proportions almost to the ground—all tend to impart a clumsy and heavy appearance to this vast pile, and to mar the effect of its general magnificence of design and the great architectural beauties which belong to particular portions of the building.

The four tall white minarets, always agreeable and beautiful objects, which have of course been added by the Turks, relieve in some measure the bad effect of other alterations and additions. In entering the main edifice, we pass through two immense vestibules, separated from each other and the interior by partitions and folding doors. After passing these approaches, we entered the vast and noble area which constitutes the great and distinguishing beauty of this celebrated edifice. It is about one hundred and twenty feet in diameter, paved with costly marbles, and has for its ceiling the magnificent dome elevated a hundred and eighty feet above the floor. It is free from all the usual obstructions of fine columns, monuments, and statues, and the eye ranges freely over this sublime expanse, meeting with no obstacle but a number of insignificant lamps, and their contemptible ornaments of ostrich eggs, which are suspended from the vault of the dome and descend nearly to the floor.

Nothing can be more grand and impressive than the view of St. Sophia. I was far less forcibly struck with the first sight of St. Peter's, though unquestionably the Roman church is very superior to the Byzantine. St. Peter's is a study for many days or weeks, and the visitor can only approach the grandeur of its vast design when he has become acquainted with the amazing varieties as well as the richness and exquisite beauties of its parts. In St. Sophia the general view is sublime and almost overwhelming. It fills the spectator with sublime and high thoughts, and he feels that this glorious temple is a fitting place, if there can be one on earth, for the worship of an infinite God. Besides this area under the dome, there is nothing specially worthy of attention.

The dome is supported by four immense pillars, which, however, have nothing remarkable but their magnitude. Between these pillars are rows of splendid and antique columns, sixteen in all, which support the gallery. The pavement of the church is composed of beautiful marbles, about fifteen feet long by four or five wide. They are nearly concealed by mats, an in dispensable appendage to a mosque. The ceiling i also composed of a variety of beautiful and preciou marbles. They are sawn in very thin slabs, many of which are ten or fifteen feet in length, and are so ar ranged that the rich clouds and veins of various piece of marble harmonize, and have the appearance of one immense block. The ascent to the gallery is made by an inclined plane, which might be mounted by a coach.

This had originally the name of the "women's gal· lery," from the use to which it is appropriated. It is very spacious, and might be converted into half a dozen churches of convenient size for Protestant worship. It is paved with marble, and supported in front by rows of columns, remarkable only for the vicious style of their capitals. We were conducted, by narrow and difficult stairs, rising from the top of some of the lower domes, to a narrow gallery, running on the inside of the grand dome, only a few feet from the top. It is only used for illuminations. The view of the lower part of the edifice is very striking from this great elevation.

The dome was originally ceiled with beautiful mosaics, formed of cubes of colored glass, an eighth of an inch square. This splendid work is now nearly demolished, and visitors usually contrive to carry away a few fragments, which, however inconsiderable one by one, will soon complete the destruction of this valuable relic of ancient taste and art. The roguish guides guard very carefully against these petty thefts, but always have some fragments which they offer to the visitor for a few piastres. Just at the spring of the dome are some frightful figures in mosaic, now much dilapidated, which belonged to the original ornaments of St. Sophia. They were intended to represent the seraphim of Ezekiel. The immense roof and immense domes of the mosque are covered with lead, as indeed are all the mosques of the city. Mohammedan teachers, with groups of pupils, were sitting upon mats or carpets in various parts of the mosque. Some of our party observed a great number of trunks and caskets, which they were informed contained jewels and other articles of value, deposited here for safety—a most interesting relic of one of the most ancient as well as prevalent usages with which history makes us acquainted.

CHAPTER XL.

THE SERAGLIO.

FROM St. Sophia we proceeded to the Seraglio, distant only the width of a street. This is not included in the privileges conferred by our firman, but is very commonly opened to parties fortified with such a passport. It was opened to us without objection, and we entered these storied and almost enchanted precincts through the principal gate, which has some architectural pretensions, but is much more distinguished by being the place where, in some niches made for the purpose, the heads of traitors, unsuccessful generals, and fallen courtiers, are wont to be exhibited to the popular gaze and execration. It is or was a sort of court register, where events of this description were announced in this very graphic and impressive style.

The Seraglio is not merely a palace, though it contains several palaces. It occupies the entire site of the whole city of Byzantium, the predecessor of Constantinople, and is not less than three miles in circumference. It is inclosed by an ancient wall similar to that of the city, and appears equally ancient. Besides the royal residences, this inclosure contains several of the public establishments, extensive stables, &c., and more than five-sixths of the area is occupied with open courts, gardens, lawns, and groves. It was into one of these spacious courts, containing perhaps nearly two acres, that we passed through the first gate. On the left are buildings used for an armory and mint, and on the right guard-houses and offices for servants. Here is an immense plane-tree forty-four feet in circumference. It is hollow, and was long used for a coffee-house, but the entrance is now closed with planks.

Advancing to the entrance of the second court, we were shown the splendid saloon where the Sultan is accustomed to receive foreign ambassadors, and another apartment where he sits one day in each week to receive petitions and complaints from his people. These apartments stand in the rear of a thick cypress grove. Open galleries run along in front, and all parts are gorgeously ornamented with gilding in the oriental style. On presenting ourselves at the third gate, it was announced that the keeper was asleep, and we must wait till he had finished his nap. Fortunately for us, the sluggard was not long in brushing the poppies from his pillow, and we were, after a few minutes of rather provoking delay, admitted to view the very splendid room which contains the throne where the Sultan sits upon certain State occasions. It is approached through a cluster of beautiful columns. It is splendidly and lavishly adorned with gold, and answers well to the magnificent but ill-defined and indefinable idea which we are apt to entertain of royal splendor in the eastern world.

The apartments which I have enumerated are separate edifices, and not parts of one grand palace. In this they are like everything in the seraglio. There is no vast palace, but a kiosk there, a saloon and cluster of chambers here, without regard to order, connection, or plan. At a small distance from the throne-room is the largest structure we had yet seen, two stories high, with galleries in front, all richly painted and adorned. We took it to be the palace, but were told it contained only servants' apartments. Through a fourth gate, we entered a long covered way, which leads into an open court, containing the column of Theodosius the Great, erected in memory of his victory over the Goths. It is fifty feet high, and, with a strange perversion of taste, is whitewashed, which quite conceals the texture of the marble, and renders illegible the inscription on the base.* This court is well supplied with trees, as indeed the whole seraglio, to an extent which gives it the appearance of an extensive forest.

We next passed a long range of stables, and entered an ill kept but beautiful garden, well supplied with shrubs, flowers, and trees. In the centre is a circular basin of green water, around which are built greenhouses for preserving exotic plants in winter. Here are by far the most extensive and beautiful ranges of buildings in the Seraglio. They consist of several very large halls, designed for public or convivial occasions. One is supported by a great many beautiful marble columns, and all are adorned with rich

* According to Mr. Hobhouse, the inscription is, *Fortunæ reduci ob devictos Gothos.*

chandeliers and gilding. One of these halls has a beautiful marble fountain in the centre, with more than twenty little jets of water. At the distance of a few yards is an alcove looking out upon the sea, furnished with a divan, where the sultan may at once enjoy the refreshing coolness of the playful waters, and the pleasure of a fine view. We were led into three beautiful baths, all constructed of fine marble, and fitted up in the luxurious style which the Turks are wont to employ in these establishments. The apartments of the women are extensive and commodious, but less splendid than the State-rooms. There is but little furniture, and that little chiefly European, which always appears out of place in their oriental palaces. One wishes to see nothing but carpets and divans. Upon the whole, considered as the residence of a powerful prince, the Seraglio is poor and mean in its accommodations and style. It is a heterogeneous and tasteless assemblage of buildings meanly constructed at first, ready to fall into ruin through neglect and want of repair. The site alone is of surpassing beauty.

We returned towards the gate of entrance by a different route from the one already described. It led us past the Treasury, an ordinary-looking building, but said to be of Byzantine architecture, and through the park which contains many fine trees and rich lawns, well stocked with deer, which seemed quite gentle. We visited the different apartments of the mint, where all the various processes of coining are carried on in a most imperfect manner by clumsy and worn out machinery. The silver coins of Turkey are only white-washed copper, having no intrinsic value. We saw two or three bushels of these worthless pieces in a solution of silver, and a man raking them to and fro to give them a shining exterior of the more precious metal. The piastre of Turkey, formerly equal in value to a Spanish dollar, has been reduced, under the preposterous financiering of the government, to about four cents. We heard of an improved machine, constructed by an American artist, who belongs to the mint, by which the work of coining is performed in a very superior style, but were unable to get sight of it.

Our visit to the Seraglio terminated at the Armory. We were at first refused admittance, and had to wait nearly an hour for the superintendent. Our impatience at this unreasonable delay, was a little diverted by a gentleman present, who assured us that he had waited at the Custom House on one occasion full four hours for the proper officer to examine his trunks. The functionary was asleep, and the employés, instead of rousing him, spoke and stepped softly. When at last he awoke, two attendants aided him in descending the stairs, and having seated him on the soft cushions of his divan, served coffee and the chibouk. It was after all this ceremony, that he at length engaged in the business of his office, for which hundreds were waiting. Such abuses become more tolerable in their excess, than in their lower degrees, as they then assume a character of amusing absurdity, which provokes the sufferer to laugh away his vexation.

When at length the great man made his appearance,

he demanded our firman, which gave us no admittance, even through the outer gate of the Seraglio, and having read it with great apparent carefulness, and no little pomp of manner, he signified to us that we were permitted to enter the Armory. It turned out to be not worth seeing. There were a few thousand muskets placed in frames in the usual manner, all badly kept. There were also a few suits of ancient armor and coats of mail. A pretty good assortment of the fire-arms of different epochs, shows that the Turks have about kept pace with other nations in the skill they have employed in forging these instruments of death, having advanced from the immense unwieldly instrument, which made a load for a strong man, to the common matchlock, and at last to the musket now in common use. Many swords and pistols, richly inlaid with gold, and variously fashioned, are tastefully arranged in suns, stars, and crescents, along the walls. The most curious objects here are the brazen camp-kettles of the annihilated Janissaries, which they used to turn upside down, in token of those terrible revolts which so often imparted to the government a corresponding change of position. This edifice, now the depository of weapons and munitions of war, is said to have been a Christian church, consecrated by the Byzantines to St. Irene.

This was the last day spent in the society of my valued friends, the Rev. Mr. and Mrs. Hamlin, whose residence in Pera had been my home during my stay in the city of the Sultan. With them and with the other American missionaries, I had enjoyed hours of delightful intercourse. Their cordial hospitality and kind considerate attentions, had contributed greatly to my comfort, as well as facilitated my objects in visiting this Oriental city, "beautiful for situation" above all I have seen in any part of the world, and it was with lively regret that I bade adieu to them and to the Golden Horn, and embarked in the Ferdinando Secondo for Vienna.

www.ingramcontent.com/pod-product-compliance
Lightning Source LLC
LaVergne TN
LVHW010207110826
845151LV00002B/625

* 9 7 8 1 4 2 5 5 3 5 5 7 5 *